D0207974

CASS SERIES: STUDIES IN INTELLIGENCE
(Series Editor: Christopher Andrew)

CODEBREAKER IN THE FAR EAST

Aerial photograph of Insein Jail, near Rangoon, taken on 1 May 1945 by Wing-Commander A. E. Saunders, CO of 110 Squadron, flying a Mosquito VI

CODEBREAKER
IN THE
FAR EAST

ALAN STRIPP

With an Introduction by
CHRISTOPHER ANDREW

FRANK CASS

First published in Great Britain by
FRANK CASS & CO. LTD.
Gainsborough House, Gainsborough Road,
London E11 1RS, England

and in the United States of America by
FRANK CASS & CO. LTD.
c/o Biblio Distribution Center
81 Adams Drive, P.O. Box 327, Totowa, NJ 07511

Copyright © 1989 Alan Stripp

British Library Cataloguing in Publication Data

Stripp, Alan, *1924–*
    Codebreaker in the Far East
    1. World War   2. Military Cryptology
    I. Title
    940.54'85

    ISBN 0-7146-3363-1

Library of Congress Cataloging-in-Publication Data

Stripp, Alan, 1924–
    Codebreaker in the Far East
        p.   cm.
    Bibliography: p
    Includes index.
    ISBN 0-7146-3363-1
    1. Stripp, Alan, 1924–   . 2. World War, 1939–1945—Cryptography.
    3. World War, 1939–1945—Personal narratives, English. 4. World
    War, 1939–1945—Campaigns—Burma. I. Title
    D810.C88S76   1989
    940.54'86'41—dc19   89-741
                                                                CIP

Printed and bound in Great Britain by
BPCC Wheatons Ltd, Exeter

Contents

CONTENTS

PART THREE: A TANGLED WEB

List of Illustrations

Author's Note

This book is meant for the general reader, and no technical skills are needed. I have tried to show how Allied codebreaking helped to shorten and win the war, perhaps by three years, and especially how British codebreakers contributed to the victory against the Japanese in Burma three months before Hiroshima – a subject that nobody has done more than hint at before. I wanted also to convey the feel of a place like Bletchley Park, and the excitement of working against the clock on reading the enemy's mind, without nostalgia or jingoism.

This is mostly a success story, with some surprises. How many people realise that Bletchley was not exclusively devoted to solving the Enigma and other German signals? Who would have expected Japanese Ultra or Magic signals to reveal not only what they were up to in Asia, but details of the Normandy beach defences and the German development of jet aircraft and deadlier submarines?

The idea has been taking shape for forty-five years. Why bring it out now? One reason is that the British government, far from lifting the veil from quite harmless facts which – in the words of a former head of Hut Six – 'must seem to present-day cryptanalysts rather like fighting with bows and arrows', is proposing to clamp down on them, although some were described in best-sellers up to 200 years ago. Some have appeared in thrillers and children's books. If the new Official Secrets Act, Section 2, comes into force, none of us will be permitted to write *anything* about our wartime work, even when the censors agree it is innocent. The ban will be indiscriminate and absolute, depending not on what is written but on who writes it. It will be an offence for those who did this work during the war – but not, curiously enough, for those who did not – to write about it 'without lawful authority'. All the evidence suggests that this author will be very hard to obtain. I must emphasise that this is not a military but a political decision, and that the Secretary of the D Notice Committee has again been most helpful and constructive.

Our American cousins have reformed in the opposite direction. They are keeping the lid on those wartime secrets that still matter, but have already released half a million Japanese decrypted signals, clearly understanding that the Allies knew their contents because we broke and read them, and the Japanese knew because they sent and received them. Who is there left to hide them from, and why? Without generous American help, and access to their store of signals revealing Japanese troop and convoy movements, reinforcements, casualties, supplies, plans and orders – the raw material that guided our commanders in their decisions – Chapter Eight, for a start, could not exist.

The other reason for publishing the book now is personal. All of us who did this work are at least in our middle sixties, and our memories are not improving. 'Three can keep a secret, if two of them are dead.' What about the third?

What is on the menu? The hors d'oeuvres is autobiographical, though less one man's Odyssey than a picture of what happened typically to most people 'in the racket', whether they started at Bletchley as I did, or in the Far East where most of us finished up. The main course reveals the various ingredients of signals intelligence – codebreaking – and one or two spicy side-dishes. The dessert brings in some unexpected titbits. There are no forbidden fruit.

I have been fairly discursive, because good intelligence comes from combining every source there is: captured documents, espionage, prisoner interrogation and photographic reconnaissance. The job of 'setting Europe ablaze' – and Asia too – also depended on codes and ciphers. The unknown but approaching deadline, the 'last boat from Tokyo' feeling, decided me to pack all I could carry aboard, and I have not had time to check the contents as thoroughly as I should have liked. With luck this interim report may encourage younger men and women, not restricted by the accident of their professional background and their date of birth, to get to work on a comprehensive and well-researched account to match the excellent books on German Enigma and other Ultra cipher-breaking. Meanwhile I hope that those who notice errors and omissions will forgive and tell me.

A.S.
Cambridge, January 1989

Acknowledgments

The first of my moles to surface was Robin Gibson, of Delhi and Singapore days, with a host of memories and perceptive ideas. Barry Smallman and Hugh Melinsky, both of my Bedford Japanese course, not only gave me their comments but set me on the trail of other course-members, their colleagues and *their* colleagues. It has been a pleasure to re-live Abbottabad days with another colleague whom I must not name, though his staying on at GCHQ prevented our discussion from becoming detailed. John Evans, also of Abbottabad, has given me expert guidance on signals and other topics. Dr Tony Clayton, of the Royal Military Academy, Sandhurst, kindly allowed me to consult his unfinished manuscript of the official history of the Intelligence Corps, and has helped with several conundrums. Louis Allen exhorted me to further efforts and pencilled in the question-marks which provoked Chapters Fifteen and Sixteen: one 'Not Guilty' and one 'Not Proven', perhaps. Above all I owe a special debt to Eric Copson, who was at Delhi with me without our discovering it until 1987. His lucid reasoning and patient advice on my wilder shots have steadied my aim; he has added much valuable material of his own, and his range of contacts borders on the miraculous. Other contributors, too many to name here, are mentioned in the notes for Chapter Seven.

My second debt is of a different kind: output rather than input. Eunan O'Halpin and Keith Jeffery first encouraged me to put pen to paper and seek a wider public for a subject which I had neglected over forty years of lecturing on music and doing other odd jobs abroad and at Cambridge. Christopher Andrew, Michael Handel, Ralph Bennett and Professor Sir Harry Hinsley, together with many members of the Study Group on Intelligence have, perhaps without knowing it, helped me to see how intricately interwoven the various aspects of intelligence are, and how methodical any proper study of it can and should be. Although this book falls short of their standards, it would have fallen shorter without their example and encouragement.

In the USA not only Michael Handel but Edward J. Drea

and John J. Slonaker have helped me generously, and I have to thank Professor Handel and the US Army War College at Carlisle Barracks, Pennsylvania, for permission to quote from a paper on 'Intelligence, Deception and the Victory in Burma, 1945' which I presented there in May 1988 for the Third International Conference on Intelligence and Military Operations.

I am grateful to Aerofilms Ltd for permission to reproduce the aerial photograph of Bletchley Park.

Many friends, and particularly Michael Herzig and Paddy With, have helped me by finding and offering photographs, and sometimes identifying their subjects, which I have been very glad to use. Ted Harrison kindly found me the special edition of the *Rangoon Liberator* announcing Japan's unconditional surrender. John Murphy and Michael Southgate, of British Telecom, hospitably showed me what remains of the Bletchley Park I left in 1944, and British Telecom have kindly allowed me to use their site plan as a basis for my sketch-plan. Frank Cass gave this book an encouraging imprimatur and a green flag when the need for urgency became clear, and of his colleagues I have to thank Norma Marson in particular for her cheerful and expert help in getting it into print.

I must pay a special tribute to my wife for her help and encouragement and for patiently enduring the results of my being engrossed in the completion of this book against an unknown but approaching deadline, and to my friends and colleagues for good-humouredly tolerating the many snippets or anecdotes which caught my imagination and which I thought should catch theirs. To all of them I am extremely grateful.

Introduction

Without the Ultra intelligence obtained from breaking enemy codes and ciphers, the Second World War, at least in the West, could scarcely have ended as early as 1945. So much has been published about Ultra since the early 1970s that it is often forgotten how much of the story has yet to be told. Though the breaking by Bletchley Park of the Enigma machine ciphers used by the German armed forces is by now well known, the breaking of the German diplomatic ciphers still — remarkably — remains classified. Ultra also provided much more than German intelligence. The breaking of Japanese wartime codes and ciphers was not, as is sometimes supposed, an American monopoly.

Alan Stripp advances our knowledge of signals intelligence during the Second World War in two important ways. His is the first book to describe how Bletchley Park and its outposts in India and the Far East broke a series of highly complex Japanese code and cipher systems. Mr Stripp argues persuasively that the intelligence thus obtained made a major contribution to the victory in Burma three months before Hiroshima. It appears likely that when General Slim, commanding 14 Army in Burma, denounced 'the extreme inefficiency of our whole intelligence system', he was condemning only the 'human intelligence' he received. Signals intelligence, by contrast, he seems to have regarded as a 'real triumph'.

Alan Stripp also makes a notable contribution to the history of the signals intelligence alliance among the main English-speaking states, formalised after the war in the still secret UKUSA agreement of 1948 between Britain, the United States, Canada and New Zealand. Though India lost its role in that global alliance after independence, it played a major part in the alliance's earlier development. During the decade before the First World War, at a time when Britain and the United States, sticking virtuously to the principle that 'Gentlemen do not read each other's mail', still lacked signals intelligence agencies, a small Indian Army unit succeeded in breaking a number of Russian and Chinese ciphers. Between the wars India was part of an imperial signals intelligence network which stretched from Britain to the Far East. Colonel John Tiltman, who played an important part in expanding the Japanese section at Bletchley Park and to whose 'brilliant pioneering work' on Japanese codes and ciphers Mr Stripp pays tribute, began his career as a cryptanalyst in India. Alan Stripp's book is the first to describe the remarkable achievements of the signals intelligence units stationed in India during the Second World War.

Codebreaker in the Far East also has its lighter side. The wartime recruitment of Japanese cryptanalysts provides an entertaining study in last-minute British improvisation. Alan Stripp himself was recruited in 1943 as a first-year undergraduate on the strength of a classics scholarship to Cambridge, an ear for music and a talent for crossword puzzles. The crash-course on Japanese which prepared him for his work as a cryptanalyst was devised and run by Oswald Tuck, a retired naval captain who had left school at fifteen and taught himself Japanese while serving on the China station before the First World War, but had no experience of teaching others. The School of Oriental and African Studies at London University, then the only British university department teaching Japanese, when approached by Tiltman, claimed that no worthwhile course could be completed in less than two or three years. Tuck said he could do it in six months. After only five months in an improvised classroom in the Bedford gas showrooms, he was able in the summer of 1942 to send some of his students (most of them Oxbridge classicists like Alan Stripp, who was recruited a year later) to translate the recently captured Japanese Air Force code.

Despite its failings, the achievements of British intelligence during the Second World War were probably the most remarkable in the history of warfare. One of the keys to Britain's success was the willingness to employ the unconventional talents of what Whitehall called 'professor types'. Alan Turing of King's College, Cambridge, and Bletchley Park, perhaps the ablest codebreaker of the war, kept his mug chained to a radiator to prevent theft, cycled to work in a gas-mask when the pollen-count was high, buried his life savings in the Bletchley Woods and failed to recover them when the war was over. It is difficult to imagine him fitting easily into the German or Japanese intelligence services. It is equally difficult to imagine the enemy intelligence services putting the youthful talents of Alan Stripp and other classicists fresh from school or first-year university courses to such remarkable wartime use.

Christopher Andrew

PART ONE

TOURS OF DUTY

1

Cambridge, Bedford and Yorkshire

How do people become codebreakers?

The turning-point for me came at Cambridge in the spring of 1943. My college Tutor, Kitson Clark, had sent round a note about an officer who was coming to interview people at the Appointments Board, now less confusingly called the University Careers Service; it might have something to do with languages. Was I interested?

I was. I had been studying Classics, having arrived at Cambridge by a roundabout route. My father had been at London University but thought I should try for Oxbridge. Our Boat Race loyalties had favoured Oxford – I think purely from colour prejudice – but in any case many schools encouraged their pupils to back both horses; if unlucky at the first, regard it as a trial run for the second. I spent several interesting days at Exeter College, Oxford, in 1942, and am still waiting to hear if they have a place for me. Some months later Trinity College, Cambridge, offered me a place and a scholarship. That settled it.

I knew that when the course ended that summer I should be called up. Few of us had any clear idea what we would be doing. The RAF beckoned, especially after the film *First of the Few*, but it seemed that the Army needed far more men, and the Navy practically none. At wartime universities everyone except the scientists and refugees had to do some form of military training. Even they were in Fire and First Aid parties, dizzily trailing their cumbersome hoses and stretchers over the medieval roofs – an authorised version of the traditional night-climbers. On Thursday nights I was one of the fire-watchers that Trinity provided as observers from the top of St John's chapel tower, which looked out over both colleges. We slept in a tiny wooden hut perched on top of the tower, and hoped all three telephones would not ring at once.

In the so-called Senior Training Corps we had been spending many mornings in khaki: drilling ('square-bashing'), violently exercising, learning to fire rifle, Bren gun and Sten gun, or more

3

often Naming Parts: 'This 'ere is the barrel locking-nut retainer-plunger'. There were tactical exercises across the fields towards Madingley by day, or about the Fens near Quy by night, usually defending an unspecified object against an unseen enemy. Anything was more attractive than prolonging this repetitious and often time-wasting routine.

The interview was friendly but searching. There was none of the expected emphasis on proficiency at sport, or on grit, gristle and leadership. What had I done at school? What languages had I studied? Latin, Greek, French, a little German. With what result? What were my motives? Then odder questions: did I play chess? Yes, with my father, not very well. Crossword puzzles?

Here I had a trump card. My father, a mathematics teacher, not only solved difficult ones in the weekly reviews but actually set some himself in the notoriously hard *Listener* series under the pseudonym Neon. These were impressive affairs of which I remember only one, made up of triple anagrams such as ADROITLY, DILATORY and IDOLATRY. He also solved and compiled stiffish competition problems, one of which, 'Robinson's Rendezvous', had won him £30, a small fortune in the 1930s.

The interviewer pricked up his ears. What about music? Here too I had my parents to thank. I grew up in an atmosphere of broadcast and sometimes live symphony concerts, and a favourite family pastime was to challenge one another either to identify a few hummed bars ('Brahms 2, third movement; easy') or, much harder, to hum a specified fragment. My mother played the piano quite well; my father extemporised, none too well, but he had recently learned to play the cello. He had even written a Mass ('Nothing more advanced than Gounod', he claimed) in his enthusiasm for the high Anglican services at All Saints, Margaret Street, where he sang in the choir. I had played the tuba in the school orchestra, and at Trinity was in the chapel choir and a madrigal group. Could I read an orchestral score? Yes, if not too complicated.

These activities seemed to be high on the interviewer's shopping-list – though not higher, I hoped, than languages. I had no wish to be conscripted into a military band, even one that played chess off duty, for the duration. All was well. I cannot be sure how the question was put, whether I wanted to be considered for a Japanese language course, but there was never any doubt about my answer. Nothing was said about the ultimate purpose of the course.

Two months later I received a letter telling me that I had been selected for the next six-month course, starting at Bedford at the end of August. This was run by the 'Y' Service, and I should be found lodgings and paid £5 a week as a civilian.

The course was held in a large room in a detached house in De Parys Avenue, a tree-lined road not far from the town centre. There were about 35 on the course, including two girls, all of us aged about 18 or 19, and most from university Classics courses. We eyed each other sheepishly. We realised later how sensible the intelligence service had been in choosing classicists and a few other dead-language students – for example embryonic theologians working in Aramaic – for these courses in written Japanese, and modern linguists, more accustomed to spoken languages, for spoken Japanese. If the legends are true of chefs being retrained as electricians for the Army, while electricians were turned into chefs, this was no mean achievement.

We had two instructors. The first was Oswald Tuck, a retired naval captain in his sixties, who had been persuaded to teach the first course, starting in February 1942. A bearded, spectacled, quiet and benevolent man, he had taught himself Japanese nearly forty years before, and was now in his element teaching it to others. The other was Eric Ceadel, another classicist and a student on that first course; quick, cool, lucid and methodical. Inevitably he became known as 'Chūi', the Japanese for lieutenant. Later they were helped by David Hawkes.

We worked every weekday, with just enough time at coffee and lunch breaks to prevent our going stale. Most evenings and weekends were needed to learn the language and above all to memorise the characters. Japanese is so completely different from almost every other language that I have tried to give a detailed description in Chapter Thirteen both of the language and of the language courses.

Given the size of the group, the atmosphere was fairly informal, and we were encouraged to ask questions and discuss difficulties. Sometimes we worked separately or in smaller groups; teaching became supervised learning, and we were given individual translation jobs. The vocabulary was specialised but not stiflingly narrow. Our material was Japanese war communiqués or press releases, or sometimes diplomatic telegrams, which often carried not only the expected messages but personal appeals: 'Please send pearl buttons (*"kai-botan"*) for shirts to wear with evening dress'. I suppose we must have asked ourselves what all this was for and how the texts of these telegrams were obtained, yet I cannot recall considering or

5

discussing the implications. We were, after all, conditioned to sixth-form and university study in which the examination is the goal and the yardstick, and the ultimate destination is not meant to weigh too heavily.

I shared digs in Stanley Street with an older man who was studying Arabic on one of the parallel courses run from Albany Road, Bedford. He was an English Mohammedan, and during the fast of Ramadhan our landlady had to bake him 'night pies' to eat after sunset and sometimes well into the night.

Many of us were music-lovers; I learned much later that chess, crossword puzzles and music had long been considered pointers to a possible proficiency in codebreaking. Several played instruments, and I believe Michael Herzig was the accomplished horn-player whose arpeggios from the Mozart concerto finales often formed fanfares for the start of our classes. We were lucky in having the BBC Symphony Orchestra and the BBC Singers evacuated to Bedford and we could often get passes for the orchestral rehearsals; I remember sitting in while Henry Holst was the soloist in the Walton violin concerto, and realising for the first time that if you can sit behind the orchestra you can learn much more than from in front. One evening we persuaded Sir Adrian Boult to give an informal talk about conducting. A more modest venture was Bedford School's performance of Bach's Christmas Oratorio for which we were recruited as tenors and basses – both scarce in wartime. This was sung in English and apparently conducted by a sports enthusiast: there was more of the rugby scrum than the concert platform in his encouragement to 'Fall on it'.

One weekend, on my way to the railway station, I was hailed 'Hello, young man' by Arthur Wadsworth, who taught French at the same London school, now evacuated to Godalming, as my father. With him was his daughter Mary, whom I already knew a little from the various school events to which the staff brought their families. She was now undergoing teacher-training at the Froebel Training College in Bedford. We arranged to meet, we liked each other, we continued to meet, we went to concerts together, and eventually we became unofficially engaged. Formal engagements were rarer in the uncertain days of wartime, and it was not until 1949, more than five years later, that we were married – and then in Portugal.

I understand from John Prentice, who was on the next course (February – July 1944) that by then 'we had a very good cricket team which terrorised the neighbourhood. Its captain was Francis Dashwood, now Sir Francis Dashwood, Premier Baronet of Great

Britain, and he was by then the only civilian member of the course'. I doubt if we had any talent to match that, except that Denise Newman was a champion swimmer. Generally we formed friendships in twos and threes. I got to know Barry Smallman and Hugh Melinsky, who were billeted on the far side of Bedford, and I recall a furious and embarrassing scene when all three of us were invited to sit in on an ouija-board demonstration by their landlady and her daughter. We were sure that we could see her pushing the planchette – or possibly it was a tumbler – and were tactless enough to say so when asked what we thought of her supernatural powers.

I also remember running across the town to tell them the news, which I had just heard on a BBC bulletin, that Italy had capitulated; that fixes the date as 8 September 1943, since the armistice was kept secret for some days. Most of us believed that the Allies would rapidly occupy Italy and that the war in Europe would soon be over, releasing much-needed troops for the war against Japan, and perhaps even meaning that we should not be sent to the Far East – a possibility we viewed with mixed feelings. We need not have worried.

A colleague reminds me that we met as usual on Christmas Day 1943 but were considerately given only one short piece of translation. It contained Christmas greetings from, in strict hierarchical order:

'Taku kaigun taisa kideru rikugun chui hokusu si'
(Tuck Navy Captain, Ceadel Army Lieutenant, Hawkes Mr)

Many of the messages we were translating were communiqués on recent fighting in Burma. The first press release jubilantly announced the fall of Rangoon and 'the destruction of the main enemy forces'. There were allegations of an Allied air attack on a clearly-marked hospital ship, and stirring messages of confidence in approaching victory despite the American island-hopping in the Pacific. All this material had been well graded, and it grew steadily harder. It had started in romanised form, with an increasing number of texts in characters; we also had to use our ingenuity to fill gaps or correct errors in the texts. Now we graduated to a Japanese textbook, entirely in characters, on the principles of flight, with umpteen technical terms: lift, drag, aerofoil section, gliding angle, stalling speed and dihedral. Increasingly we worked on our own, each with a small pile of messages and always able to consult Tuck or Ceadel when we were baffled.

Ceadel was above all a man of logic and pattern. It was said that the two elderly sisters on whom he was billeted were addicted to Fair Isle knitting, which he conceived and improvised for them, and that in the manner of chess masters playing several matches simultaneously he would close his eyes, meditate and then dictate to each in turn the colours and arrangement of stitches needed for the next row of each garment. He now unveiled his masterpice, a code-breaking exercise.

We felt fairly safe in assuming that the hidden text would be similar to those of the communiqués already familiar to us, many of which started with the date of some military success. For example 'On February 15 Imperial land, sea and air forces occupied Singapore', or 'On September 27 our bombers raided enemy air-fields near Calcutta'. The Japanese language made a neat pattern of this by calling January 'No 1 month', February 'No 2 month' and so on, and since they put the month before the day it was likely that the hidden message began 'Number X month, number Y day', or in Japanese 'X gatsu, Y hi...'. Moreover the numbers themselves form patterns, as there can be no more than twelve months or 31 days, so that we could begin to build up a speculative picture of the opening phrase of the coded message.

Ceadel had been kind to us, as befitted a group facing this task for the first time. Although any reputable codebook assigns its code groups to words or phrases in random order, he had classified all his under their first syllable, in the order of the kana syllabary, which I describe in Chapter Thirteen. The code was in groups of three digits, making a thousand groups from 000 to 999, and as there are fifty kana syllables it was easy to guess that 000–019 stood for words beginning with the syllable 'a', 020–039 those beginning 'i' and so on, in the traditional order of the syllables. I forget how final 'n' was fitted in.

How long did they allow us? How well did we do? I think everyone succeeded in breaking most of the message and some of us worked it all out; nobody was disgraced. It was also self-evident what we should be doing when the course finished. We had heard of the existence of Bletchley Park, the Government Communications Headquarters (GCHQ), because we knew slightly older contemporaries who had been on earlier Bedford courses and gone on there. The implication, without any breach of security, was straightforward. Early in 1944 rumours began to circulate. Some of us were to go to a naval unit in Ceylon, some to Australia, some to Bletchley Park, one or two to Berkeley Street. With the rumours came speculation: who looked most nautical, military or diplomatic?

8

Fifth Japanese language course at Bedford, 31 August 1943 – 18 February 1944.

Martin Parfitt McLaren Sumner Booth — Chalmers — Mitchell
Herzig Wolfe McKean Goldberg Collingwood Skinner — Turner
Stripp Fletcher Warmington Smallman Polack Eddolls Smart James Newman
Fenn Webster Bellingham Hawkes Tuck Ceadel Hall Melinsky

In February 1944 thirteen of us were called up into the Army Intelligence Corps, whose badge has been irreverently described as 'a pansy resting on its laurels'. (Why has it never become 'Royal', when vets, caterers, paymasters and dentists, among others, have?) We collected uniform, equipment, vaccinations and inoculations at the nearby Kempston Barracks, along with our Army numbers. Mine was 14429743, which my father helpfully suggested I could memorise because it was the product of two large numbers, *each of them prime* unless my memory deceives me. I found it simpler to learn it parrot-wise. Our last night in Bedford was spent blancoing equipment, polishing cap-badges and burnishing our boots to mirror-like perfection. We were due to report to the Intelligence Corps Depot and the rumour was that discipline there was rigid and the instructing staff thugs. That proved to be an understatement.

The Depot was at Wentworth Woodhouse, a grandiose mansion in spacious grounds near Rotherham in south Yorkshire. Officers lived in the house itself; we, as mere private soldiers, were quartered in the stables or in huts nearby. Very early each morning a distant bugle would sound reveille, and soon afterwards boots would clump outside, our hut door would be flung open and we would be ordered up and out. For washing and shaving there was only icy water and hardly any time; moving at the double we paraded for breakfast, each carrying knife, fork, spoon and mug, and then began drilling and weapons instruction. We had done it all before and would have needed at most an hour's reminder. That was of no account: what mattered was to keep us on the move with no idle moments; 'idle' was one of the principal terms of abuse. 'Twenty-four hours a day, seven days a week, fifty-two weeks a year. That's your duty. Leave is a privilege, not a right; time off for meals is an act of grace, and don't you forget it.' The other Supreme Principle around which all life revolved was that well-known maxim 'If it moves, salute it; if it doesn't, whitewash it'.

At Cambridge our Training Corps instructors had been tough, efficient but recognisably human. Here the specialists were passable but the rest were bully-boys. When the Intelligence Corps was re-estabished – having disappeared between the wars – nearly a year after the second world war began, it had no instructing staff of its own and non-commissioned instructors had been sought from any unit that could spare them. This lot could obviously be spared. The Guards, not very choosy themselves over the quality of their NCOs, had flushed out their most disposable corporals and sergeants and despatched them to the I. Corps Depot with a sigh of relief. They were not so much skilled at instructing as at catching people out. They would bellow or scream an unintelligible order and at once countermand it with 'As you were' before anyone had moved more than an eyebrow. If, in answer to a catch-question, anyone volunteered an answer, he was ridiculed. If none of us did, we were sworn at.

One of our group was put on a charge for appearing with 'dirty cap-buttons on parade' after an all-night exercise in which all our highly-polished buttons had had to be dulled so as not to reflect light to 'the enemy'. He was marched in before the Adjutant, one Captain Rankin, widely known as 'The Blonde Brute'. As he was marched out again, sentenced to several days' 'confined to barracks', he could just be heard muttering 'Rankinjustice'.

Why it is thought necessary to cross the border-line from firm control to brutishness in order to achieve proper discipline, nobody has ever explained. Recruits do not expect to be feather-bedded, but anyone who treats them as less than human demeans himself and forfeits the respect and efficiency which he might otherwise expect. The Army, and not least the Guards, have yet to rid themselves of the 'breaking-in' and 'breaking-down' attitudes which the worst types of NCO still embody.

While we were there we had two outings which stood out in happy contrast. One was a cross-country run in full uniform and boots, which Barry Smallman and I, to our surprise, led for most of the way. Another was a much-needed trip to the Elsecar Colliery pithead baths. Less pleasant was a route march, with full equipment, across the snow-covered waste north-west of Sheffield: Wharncliffe Crags. The ground was strewn with small rocks, but the snow covered all natural features so that alternate steps could either jolt your boot on a rock just below the surface, or wrench your ankle when the crust gave way into a hidden hollow of bracken a foot deep. But at least these were natural hazards, and the march could have had some point.

Most of the others undergoing training were in the Field Security branch, which made up a major part of I. Corps duties: somewhere between Military Police and Special Branch. They were on their way to the course at Matlock. We were the odd ones out; we conformed to no pattern – almost always a dangerous condition in an organisation which looks for all-round conformity.

One thing which helped our morale was the discovery that on our occasional free evenings we should be welcome at the nearby vicarage. The vicar, his wife and their two daughters gave us coffee, played us records and offered us comfortable chairs to relax in. They reminded us that there was intelligent life beyond Wentworth Woodhouse. Another reminder followed.

We were told that twelve of our thirteen would shortly be promoted to Warrant Officers, Class 2 (Company Sergeant-Majors) and would leave by air for Brisbane the day afterwards. The instructor-corporal's face, as he contemplated the awfulness of having us, of all men, leapfrog his hard-won two stripes at the whim of higher authority, was a picture. I forget when I learnt that I, as the youngest and possibly the least efficient, would be the reserve.

Our status rose by several notches, and each of us took turns in drilling the other twelve. The toughest test was to project your voice across the enormous parade-ground, competing with nearby motor-cycle exercises, so that the words of command could be heard at the far side. The corporal clearly doubted if we could cope. But our group loyalty paid dividends. For once, the commands were not going to be delivered in a barely-comprehensible scream at a moment chosen to catch us out; nor were any of the squad anxious to disgrace either themselves or their colleague who was temporarily in charge. The standard of drilling was admirable, and far above what the corporal had achieved.

Eventually the thirteen were mustered to be inspected before departure by, it was said, the DDMI (Deputy Director of Military Intelligence). I remember the red tabs and, to my surprise, the strong glasses – which would have earned a string of abuse if one of us had needed them: 'You there, you 'orrible little man with the big glasses. Pick yer feet up.'

The next morning the twelve were gone, and I was given a rail warrant to GCHQ, Bletchley Park. I must say something about the background of this remarkable place before resuming my personal account.

2

Bletchley Park

After the First World War the British government reviewed the lessons learnt in breaking German codes. It decided to establish a new unit called the Government Code and Cypher School (GC&CS), ostensibly 'to advise as to the security of codes and cyphers used by all Government departments and to assist in their provision' but also, in a secret clause, 'to study the methods of cypher communications used by foreign powers': in other words to break and read their signals traffic. GC&CS, an inter-service unit, was to operate under the overall control of the Admiralty in the person of its Director of Naval Intelligence, Commodore (later Admiral) Hugh Sinclair, nicknamed 'Quex'.

The connection with the Royal Navy was no accident; their Room 40 had been notably successful in breaking German naval codes in the 1914–18 war and was anxious not to lose its expertise in peacetime. The operational head was to be Alistair Denniston, a former member of Room 40, with Edward Travis as deputy and a team which included William Clarke, Dillwyn Knox, Oliver Strachey and the Russian and Japanese experts Felix Fetterlein and Ernest Hobart-Hampden. It also contained Leslie Lambert, better known as the short-story writer A.J. Alan. The establishment was twenty-five, with forty-six assistants.

In 1923 Sinclair was appointed head of the Secret Intelligence Service (MI6) and Director of GC&CS, though Denniston stayed in charge. By then its overall control had passed to the Foreign Office, and the appointment of an Admiral went some way towards meeting the grievances of the armed services at what they believed to be the stifling grip of the FO. GC&CS worked in various buildings in London, moving from the interestingly-named Watergate House to Queen's Gate and finally to Broadway Buildings, which also housed SIS.

Bletchley was bought in 1938 on Sinclair's initiative, since it was widely expected that if war came London would be heavily bombed.

It consisted of a gross and unlovely Victorian twenty-roomed mansion, red-brick with timbered mock-Tudor gables. There had been wide lawns, a lake with swans, a croquet pitch and the traditional ha-ha to keep cattle out without spoiling the view. During the Munich crisis of September 1938 GC&CS was evacuated down there and acommodated in the house, in small buildings in and around the stableyard, and in wooden huts hurriedly erected in the grounds. I cannot better Peter Calvocoressi's description in *Top Secret Ultra* of the impression the place made on new arrivals:

'The house had been built ... in a style which, up to a few years ago' (he is writing in 1980) 'has been adjudged ridiculous ... inside it was dreadful. I remember a lot of heavy wooden panelling enlivened here and there by Alhambresque (Leicester Square, not Granada, Andalusia) decorative fancies ... In a pond in front of the house a few ducks had survived the transfer of the property to government ownership.'[1] Teleprinter links were set up to link it to the main intercept stations, and inevitably the young women who tended them were called teleprincesses. By 1 August most of the regular staff were installed there and ready to receive the newcomers, who arrived in the guise of 'Captain Ridley's hunting party'. Captain Ridley was in charge of administration, and this apparently inappropriate cover-name was chosen because the contractor who built the huts, Captain Faulkner, was an enthusiastic rider and would often come over to supervise wearing jodhpurs.

In November 1939 Sinclair died and Menzies succeeded to his throne as 'C', head of SIS. Denniston was now Director with Travis as Deputy Director, virtually as in 1919; Travis also ran the Communications Security Section, responsible for advising on the security of British codes and ciphers. In 1942 he took over the direction of Bletchley Park while Denniston was relegated to running the small diplomatic section in Berkeley Street.

The administrative offices were in the mansion itself, which also housed Nigel de Grey, one of the team which had solved the Zimmermann telegram of January 1917, and at one stage Colonel John Tiltman worked there too; he had already done brilliant pioneering work on Japanese and other military codes and played an important role in expanding and recruiting for the Japanese section. At first most of the rapidly expanding staff worked in the huts, in fairly Spartan conditions, with trestle tables and folding wooden chairs. More and more huts were built until they sprawled over most of the grounds, whether singly, in pairs or grouped in T or

H patterns. They were urgently needed, because the number of staff was growing out of all recognition. In 1939 the official budget had provided for Head, Assistant Head, three Chief, 14 Senior and 16 Junior Assistants, together with clerks, typists, telegraphists and others making some 150 in all, plus a handful of ancillary staff. Very probably there were some extra staff whose salaries were borne on the budgets of other departments. By late 1942 the total had risen to about 3,500, and by early 1945 to over 10,000.

Recruitment was directed particularly at the universities and the professionals. 'During the summer vacation of 1939 Denniston wrote to the heads of about ten Cambridge and Oxford Colleges, asking to interview half a dozen of the ablest men in each for war work.'[2] The work was said to be associated with the Foreign Office, which was true so far as financial accountability went, but shed no light on what duties to expect. This contingency list included able undergraduates as well as 'professor types': linguists, historians, an art historian, a lawyer and even, despite earlier prejudices, two mathematicians: Alan Turing and Gordon Welchman. The 'professorial type' salary was £600 a year.

Cambridge far outnumbered Oxford in its representation at Bletchley Park, perhaps through the accident that there had been more from Cambridge several decades before. Sir James Ewing, a Fellow of King's and Professor of Mathematics and Applied Mechanics, had worked in Room 40 in the 1914–18 war and had recruited three other King's men then: Frank Birch and Frank Adcock as well as Dillwyn Knox. After the war Birch took to the stage but returned to Bletchley in 1939, canvassing several others to join him. Adcock, by then a Fellow of King's and Professor of Ancient History, was urged by Denniston to sound suitable people before the war. In Denniston's words, 'It was naturally at that time impossible to give details of the work, nor was it always advisable to insist too much on the imminence of war. At certain universities, however, there were men now in senior positions who had worked in our ranks during 1914–18. These men knew the type required.'[3]

Adcock was an enthusiast, and of the first sixteen 'professor types' eleven came from Cambridge, two from London and three from The Other Place. It is not surprising that this should happen, given the success of Ewing's original trawling operation and the emphasis placed on recruitment by personal contact and recommendation. Not only that: so many Kingsmen arrived that in 1941 Bletchley was more than once called 'Little King's'. A little later the sister of one of the early members of Bletchley was able to recommend some bright undergraduates from Newnham, and the same thing happened at Oxford, with 'a massive exodus from Lady Margaret Hall to Bletchley'.

As well as Turing and Welchman, recruits from Cambridge included Jack Good, Max Newman, Noel (now Lord) Annan, a future Provost of King's College; Shaun Wylie, who in Lewin's words was already 'an international hockey player, winner of the unarmed combat competition in the local Home Guard, and President of the Bletchley Dramatic Club';[4] and Dennis Babbage, a descendant of the Charles Babbage whose Analytical Engine, conceived in the 1830s, had been the first step towards the creation of a machine which could tackle *any* mathematical operation, and that not in any narrow arithmetical sense. Harry Hinsley was one of the first of the 'able undergraduates' to be sounded a few months before the war began, and a Cambridge figure who made an indirect contribution was Wynn-Williams of the Telecommunications Research Establishment, whose pre-war work in electronics was valuable in the development of the Bombe and the Robinson family of machines in use at Bletchley.

There was no shortage of figures who were colourful as well as distinguished. Josh Cooper, head of the Air Section, short-sighted, absent-minded and cordial, was said to have been called in to help with the interrogation of the first captured German pilot. No organisation had yet been set up for this purpose, and Cooper, with his rational and enquiring attitude towards the discovering of intelligence, seemed an excellent choice. The pilot was marched in and proudly gave the Nazi salute and a loud 'Heil Hitler'. Not to be outdone in politeness, Cooper instinctively rose and did the same, immediately recognised his error, sat down in haste, missing the chair which he had pushed back, and slid foot-first under the table.[5] On his visit to Buckingham Palace to receive a decoration he was asked what his work was. He pondered at length, scratched the back of his head – a favourite gesture – and at last replied, 'I really don't know, Ma'am'.

The head of the Army section, John Tiltman, was just as unconventional, and was celebrated for his unusual mixture of Army and civilian dress. On one occasion he was strolling across the grounds clad in a nondescript jacket and a perfectly proper but strikingly coloured pair of trews, the narrow tartan trousers of his regiment. Two Free French officers goggled at this apparition; one clutched the arm of the other and asked 'Ce pantalon-là, c'est de rigueur ou de fantaisie?'[6]

Turing suffered from hay-fever and was known to cycle to work in his gas-mask when the pollen-count was high. He would chain his mug to any fixed object like a chair or a radiator to prevent its being stolen. He converted his life savings into small bars of silver, which he shrewdly predicted would rise in value, and buried some in the nearby woods and some in a stream. When he returned to find them after the war, the landmarks in the wood had disappeared and the stream bed had been cemented over.

Alexander, Golombek and Milner-Barry formed a striking trio of a different kind. All three were representing Britain in the International Chess Olympiad in Buenos Aires when the war broke out, and all three were eventually recruited to Bletchley. Finally there were several husband-and-wife teams, starting with Denniston and his wife – though they were often split between different departments.

It was a happy characteristic of Bletchley Park that differences of age, rank or background, as well as departures from convention, were largely disregarded. The atmosphere was often likened to that of an Oxford or Cambridge college. Discipline or hierarchy in the normal sense hardly existed, and in return GCHQ was rewarded with men and women who 'hated to take leave or rest days'; a cautionary notice exhorted them to 'take at least one day off every week'. The 'long-haired intellectual', far from being a figure of fun, was at the centre of the imaginative and flexible approach needed for successful codebreaking. Denniston, Travis, Tiltman, Cooper and others put their faith in 'the ability of the highly intelligent amateur to grapple successfully with very complex problems'.

Neil Webster, an old hand, puts it like this:

> The cryptographic organisation at Bletchley was highly efficient. Indeed it was the most efficient working organisation I have met ... It was run neither by business men nor by civil servants but by mathematicians and chess players who brought detached and decisive minds to the solution of cryptographic, organisational and human problems. Contributory factors were the devotion, high morale and esprit de corps of the picked band of workers. Gifted people were willing to work on boring and repetitive tasks if it was important that these should be done by people capable of spotting the occasional small nugget which might turn up in the sieve.[7]

David Kahn, the author of the still unrivalled book on the history of codebreaking, waxes lyrical: 'An unbelievable galaxy ... white-hot with talent'.[8] A further tribute comes from George Steiner, surely one of the last men to join in any popular ballyhoo: 'It looks as if Bletchley Park is the single greatest achievement of Britain during 1939–45, perhaps during this century as a whole'.[7] Lord Dacre, formerly the intelligence officer Hugh Trevor-Roper, adds that 'The state of friendly informality verging on apparent anarchy was Denniston's particular contribution, that enabled these clever and sometimes anarchic men and women to develop their talents and carry out their work.'[7] One ironical comment attributed to Churchill, a passionate supporter of Bletchley's work, and one of its best customers, sums up the motley and unsoldierly aspect we must sometimes have presented: 'I told you to leave no stone unturned in your search for suitable staff. I didn't expect you to take me so literally.'

Bletchley Park had changed its title in 1942 from Government Code and Cypher School to Government Communications Headquarters, as it remains today despite its move to Cheltenham. Oddly enough it kept its original name in the USA, at least in exalted circles. A memorandum for President Harry Truman, dated 12 September 1945, points out the 'profitable collaboration' between the two countries, recommends that it should continue in peacetime 'in view of the disturbed conditions of the world and the necessity of keeping informed of the technical developments and possible hostile intentions of foreign armies', and is signed by Acting Secretary of State Dean Acheson, Secretary of War Henry L. Stimson, and Secretary of the Navy James Forrestal; it still mentions 'the British Government Code and Cipher School'. Despite the change of name on the gates, any casual passer-by could see that the clientèle had not changed, though it continued to grow. Security passes were still needed to satisfy the men of the RAF Regiment at the gates. Was it really likely that a nation fighting for its life would need the codes and ciphers mentioned in the original name any the less? What were all the despatch riders and tall aerials for? Why were men and women of all nationalities and every sort of uniform coming and going, often on night shift?

Yet the extraordinary fact persists, that throughout six years of wartime growth to a maximum strength of over 10,000 with Free Poles, Free French, Americans, and British Army and ATS, Navy and WRNS, RAF and WAAF, and countless varieties of civilians, no leaks seem to have occurred. Lord Camrose is said to have stumbled on the secret in 1941, but to have promptly sat on it. Any enemy would have taken it for granted that we would have such an organisation, especially after the success of Room 40 in the previous war – just as they had themselves. It seems impossible to believe that none of those working there ever told the secret to a wife, husband, lover, friend or parent; yet it never emerged. This is all the more striking in view of wartime tensions, enforced departures and family separations, and above all the personal tragedies of many of the European refugees.

Lewin tells the story of Judy Hutchinson, who had been in charge of Field Marshal Alexander's War Room in the Italian campaign, who faced a severe brain operation in 1970, twenty-five years after the war ended, not at all afraid of the consequences of the critical operation but with 'the terror, over-riding all other concerns, that in delirium she might give away the secret of ULTRA' – the breaking and reading of the German Enigma machine signals.[9]

On the face of it this silence seems all the more astonishing since the security precautions at Bletchley Park, though strict, were never ridiculously oppressive. No doubt the many other secret activities going on in the British Isles made tight security more palatable – but there were whispers about some of them, whereas Bletchley and its offshoots seem to have been leakproof. Presumably people capable of seeing the point of breaking the enemy's signals, and of doing it, could readily understand why it was important not to jeopardise the whole affair; very logical, yet logic is not always put into practice, as the unlocked car door, the lost credit card with the PIN-number scribbled on it, the key left under the front doormat, all testify.

One part of the explanation must have been that we could all see that this was a true secret. It is when attempts are made to keep everything secret, regardless of commonsense, that leaks occur. The more indiscriminate the embargo, the less effect it has. The other point is that we were trusted; we willingly lived up to a trust placed on us and were not subjected to lunatic, draconian and ultimately counter-productive measures.

Yet another factor was the long tradition of 'the need to know' principle; only someone who needs to know a secret can be told it. That rule was enforced very rigorously in sigint units. As Kozaczuk puts it: 'Few people, even at the top, had a clear overview of the totality of the operation, from interception of ciphered German messages, through their breaking, translation, editing and annotation, to the distribution of decrypts and intelligence summaries. The operation was so compartmentalised that hardly anything that any one person could have divulged about it would have given the secret away.'[10] But that is a different form of security: what mattered was not that no unauthorised person could know the whole story, but that Bletchley Park was not identified as the British codebreaking centre, even though the German Black Book listed at least one member of the security services as having gone 'to Bletchley'. There were no air raids, no suicide squads, no sabotage. This is not solely due to the guards and the perimeter fence: when the civilians in the Home Guard took on the military in a friendly exercise, they breached the wire in a few minutes by tunnelling under it.

The 'need to know' principle was reinforced by the 'once in, never out' rule. There was no escape, unless you were going on to another sigint unit overseas. Otherwise, however genuine and compelling your plea, it was almost impossible to convince the authorities that they should release you to move on to other work.

The internal compartmentalising that Kozaczuk mentions was certainly strict. People might live in the same lodgings, eat together and know each other very well indeed; but if one was working on army and the other on navy Enigma, let alone on Japanese material, then no discussion took place outside. Again I cannot believe that was 100 per cent true, but nothing leaked out as a result.

We rarely knew what was going on in the next room, unless that was literally sharing the same work with us. To judge by the number of rooms in Block F, many other Japanese crypto systems must have been worked on. A few yards along our corridor, nicknamed 'The Burma Road', was a team that included Herbert Murrill, later the BBC's Director of Music. He was another lively character: a senior officer who visited us without warning found him standing on the table using the single overhead light socket, the only power available in the room, for his electric razor. We used to discuss music while we were both off duty, but to this day I have not the foggiest idea what he and his colleagues worked on. One night shift I was called on to do some key-breaking, an activity I had never heard or dreamed of until then, though it had been going on all the time I had been there.

It can be argued that this was overdone. When a codebreaker gets stuck he appeals for guidance to colleagues in his own room. If that fails, he has to fall back on his own wits again. Very probably there is someone in another room who has met and overcome the same problem. Some of the Hut 3, 6 and 8 Enigma experts who had worked together before coming to Bletchley did pool their wits. The girls who tended the Bombes were encouraged to discuss difficulties and exchange ideas. The 'Sunday Soviets' at the radar research unit at Malvern existed for this very purpose. Not only was security unimpaired: quantum leaps forward in their research resulted.

I joined a roomful of twenty or so young men, mostly undergraduates like myself, presided over by two slightly older men, Maurice Wiles and Alexis Vlasto. We were all working on the Japanese Army Air Force code system, called 6633. David Nenk, in a small room nearby, was one step higher but was generally busy with key-breaking. (See the Glossary for this and other technical terms.)

As a newcomer I was set to work on translating signals which had already been stripped of their key and been decoded. I was at once staggered by the volume of useful information most of them carried. They told us the movements of squadrons, described Allied air attacks on airfields and aircraft, fit and unfit airmen, fuel and ammunition stocks, requests for spare parts, and occasionally the impending visit of a senior officer on a tour of inspection. Most of the messages came from Burma, but others were from the areas of south-east Asia or further afield: the East Indies to the south of Burma, and the Philippines to the east. Even those which mentioned only low-ranking personnel were passed on to the indexing staff, and helped to build up a remarkably detailed picture of the enemy's organisation. Even after my brief apprenticeship at Bedford I was dazzled by the picture which this one code painted of the Japanese military machine in action.

Its clear relevance to the bitter fighting now going on had one curious result: although Burma was over 5,000 miles away, Tokyo 6,000 and Singapore 7,000, Block F felt closer to the Japanese war than to Europe and the Mediterranean. It was almost a shock to leave the building at the end of a long shift and emerge into the humdrum Midland landscape with not an Oriental face in sight.

There is so much to say about this and similar code systems, both from the signals and from the intelligence aspects, that I shall give a much fuller description in later chapters.

To return to 1944: the undergraduate tradition led our room to compose a special message on 1 April, purporting to have been sent from Rangoon to signals units throughout Burma to remind them that 'all 6633 signals with the following call-signs are bogus messages'. We dressed it up coquettishly with the proper clerical paraphernalia, put it in the middle of the pile marked for the attention of Maurice or Alexis, and awaited the outcome. An hour or so later Maurice worked down to it. There was a long, tantalising silence, and he asked Alexis to have a look. Both seemed thoughtful, as befitted men who were being told that much of the work they and we had been doing was a waste of time. It was Maurice who noticed the significance of the call-signs above the message: from BI PI I to MO RI SU. I have since learnt that one of Anthony Fitton Brown's team in the next corridor fabricated a similar spoof message which he planted 'on one of our more gullible colleagues'.

Most of the people at Bletchley Park were busy breaking, reading and assessing German signals traffic, primarily that of the Enigma cipher machine in its varied forms, and this has been widely described. The Germans also developed, somewhat later, the *Geheimschreiber* on-line machine, for a small volume of important traffic, and it was a relief that they were not able to switch more signals over to it. There were further signals using hand ciphers, which have been well described. The number of people engaged in Japanese military traffic was much smaller.

As the total numbers increased not only were new huts erected but some began to be replaced by new and solider buildings, designated by letters instead of figures; some of them were large enough to swallow up several different sections. Hut 3, dealing with the intelligence derived from German Army and Air Force Enigma, moved from its first tiny hut to a bigger one next to Hut 6, which did the actual breaking, and a primitive wooden tunnel connected the two huts so that decrypts could be shunted through on a tray without delay. Nearby was Hut 8, for naval Enigma. By summer 1943 the staff of all three huts moved to a large brick building, taking their original hut numbers with them 'to avoid confusion'.

These new buildings were much stronger. Some were made not of brick but of prefabricated concrete slabs, but the structural members in walls and roof were not the usual concrete beams and rafters, but rolled steel joists and uprights, bolted together.

Our part of the Japanese section worked in the second spur of Block F, one of the single-storey blocks, and I do not know far along this long building it extended. I learnt recently that the first spur was 'The Testery', named after Major Tester's unit, including Roy Jenkins, which did much of the early cryptanalytical work on the *Geheimschreiber* and its cover-named FISH traffic. On the other side of the arch, nearer the mansion, was 'The Newmanry', Max Newman's team which attacked FISH by means of the ROBINSON machines. Some of the buildings which housed the later ROBINSONs and the COLOSSUS computers were massive, somewhat in the style of surface bunkers, with even more heavily reinforced roofs. Most of these have only recently been demolished, apparently with great difficulty and to the wonderment of the workmen.

Security within GCHQ was tight in physical as well as personal terms. When pieces of apparatus had to be moved the short distance from Block F to the extension in Block H, everything had to be hidden in brown paper sacks. Things too large to go in a bag, for example the standard 19″ Post Office racks which were widely used, had to be carried at the run, so that no prying eye could see what was afoot, even though the only eavesdroppers who might catch a wondering glimpse of the move would be already inside the security area.

The more massive buildings seem to have been built not merely with air raids or V-weapons in mind. Even the upstairs windows of the two-storey part of Block G were closely barred; the sockets are still visible. The next block, also reinforced, was still in use until 1987, and the group of tall aerials came down about the same time; GCHQ had been there until then. Now most of the former GCHQ site is used by British Telecom.

I never heard of any anti-aircraft defences set up specifically for GCHQ, even though it had been brought out of London for fear of air raids. The original flimsy Huts 3, 6 and 8, in which work of such crucial importance in avoiding defeat and later in helping to ensure and hasten victory was done, would have been wrecked by any bomb falling nearby. It may be relevant that by 1944 the thickly-wooded country to the east, near Woburn, was filled with almost continuous ammunition dumps hidden in shelters under the trees, so no doubt some special precautions were taken for the whole area.

We did occasionally visit the Hollerith hut, which had been moved inside the area at last. Hollerith machines handle punched cards, each containing a wealth of carefully-tabulated information within a small space. If you wish to try a signal against each of 10,000 possible starting-places in a known key, the machine will do that for you at high speed, though you will still have to see which of the 10,000 results makes sense. Provided that there is some way of doing this, the task is worthwhile. The Hollerith machines were always in demand, and Freeborn, who was in charge, was sometimes cast in the role of a prima donna accepting or rejecting suitors. It is not clear whether he was personally ambitious or because he had to protect his machines from overuse and himself from being dictated to.

I must digress here to emphasise that the Hollerith machine was

Aerial view of GCHQ, Bletchley Park, seen from the south-west   (Aerofilms)

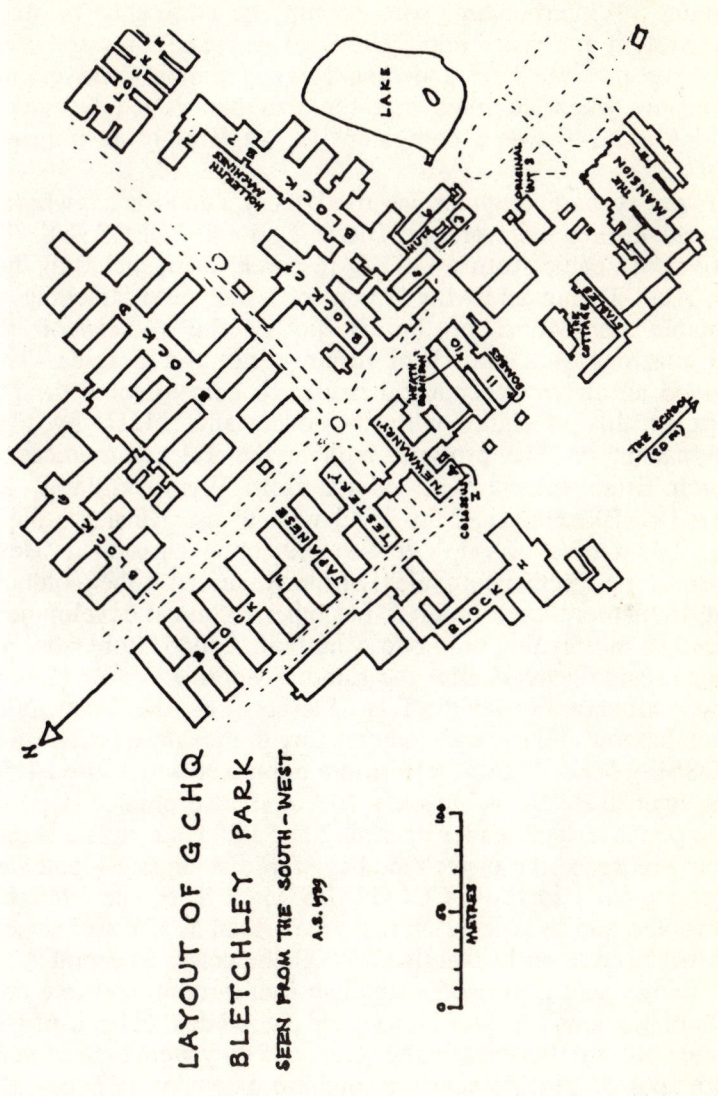

LAYOUT OF GCHQ
BLETCHLEY PARK
SEEN FROM THE SOUTH-WEST

A.S. 1979

Lay-out of Bletchley Park

25

not a computer. This has been widely mis-stated and misunderstood. The confusion arose because similar punched-card machines, produced by IBM among others, were often used in the USA, and the term 'IBM machine' has since become synonymous with 'computer'. Winterbotham, who set up the admirably swift yet secure system for distributing Ultra to overseas commands, and who never pretended to understand cryptography, inadvertently misleads us when he hints that the machine which he saw at Bletchley in 1940 was a computer.[11] It was simply an improved Bombe.

Only one type of computer was used in cryptanalysis anywhere in the world during the war: the Bletchley Park COLOSSUS. The initiative first came from a GCHQ research team, including Jack Good, Alan Turing and Max Newman, which was attacking the formidable non-Morse on-line traffic of the *Geheimschreiber* cipher machine – a ten-wheel affair – not the Enigma. They conceived an electro-mechanical device to help to solve the new settings of this machine, with its cover-name FISH, by high-speed machinery. The protype, built at the Telecommunications Research Establishment with advice from Wynn-Williams, and delivered to Bletchley in May 1943 was, to use Hinsley's happy phrase, 'a bit of a lash-up'. It was thereupon christened 'Heath Robinson', the English equivalent of the American Rube Goldberg. Twenty-four more were ordered, but other technical developments followed so rapidly that only two were built, called 'Robinson' and 'Robinson and Cleaver' after the London store.

Close collaboration with T.H. Flowers, of the Post Office research laboratories, was already leading to the construction of the COLOSSUS Mark I, an all-electronic computer which used 1,500 valves against Heath Robinson's 100, and incorporated a photo-electric punched-tape reader operating at 5,000 characters a second – above this speed the paper tape began to disintegrate – and went into service early in 1944. COLOSSUS Mark II, of late 1944, had 2,400 valves, and by processing tapes in parallel its effective sensing speed had risen to an impressive 25,000 characters a second.[12] The whole thing was the size of a smallish living-room, and like most early computers with valves it produced a good deal of heat. At least ten were built, no two exactly the same, and they were housed in the western spur of Block F and the southern extension of Block H.

The Americans had been working along broadly similar lines. IBM had built an electro-magnetic machine for the Navy which began working in 1944, but it was neither intended nor used for cryptanalysis, and it was inflexible in application. The more flexible ENIAC machine had been designed for Army ballistic calculations. It used 19,000 valves but suffered from some cumbersome storage features, and was still incomplete at the end of the war.[13]

Once off duty we dispersed. In 1939 and 1940 most of the newcomers had been in their twenties or older; many of them remained civilians and were billeted in and around Bletchley. We in the Army were housed at Shenley Road Military Camp, at most half a mile from GCHQ; each of us had a bunk bed and a cupboard to store our belongings. There were always some people asleep who had just come off shift and we tried not to disturb them. We shared the camp with women of the ATS (Auxiliary Territorial Service) who also worked in GCHQ, and as military camps go it was reasonably civilised: a large mess, library, games room, music room and so on. Most of our colleagues were from those sections that so outnumbered ours, modern linguists who like us had been recruited from the middle of their studies. Their quotations from Goethe and Schiller, spoken or sung, left little doubt of their speciality.

Because people were always coming and going, and those off duty were under no compulsion – or at least no enforceable compulsion that we could discover – to stay in camp, it became a sub-standard hotel with no reception desk and nothing to pay. More than once a soldier on night shift or on leave let a personal friend, or a civilian colleague temporarily without lodgings, use his bunk in a Box and Cox arrangement. The one feature not to miss was the weekly pay parade.

The camp commandant was Colonel Fillingham, of the Durham Light Infantry, and the DLI provided the camp staff who kept the place more or less clean and tidy. They can hardly have been the pride of the regiment, most of whom were in Burma with 33 Corps, and there was a culture-gap between them, condemned to this servile role, and us with our hoity-toity ways, our lah-di-dah talk, our regrettable tendency to wear shoes, not boots, and our constant comings and goings between the camp and the mysteries of the security area.

Fillingham was determined to give his guests some semblance of good order and military discipline, though his room for manoeuvre was limited; he was not our employer but our hotel manager. He was, I think, not so much unjust as unimaginative, and he had a bee in his bonnet about the need to preserve the military orthodoxies. He had a very short fuse and could explode if provoked. Michael

Dealtry, from the Bedford course after mine, made 'a witty but ill-judged speech about the day he joined the great unwashed' – perhaps too much in earshot of the DLI, who may have thought they were meant. He was sent for three days' punishment under the command of Captain Blackman, the Adjutant. It was very cold, but 'Dealtry shot a grouse with his rifle, which was entertaining' – and which I should have expected to lead to three more days, or worse.[14]

Towards the end of my stay at Bletchley Park several of us were told that we would be commissioned and sent away for further training. Immediately Fillingham and Blackman sprang into action to ensure that Shenley Road Military Camp should not be disgraced. Before breakfast each day we had to carry out 'Purposeful PT', which meant climbing trees and swinging across rivers on ropes. At least this lacked the sheer corrosive malevolence of Wentworth Woodhouse.

By 1945 Fillingham had managed to insist that students on the Bedford course should spend some time doing PT and military training. This went against the belief of staff and students alike, that the intensive language syllabus demanded exclusive priority and no outside interference. The PT was reluctantly swallowed, but the arrangements made for training on Wednesday afternoons were often erratic and sometimes non-existent, and this pointless waste of time caused a lot of resentment.

I was able to get over to Bedford a few times to see Mary, sometimes by the slow train which still linked Oxford and Cambridge via Bletchley Junction, and at least once, on an unforgettably hot day, by bicycle.

An important feature of Bletchley Park was the music. There was a choir which raised the standard of singing in the local church to extraordinary heights. There was always a Christmas concert and a revue written, sung and acted by those off duty. String quartets regularly visited to give recitals of chamber music, and perhaps the most memorable event was Purcell's *Dido and Aeneas*, put on for four nights in September 1944 by the Bletchley Park Musical Society, with Herbert Murrill directing a baroque-sized string orchestra, a harpsichord smuggled over from Cambridge, six vivacious dancers, an affecting Dido, a good chorus of courtiers, witches and sailors, and scenery made at the military camp. Costumes were borrowed from 'the Cambridge University Greek Play Committee, Girton College, and Oxford University Dramatic Society'.

3

Marching Orders

By now I had unexpectedly become a Sergeant and ate in the Sergeants' Mess; only at an establishment like GCHQ could one leap the two intervening ranks in one go. Mary had scarcely sewn on my three stripes when I learnt that the commission already hinted at was on its way for me and for eight others: Jock Anderson, Marcus Crowley, Joe Cunningham, Tony Fenn-Wiggin, David Jones, Peter Soskice, David Warwick and Tim Whewell. To make us still more military we were to go on a course at Rushden Hall.

We arranged to meet. The Japanese linguists just outnumbered the German, but we were united in our ignorance of Rushden Hall, and consulted the Adjutant. It was in Northamptonshire and was 'something to do with REME, the Royal Electrical and Mechanical Engineers'. Curiouser and curiouser – but we were given a few days' leave to get our uniforms and get ourselves organised. A new personal number also arrived, much easier to remember: P 329137.

One difference between the commissioned and the non-commissioned is that the uniform for the latter, shabby and ill-fitting though it may be, particularly in the British Army, is provided free; officers buy their own. There is much more to get: service dress as well as battle-dress, shirts, ties, an immense greatcoat instead of the absurd gas-cape of the private soldier, a hat, more comfortable boots that actually fit, khaki handkerchieves by tradition, a short swagger-stick, and a pair of pips. Most people, knowing that the transition from second lieutenant is only a matter of time, buy two pairs. Optimists get three; only the immodestly ambitious buy a pair of crowns as well. My prospective father-in-law kindly gave me his Sam Browne belt from the 1914–18 war, in which he had won a Military Cross.

I forget where I first tried the complete ensemble, feeling that I was impersonating someone else, and getting used to being saluted, yet still having to look out for officers of field rank (Major and above) to salute. It's easy to see that someone is an officer, but are

Course at Rushden Hall, summer 1944

Soskice   Jones   Warwick   Anderson
Whewell   Cunningham   Fenn-Wiggin   Stripp   Crowley

the two things just visible on the shoulders of that tall middle-aged chap two pips or one pip and a crown? Better play safe and salute. He returns it, looking amused: he was a mere lieutenant. Next comes a tall boyish fellow, surely a one-pipper like me? He looks put out; it was a crown. Short men are no problem.

Rushden is just east of Wellingborough and some 12 miles north-west of Bedford, and the Hall was a small manor-house, built in the local stone and used as the REME training centre. We were expected and made to feel at home. What exactly had we come to do? We were nonplussed.

'To take part in the special course.'

'Naturally; but which special course? What do you want us to train you for?'

'Very difficult', we told him. 'We aren't allowed to tell you. It's Top Secret.'

'Of course. But we can't help you unless we know what it's all about.'

We explained that this Top Secret really was inviolable. We were sorry, we trusted him, but the decision was not in our hands. Could he get on the phone to GCHQ?

He retired, looking shaken, and returned half an hour later, having got nowhere.

'The War Office say they will write and tell us as soon as they find the right person to ask. I see your point about the secrecy. It's not your fault. Come and have a drink. Then we'll find you some rooms and have dinner.'

They did their best for us. In the end they laid on a typical officer-training programme. Each man takes it in turn to lead the rest ('I am in command; follow me') in surmounting some unnatural hazard: getting a heavy metal drum across a river without dropping it in, hauling it over a brick wall fifteen feet high, or using an odd collection of planks to make a bridge. As with our drill at the unspeakable I. Corps Depot, this team worked together and tried to cover up the inadequacies of each leader in turn. Fenn-Wiggin, I think, carried it off best, having a natural authority that the rest of us lacked; he knew when to relax. We learned to ride motor-bikes and, working in pairs, made for some capricious map-references; each had a feature that we had to note down to show we had been there.

One night there was a dance, to records on a radiogram. The permanent staff, who throughout our stay put themselves out to welcome us, brought their wives, who gave us kind smiles and thanked us when, duty bound, we invited them to dance. They may already have guessed that none of us was much good at it, but they bore it graciously and we lamed none of them. Slow waltzes seemed to be the safest. My memories of Rushden Hall, such as survive, are warm.

We were sent on, inexplicably, to their depot near Nottingham: larger, more formal, but still keen to fit us in. 'The War House tell me that you do Japanese crossword puzzles. That's beyond our resources. We can train you in sabotage, which is presumably what this Top Secret stuff is about?'

We protested. 'We aren't going to be saboteurs. The Japanese crossword puzzle idea is warmer but we can't tell you more than that.'

'The sabotage it will have to be. There's no danger. Come and have a drink.'

We spent the first two days on further motor-cycle excursions, and Joe Cunningham and I managed to convert one mission into an unforgettable visit to the stone leaves of Southwell Minster. Few if any of us had flown before, so we had a practice flight in an ancient and creaking Anson – a sensible precaution for a budding parachutist. Less obvious was the reason for our being taken to Bulwell where we were shown, under strict vows of secrecy, the 'swimming' tanks that could be used in an invasion.

Next we were taught how to blow up railway lines and bridges. Nottinghamshire County Council had apparently produced a list of derelict objects that they would like to have removed, free of charge, and our explosives expert trained us in using Amanol and 808, anti-tank mines, sticky-bombs and slow and quick fuses. The dreary countryside echoed with the sound of our explosions and our ears rang. We took it in turns to booby-trap a ruinous cottage, using push *and* pull detonators to fox the opposing team, but with a gentleman's agreement not to connect them to explosives. Neither team could defeat the other. Finally we practised abseiling down the side of a three-storey building, on the assumption that we had landed on the roof and had a long rope handy. It seemed a little far-fetched – but our instructors in all these skills knew their stuff and were a pleasure to try to emulate. It is the drill-sergeant and his underlings who are so often, as one of our squad pointedly remarked, rancid. On our last night there was another informal dance, dominated by the safer slow waltzes; someone must have rung ahead from Rushden Hall.

The next day we were told that travel warrants had come through for all of us. A couple were to go back to GCHQ, one to London, one or two to the Mediterranean. Soskice and I were to join 'Group Marr-Johnson'.

'That snob', said someone in the know. 'Bad luck. It means New Delhi.'

We were given a week's embarkation leave. When it ended I travelled up from London to Yorkshire and made my way to Wentworth Woodhouse, remembering to avoid the tradesmen's entrance this time, and make for the mansion itself. They searched their files.

'You've another week's leave. Go back home and enjoy yourself.'

I spent a night there first. It was a cheerless dinner despite some merriment among the permanent staff: the Earl of Northesk and others. The next morning I slipped away unobtrusively; in the distance the staff corporals were still ranting at their squads. After a further week in London, with renewed greetings and renewed farewells, I took the precaution of telephoning.

'Yes, this time it's on. Get up here as quick as you can.'

Almost predictably, when I arrived I was told to stay within reach; there might be several days to kill, and they would try to arrange something interesting for me and three others who were killing time. The next day was spent on the 'something interesting': we were to impersonate enemy agents and make our way to a nearby reservoir where we must drop an imaginary packet of poison into the Sheffield water supply without being observed. So even our own Corps didn't know, or care, what we were doing and what we needed to be trained for.

We had a small truck at our disposal and were pleased to see four oafish corporals, including my pet abomination, following us in a car, trying to look like civilians. We told our driver that he was free for the day but was to pick us up at 1700 hrs. Two of my colleagues were about my age; the other was older, unassuming and studious in appearance. He offered no suggestions but fell in readily with ours. We had coffee, studied our maps, and decided to have a leisurely day while the corporals waited; by late afternoon they should have become bored and careless. We observed with malice that it was beginning to drizzle. After lunch it started raining more heavily, so we went to a cinema, had tea, and split up to make separate detours, approaching the reservoir from different directions and at varying intervals. Each of us in turn saw the four loafing about, trying in vain

33

to merge into their surroundings, and looking very damp and dejected. Serve them right.

We had no difficulty in mingling with passers-by, strolling past a far corner while the watchers were watching the one obvious approach, almost shoulder to shoulder. We jettisoned our imaginary poison, met at the truck and told the driver to take a circuitous route back to the Depot, entering by the back gate. He entered into the spirit of it. Much later the corporals returned by the main gate, looking furious.

The Training Officer summoned us to hear his verdict on the day's events: we had all been recognised.

'When and where?', we asked. He refused to be drawn.

We guffawed. 'They're pulling your leg. They haven't the foggiest idea how or when we did it.'

He persisted. The monosyllabic man broke his silence. 'Are you seriously saying that you accept the word of those detestable buffoons in preference to ours?'

The Training Officer capitulated.

The following evening half a dozen of us were invited − a new word − to join a team looking out for heath fires near Penistone. It had been a warm summer and the parched heather in the peaty soil could smoulder underground for days. It was a pleasant evening and a good cause, so we accepted. We waited half an hour for the truck, and eventually ran it to earth. To use John Trench's immortal phrase, 'The lorries, by a mischance that will surprise no one who has served in the Army, were waiting for us at the wrong gate'.

We drove up to the gaunt moorland, grey and tawny except where the Ewden Beck made a vivid green oasis, and as the light faded we could see occasional flickers of flame, mostly on the far side of the valley. We each had a beater to deal with any fires within reach, but few were; each flame burned for only half a minute or less, and by the time we reached it there was nothing but a smoking patch of heather. From time to time a grouse would burst from cover almost under our feet with a shockingly loud chortle. As an untravelled Southerner I had never heard them before.

Next day I was told that I had one more night before going to join a convoy at Glasgow. I was able to take the train across to spend it at Bradford, where Mary was staying with her aunt and grandmother.

At Glasgow I found a hotel where I had a bath and a princely breakfast, and made my way, as directed, to King George V dock.

The officer in charge was scornful. 'You should have been here two days ago.' No co-ordination, as usual. But what was I wanted for? 'You're Security Officer for your ship. You know what to do?'

The same old story: they too had assumed I was in Field Security. I received an armlet with 'Security Officer' in large red letters, and invented a job for the next day or two. The lists told me which troops were due to arrive; when they turned up I told them impartially that they were too early or too late but I would do my best to fit them in. I checked them off as impressively as I could and told the Purser, who told another officer where they should go. When they got there they were told it was the wrong place. 'But for me', I told myself, 'they would be standing on the quayside still.'

Eventually most of the list was complete, but for a few would-be deserters and some who were genuinely ill, and I reported the omissions, which the real Field Security would have to look into. 'You don't board the ship here', I was told. 'Take your kit, have some dinner, and go down to Gourock, the Tail of the Bank. The convoy is forming up there.'

It became more Alice in Wonderland all the time: was I now to navigate as well? We drove down to Gourock and on to a pierhead, where a launch was moored with the crew standing ready.

'Quick, the convoy is waiting.' Impossible. 'Where's your kit? Get on board as quick as you can.' I scrambled on, the lines were cast off, and as the coxswain went Full Ahead another figure rushed out of the tiny office.

'He's not for Q3. He's for Q13. She's right over there', pointing far out towards Holy Loch.

I learned later that Q3 went only as far as the Eastern Mediterranean, and I wonder how different the rest of my life might have been if the message had arrived a few minutes later. Would they have passed me on to Delhi or found it simpler to retrain me for some Middle East post? I also wonder how we ever succeeded in sending our invasion troops to the right place at the right time.

Meanwhile I scrambled aboard, and again it seemed that the world had been waiting for me, not the opposite. The Ship's Security Officer was needed for this and for that awkward decision, and above all for censorship.

I can still remember that job, for which no doubt other Field Security officers are trained. Every umpteenth letter had to be sampled, and all letters not in English had to be handed to me unsealed. The *Strathnaver*, the P and O ship on which I had at last arrived, was supposed to carry over 1,000 passengers in normal times, and it now held about three times as many. Sacks of mail awaited my examination. Nobody had told me on what basis to sample, so I started on the foreign-language mail.

'Cher M. Duparac', 'Exmo Sr Antonio Ferreira', 'Kjaeledegge', 'Sevgili Bayan Arda', 'Muy señor mio', 'Liefje' – an avalanche of letters, and none of those which I could understand looked in the least suspicious. No stilted phrases suggesting hidden messages, no traces of invisible ink that the amateur could see, no suspicious dots under selected letters. I passed the first batch. Many of the ones in English, which I decided to open only if they aroused my suspicions, bore those pathetic acronyms on the back of the envelope: ITALY 'I Truly Always Love You; HOLLAND 'How Our Love Lasts and Never Dies; and the curious SWALK 'Sealed With A Loving Kiss'. If this was a code it had been in force since the 1914–18 war.

Further sacks were already arriving, so I went on deck. It was a clear evening and as we slipped down the Clyde estuary there were ships in every direction, all apparently in our convoy, some dozen or so in all. They included the Polish vessel *Batory* and one of the Empress line, which was said to be carrying some VIP.

Who starts these rumours? Are they ever right?

Our course lay through the Irish Sea and for some reason we paused in Cork harbour before sailing fairly far out into the Atlantic. The Normandy invasions had taken place but some U-boats were known to be still operating from bases on the French Atlantic coast. No doubt we had an escort, but I cannot recall its being in sight very often.

The ship's routine retained some peacetime features, like estimating the daily total of miles sailed, but that was all. The sheer weight of numbers overwhelmed us. There were men everywhere: sleeping in hammocks in the 'tween-decks, taking it in turns to sleep in cabins and dormitories, making the decks invisible in fine weather. The overloaded galley, serving meals in relays, and the generally low standards of wartime rationing, made the food for the NCOs and other ranks wretchedly poor, and whenever we took turns as orderly officer we were dismayed at the difference between their meals and ours. I learned much later that a colleague of mine on another ship in the convoy had a narrow escape when he was doing his rounds. On asking 'Any complaints?' in one canteen he was shown a bowl of alleged chicken soup in which an identifiable jawbone, complete with teeth, stood out in horrid relief. He was a kindly man, and his comment 'Our chicken in the officers' mess wasn't too good' was intended to reassure, but he may have only narrowly escaped lynching. The same was true of accommodation: I shared a cabin with the ship's Baggage Officer, an armbanded amateur like myself.

A friendly and unpretentious General and his ADC joined me as I leaned on the rail and watched the sunset. I think I remember him as General Anderson – but could he have wound up affairs in First Army so soon, and if so where was he bound in so leisurely a fashion? Generals and even lesser mortals were already travelling by air. We chatted and he asked me what I was doing. Feeling absurd, I tried to explain that I was not allowed to say, and fortunately he understood the dilemma. I now realise that as an Army commander he would have been an authorised recipient of Top Secret Ultra sigint and would probably have guessed what I was up to. I was grateful to him: up to what point does a raw one-pip second lieutenant stick to his guns and decline to answer a General's questions?

The weather was passable and the Rock of Gibraltar stood out clearly as we passed through the Straits. There was a good view of Cap Bon in Tunisia, where the remains of the Afrika Korps had surrendered in May, thus enabling convoys like ours to take the Mediterranean route rather than the long crawl round the Cape of Good Hope. As we neared Port Said further sackfuls of mail built up. 'Chérie', 'Egregio Signore'; 'Lieber Franz! Ich schreibe Dir von einem Ort nicht weit von Palästina ....' Could that really be dangerous? How far is 'not far'? And where would the convoy be by the time this letter, perhaps from one Jewish friend to another, ran the slightest risk of falling into enemy hands? I let it go uncut.

The bumboat men of Port Said, clinging precariously to the tops of their masts, implored us to buy their leather purses, wallets, handbags, hassocks and knick-knacks. Frantic bargaining ensued before the convoy moved down the canal towards Suez. Mirages arose on both banks as the heat increased, and as usual there were rumours of deserters jumping overboard into the warm shallow water in the hope of making a getaway. A long wait at the Bitter Lakes while a northbound convoy passed ('Lucky blighters') then on to Port Suez and the stifling journey down the Red Sea. By now we were in tropical kit: bush jackets and those remarkable long-legged khaki shorts.

Somewhere in this stage of the voyage I developed a high temperature and was sent aft to the isolation ward with suspected smallpox. The only other patient, safely round several corners, was an Indian sergeant with leprosy. We were lucky to have more space to move and breathe in, as the rest of the ship was torrid, but the stern is too smelly an area, and too close to the rumble and clatter of the ship's propellors, to be palatial. Someone else, I reflected, would now take over as Security Officer and was welcome to the job of embarking several thousand troops on the dockside at Bombay. Meanwhile the heat was still growing, flying-fish were everywhere, and once Aden was passed – a derelict hole, we thought – the breeze freshened and the stars in the indigo sky grew enormous.

Whether it was really smallpox, its impact blunted by vaccinations from the age of fourteen onwards, or a belated dose of chicken-pox, the doctors could not agree. I spent the next ten days or so in the isolation hospital on Colaba Point, near the tip of the peninsula on which Bombay stands, and certainly isolated from its more unsavoury parts and open to the occasional sea breeze. Then there was the long train journey to Delhi, some 750 miles away.

The compartments were spacious and solidly comfortable, and the train stopped longer at the larger stations so that we could have our meals in the restaurants there. The 'mofussil', the undifferentiated Indian countryside, from desert to low hills or scrubby heaths, slid past continuously leaving no single feature to catch the eye. I began to grasp the immensity of what is not just a country but a sub-continent.

At last we reached Delhi. The Railway Transport Officer looked at my travel warrant. 'GHQ(X); that means you stay the night in the tented camp and they'll fix up transport.' Next morning a truck took me out to GHQ(X), the designation of WEC, the Wireless Experimental Centre.

4

Delhi

WEC occupied the buildings of Ramjas College, a former part of Delhi University, perched on an isolated hill some miles outside the city on the Rohtak road. The hill was idyllically named Anand Parbat, 'the hill of happiness', and was crowned by the college buildings and outbuildings which now formed the security area. At the bottom of the hill, further away from the road, was the lower camp where we lived in rows of standard-issue Public Works Department bungalows. In each were ten or so rooms opening off the long front verandah with 'bathrooms' behind; these were cubicles with a canvas bath and a 'thunderbox'. Majors and above had two rooms. In hot weather we often moved our beds on to the verandah, never forgetting the obligatory mosquito-net. The rule was to wear long sleeves and long trousers as an anti-malarial precaution after twilight, though most people preferred shorts and short sleeves during the day.

My servant or 'bearer' was Abdul Hamid, a cheerful and resourceful man who looked after me and my possessions devotedly. He must have been born about the time his notorious namesake the Sultan of Turkey died. I settled in and walked up the stony track to the security area, where I was issued with a pass and introduced to a roomful of people informally presided over by Hugh Lloyd-Jones. The room was square and high, and had a huge old-fashioned fan in the ceiling which revolved just fast enough to give a gentle breeze without swishing our papers on the floor or disturbing the fat pigeon who sat on the blade and spent most of his life placidly going round and round. When the fan stopped he stayed there, giddy or not.

In the hot weather the temperature rose to 120° in the shade, but there in central India the humidity was generally so low that it felt cooler than this suggests. When it became humid the windows were opened fully and woven screens of 'khaskhas tatti' were inserted in their place, which the local women cooled by constantly ladling

The author at the Wireless Experimental Centre, Delhi, summer 1944

water on to them. The gentle plash of the water and the low murmur of their voices blended with the heat to give a soporific effect.

When the monsoon was close the humidity went up sharply and 'prickly heat' added to our discomfort. The storm-clouds would draw nearer each day and eventually arrived and broke in sheets of water and fierce silver lightning in the thundery purple sky.

WEC numbered a little over one thousand in all, including Army, RAF, Indian and West African service personnel as well as the Indian civilian wireless operators, the intercept crews on whose skill the whole operation ultimately depended. The sections were:

- A: administration
- B: collating and evaluating of signals intelligence, and compiling of Japanese order of battle
- C: breaking and translating of intercepted signals
- D: traffic analysis of radio networks
- E: radio intercepting

of which B, C, D, and E describe the complete codebreaking process in reverse order. Our C Section concentrated on the main Army and Army Air Force codes used in Burma and the south-east Asia area, and I was again assigned to the Army Air Force code system 6633, but many of my colleagues in the same room were busy on other things.

The unit felt very different from Bletchley Park in many ways. WEC was barely a fifth of its size, but there the Japanese section had been a small exotic plant grafted on to a large and vigorous German parent. Here everyone was concerned with Japanese codes or ciphers, and it was much larger than Block F at GCHQ. Moreover the presence in the next building of B Section, which passed the tactical and strategic assessments straight on to the various head-quarters, and the fact that we all lived and messed together, should have given a sense of immediacy. It was possible to visualise our individual jobs as part of the whole and not just as separate chores on some vast assembly line.

Nevertheless in our daily affairs there were closed doors between one section and another, far more potent and exclusive than any at GCHQ. I learnt quite recently, and by chance, that B Section had a map room which could have told us the answers to questions which held us up: what and where is RABAURU (kana spelling for Rabaul in New Britain) or KABIEN (Kavieng in New Guinea, and not far from Guadalcanal and the other Solomon Islands)? We didn't know that the map room existed and they didn't know of our problems. Communications between B and C Sections took place only at the top, and section heads are not the people to consult frequently over obscure place-names. Hence needless inaccuracies and time wasted: security turned into absurdity.

This rigidity seemed to be built into the organisation. I am told that the head of WEC, Lieutenant-Colonel Marr-Johnson, was a man of charm and ability and a good friend to those who knew him well. To most of us he seemed brusque and inaccessible. One or two able men who showed dangerously independent judgement were exiled to cheerless assignments elsewhere. At Bletchley Park Denniston and Travis had been known first and foremost for their code-breaking abilities; given this professional expertise their administrative control, however casually and often charmingly exercised, was never in question. Marr-Johnson's ability as a codebreaker was unknown to us, and our dealings with him were purely of an administrative and disciplinary type.

I cannot testify to the reputation for snobbery that had, as it were, preceded him, because it was not his habit to converse with mere lieutenants, but his alleged branding of a Major who had been a businessman in India before the war as 'that Bombay carpet-bagger' lends it some credence. We readily believed the rumour that while on a liaison job in Washington he turned up in riding-breeches on a white horse that he tethered in front of the office. It is a pity that we never knew him better. Fortunately our other masters, and particularly Major Divers, head of C Section, were easy to work for and get on with. But the humdrum military ethos and banishing of the unconventional prevented WEC from ever becoming a Bletchley Park in Asia. The informality praised by Lord Dacre and others as contributing to Bletchley's success could not survive in the hierarchy of WEC.

I soon moved from Lloyd-Jones' room to Robin Gibson's, where we were concerned not so much with routine translation as with tougher problems: messages which could not be dealt with because the keybook or substitution table had been changed, or the indicator lost, or because either the Japanese operator or our own had slipped up. Such messages could play havoc with shift-working, especially when a badly mangled message seemed to contain urgent information; it continued to go round and round in your head long after you had given it up as hopeless. Sometimes light would dawn, or at least a promising line of attack would suggest itself, some hours later, and mean an unexpected return in someone else's shift to try it out.

The tide had turned in Burma during 1944. General Slim, who had commanded the Allied troops through most of the dismal retreat during 1942, and the mixed fortunes of 1943, had defended Imphal and Kohima against fanatical attacks, inflicting unusually heavy losses on the enemy in the process, and had then launched an unexpectedly vigorous pursuit as the Japanese retreated in some disorder. He was now preparing to maintain and increase the pressure so as to defeat them decisively. To win the campaign it would not be enough to push them further south and risk ding-dong movements *ad infinitum*; he must destroy their ability to operate as an organised army and air force, preferably before the monsoon brought all major military activity to a standstill in early May 1945.

The Japanese Army and Air Force in Burma now faced a totally new experience for them: approaching defeat. It was their turn to be outnumbered in the air and outfought on the ground. The change of fortunes in the air was especially striking: whereas Allied aircraft design had improved by leaps and bounds during the last two years, the Japanese were still using the same types of aircraft as in 1942–43. Their performance could not equal that of the more modern British and American aircraft in the area. Moreover, as the Americans advanced in the Pacific, Tokyo was having to move some air force units out of Burma to countries like Indo-China, which were more exposed to the US island-hopping moves towards Japan. Some reinforcements were brought in, but many units were seriously below strength. New aircraft, and even older machines, were being built or modified for *kamikaze* attacks on the US fleet – the suicidal tactic by which the whole aircraft, stuffed full of explosive, is deliberately crashed on to a naval vessel in order to cause the maximum damage.

Those enemy aircraft that were available in Burma were handicapped by their exclusive role of army support. They rarely flew offensive sorties against Allied aircraft and it was becoming harder to challenge them to do so. From time to time a sizeable formation was brought together to attack British and Indian troops who were menacing their positions, but then that formation in turn would be jumped on by Allied fighters which at last included Hurricanes and Spitfires, and by the end of 1944 the number of enemy aircraft had shrunk still further.

One of our tasks was to keep track of their position, state of readiness, ability to operate effectively, reserves of fuel, ammunition, pilots, crew, aircraft, immediate plans and longer-term intentions. There was no shortage of 6633 traffic, which interlocked usefully with BULBUL, as we called another army air force code which concentrated more on immediate tactical matters such as the detailing of aircraft for specific missions. Fuller details of these code systems and the information they gave us are in Chapters Seven and Eight.

Very few WEC officers had cars, and journeys to Delhi meant using one of the regular trips by Army truck, hiring a bicycle from the main gate for one rupee eight annas a day – no fun when it was really hot – or taking a 'ghari', a small two-wheeled horse-drawn carriage with driver in front and room for two passengers, facing rearwards, behind. By day this was safe enough, but two WEC officers whose driver took the forbidden short cut back through Karol Bagh one night were never seen again.

Several of us used to have Saturday lunch at a rather plush restaurant (the Cecil?) in New Delhi from time to time. There was no feeling of guilt at eating well provided it was European fare, but we were discouraged from eating Indian food because of the constant fear of another rice famine, caused less by overall shortage than by the immense difficulty of moving enough rice from one teeming part of India to another when a shortage was forecast.

I joined an art class in drawing from life, which met in a cellar of that gargantuan Lutyens creation, the Secretariat. It was impressive in sheer bulk, but by dwarfing everything within sight it appeared absurdly grandiose. The contrast of its vast, calculated landscaping with the crooked and crowded alley-ways of Old Delhi was too severe. Instead of elevating the spirit, as he had presumably intended, it squashed it flat. My art lessons at school had been timid affairs, with the emphasis on drawing outlines and filling them in. Now we were given a fat soft crayon each and told to make bold strokes from the start, leaving thick shadows and contrasting background to suggest shape and contour. Our models were Indian soldiers in many varieties of tribal dress. Their emphatic cheekbones and deep-set eyes made it easier to forget the prissy tradition I had been taught.

Another trip to Delhi was prompted by an unusual incident. After a routine session of paying monthly bills I had several of my cheques bounced back to me. I knew from my pay chit that I was in credit, so in some perplexity I consulted my Adjutant. He soon realised what had happened: a clerk in the Army Pay Office at Meerut had written my initial 'A' carelessly so that the two sides didn't meet at the top.

The bank had presumably read this as an 'H' and started up a new account for a non-existent 'H. Stripp'.

The Adjutant rubbed his hands. 'I was a bank manager before the war. If I were your bank manager the last sort of letter I should like to receive would run like this' – and with some relish he dictated the following broadside:

'I am surprised to have these cheques returned to me, since I believe there is sufficient balance in my account to cover them. Should this be so, action will be taken by my solicitors.'

He predicted that by return I should receive an abject apology and a warm invitation to call in and receive an explanation from the manager in person. He was right. It was the only time I have been offered sherry in a bank. I gathered that the point at issue was a possible action for defamation of character. If a bank returns a cheque it implies that the drawer is at least inept and possibly insolvent, and thus it impugns his reputation as an 'officer and gentleman' in a way that could affect him professionally. To do this to a customer who is solvent is to render the bank liable for substantial damages. Is this still true when the banks are among the first to encourage us to borrow money and live beyond our means, and when it is the possession of a 'credit' card – really a card to show their approval for getting into debt – which shows our financial status? Another time it would be tempting to refuse the sherry, and sue – but though I have often written my name appallingly badly I have never succeeded in landing myself in this interesting position again.

After the Allied victory in Burma in early May 1945, three months before Hiroshima, there was less to do but work did not stop entirely. Many Japanese had been trapped on the west bank of the Irrawaddy or between it and the Sittang and Salween rivers, and were making frantic efforts to get out. Even after Japan's surrender in August, large groups were still stranded there. Most of them did not hear of the Emperor's order to lay down their arms, and many of those who did refused to comply with it. They could not believe it. Japanese and British officers had to go forward in pairs under a white flag to convince them that the war was over, and British signals officers surprised their enemy counterparts by openly intervening in their radio networks to pass the surrender message to them.[15]

An excellent scheme, designed to occupy us profitably in our free time, was called EVT: Education and Vocational Training. All personnel, of all ranks, were invited to send in a form showing which subjects they would like to study and which, if any, they were prepared to teach. It worked well and was good for morale as well as for learning. After toying with a class in Greek tragedy, which showed me, to my chagrin, how much more Greek I had forgotten than my colleagues, I discovered that Vernon Butcher offered a class in musical composition. He was an excellent musician and teacher, and I was the only student; the subject also prospered because only a few doors away from my room lived Peter Racine Fricker (a pupil of Matyas Seiber who in turn had been a pupil of Bela Bartok), who soon after made so powerful an impression with his early works.

On the night that the General Election result, with a win for Labour, was announced, 'The Red Flag' was sung in the Officers' Mess – admittedly as a solo – while despair and horror reigned in the Sergeants' Mess.[16] By a wise and tolerant decision we were allowed to create our own 'House of C', in which all ranks could debate the burning issues of the day from any political angle short of mutiny. A good deal of steam was profitably and harmlessly let off here, and though the standard of debate varied, at least it rarely sank below Westminster's standard.

An unforgettable open-air performance of *A Midsummer Night's Dream* was put on in Delhi by the WEC Players. It was produced by Norman Gass, formerly of Oxford University Dramatic Society, and was staged in the wooded grounds of the Lodi Gardens. They revealed a Puck who darted between the trees faster than any known before, and Theseus and Hippolyta made, in the words of the SEAC magazine *Phoenix*, 'a thrilling entry along the Lodi ramparts high above our heads, silhouetted by the rushlights of their retinue'. It was intended to run for four nights but was extended for ten in all, with every house packed; 'Indian girl students, studying Shakespeare at school, were among the most appreciative in the audience'.

At a much lower level I was persuaded to play the part of a foppish young-man-about-town in *Laughter in Court*, a Wodehouse-like comedy put on at WEC; and GHQ India Command arranged a cricket match between the Airborne and the Chairborne, in which the headquarters staff were carried on, chairs and all, while their opponents arrived by parachute.

Several of my colleagues flew to Saigon and other Japanese headquarters hoping, largely in vain, to collect crypto material before they destroyed it, and other schemes were hatched to keep us busy inside WEC. Marr-Johnson launched a project to compile a history of WEC's work and of Japanese cryptography by collecting all the relevant information on enormous cardboard sheets to be stored in large wooden boxes – all specially made. Robin Gibson tells me something I had quite forgotten: that I 'rebelled against this tomfoolery and noted all the details on standard 5″ by 3″ cards'.[16]

While the Japanese were burning their records and we were trying to immortalise some of ours, others were judged expendable. There must have been millions of decrypts and rough drafts of translations which were expendable in the official view, and their destruction began. The day of the shredder had not arrived in India, and most intelligence units were ordered to burn their surplus paper. One colleague speaks of the CSDIC bonfire at the Red Fort 'which turned the sky over part of Delhi black for three weeks'. For a time I became WEC Burning Officer, a post not in the establishment, which may have been Marr-Johnson's revenge for my spurning his gross card-index. I coolly presided over a warmish Sergeant and a gang of really hot young men who shovelled whole truck-loads of paper into a poorly-designed and hastily-built incinerator, from the chimney of which, as we watched, Top Secret documents wafted, half-burnt, over the astonished western suburbs of New Delhi. It is hardly surprising that after this episode I found I could be spared to take a week's leave.

5

Naini Tal, Agra and Abbottabad

Wilfrid Noyce, also of C Section, was off to climb somewhere in the Himalayas; he was a promising climber who went twice to the South Col, once without oxygen, in the 1953 Everest expedition, and was later killed in an accident while climbing in the Soviet Union. Bernard Newman and I agreed on a more modest objective in the same area: Naini Tal, one of the hill-stations close to the Himalayas. There was a slow train across the plain to Bareilly, where we changed to a narrow gauge. The terrain altered as we reached the foothills and arrived at the terminus, Kathgodam; thence by rickety coach driven by a Sikh who worried us by gesturing at the views on the left while he negotiated hairpin bends to the right, with a sheer drop below. As the road twisted and climbed there were signposts to other hill-stations: Almora and Ranikhet.

The particular charm of Naini Tal is its setting beside an oval lake surrounded by seven hills. The first evening Bernard added to my slender knowledge of the modern English novel by lending me an exercise book which he had filled with his favourite extracts. Apart from reading, lazing in the garden or walking round the lake – there were sailing dinghies but I think they were privately owned – the thing to do was to climb the hills: Tonnochy is the only name I can remember. There, we were promised, we should have a view of the distant Himalayas; but although we climbed one or other of the hills every morning there was no view worth speaking of. On the last morning we tried again. At first it seemed no better, but then we suddenly saw the whole row of gleaming white peaks absurdly high in the sky though they were some seventy-five miles away, standing clear above the intervening foothills and the dull clouds that shrouded them: Trisul, East Trisul, Nanda Kot and, massively topping them all, Nanda Devi, 25,645 feet.

With this spectacular send-off we returned to the rest-house, packed our bags and endured again the hair-raising descent to Kathgodam. We had arranged to break our return journey with a detour to Agra. Would the Taj Mahal disappoint us, after all that had been written about it? Was it overrun by tourists, guides, touts and stall-keepers?

Mercifully, no. The buildings are so finely proportioned, and the setting on the river-bank so striking, that there was nothing jaded about it. Shah Jehan's marble tomb, Kipling's 'ivory gate through which all good dreams pass', with its long pools and slender minarets, justifies and survives the admiring hordes that go to see it. We were lucky in having enough time to return to see it by moonlight.

We had debated what we should find when we got back to WEC. I soon discovered: I was posted to the Wireless Experimental Depot at Abbottabad, near Rawalpindi in the North-West Frontier Province, and only some 120 miles from the Afghan border. My job was to replace Geoffrey Bownas in the Persian section there. He was a year older than me and had flown back to England to be demobilised.

Abdul Hamid pleaded with me to take him there, and perhaps later to England, but I knew it would not work. Each large camp has its own grapevine of regular and reserve servants, and would resent the arrival of an intruder. His family ties would tug at him and before long he would regretfully find them too strong. As for coming to England as my personal servant, he simply could not believe that the palmy Victorian days were past and that his 'officer sahib' would shortly be an impecunious second-year undergraduate: it must be one of those mad English jokes. But he took it well and we parted good friends.

The train journey via Lahore was some 400 miles and at Rawalpindi we changed to the narrow-gauge train for Havelian. On the platform I recognised two of our sergeants from WEC, and as the train was packed full I invited them to share my more spacious compartment. When the ticket-collector arrived he raised his eyebrows but connived at this infringement, and I had a long conversation with him. For most British officers in India the officers' mess was the be-all and end-all of life; contacts with Indians were rare, artificial and often tacitly discouraged. This was a tragedy: attitudes became rigid and misconceptions flourished in a country that can offer particularly warm and rewarding friendships between people of many races as equals.

At Havelian we had another breathtaking drive round a tortuous road to Abbottabad, an agreeable small town set in a broad valley with low hills nearby and mountains not far away: Jammu and Kashmir to the east, Chitral to the north and Afghanistan to the west. The Khyber Pass is only about 100 miles due west, and Kabul 120 miles further on. Gurkha regiments had long been quartered at Abbottabad and a few miles north-east was the large artillery depot at Kakul. But the town itself was a thriving hotch-potch in a mainly Muslim area dominated by the high-spirited Pathan tribesmen, Afghan in origin but long occupying both sides of the frontier and speaking various forms of Pushtu.

My job, however, was to study Farsi, the main language of Iran and Afghanistan and much closer to the languages of north-west Europe than many found in between: *dukhtar* for daughter, *madar* for mother and *pidar* for father. It is a beautiful and flexible language with a strikingly simple structure and a fine literature, written in the Arabic script and borrowing a few words from Arabic itself. My *munshi*, or teacher, was a capable young man from Kabul, and I spent the first few weeks much as I had at Bedford, hard at work learning the language, but here with the comfortable advantage of private tuition in an easier tongue.

The Wireless Experimental Depot had been established before the war or even, by one account, before the first world war, to intercept and read Persian, Afghan and probably Soviet signals, though the latter were certainly not being read now. It was a small unit, with the officers' mess numbering less than a dozen. Colonel Harcourt, who had been Reader in Persian at Oxford, was in charge of the intelligence section; the other members included John Sheppard, Pat Gibbon and me as new boy, with Ben Collins looking after traffic analysis. Ken Freeman ('Titch') was the CO, Dave Watson was Adjutant, and the signals section was looked after by John Evans, David Allibone and John Kennedy. A small group of British sergeants and other ranks, together with a very large body of Indian civilian wireless operators, carried out the detailed intercepting.

Our immediate concern was with Azerbaijan, the extreme north-west province of Iran just across the frontier from the Soviet republic of the same name. At one point in the war the Allies had taken over much of the transport organisation in Iran for fear that German influence might prevail in preventing our use of the rail network for supplies to the Soviet Union; the Russians occupied a broad control zone in north Iran while we looked after the south. It now seemed that Russia might seek to prolong its stay in the north-west corner of its temporary zone, using the argument of the undoubted common origin of the race which straddles the frontier. This was, I believe, the first major problem to arise after the Allied victory in 1945, and the 'Azerbaijan dispute' was one of the first occasions on which the phrase 'the cold war' was heard.

All this threatened to rock the boat, and Abbottabad was concerned with finding out what it could about Iran's real intentions. The traffic we studied, therefore, was not military but diplomatic, with a single code-system covering every aspect of diplomatic and consular activity from summaries by overseas press attachés of local newspaper reports on Iran, at the brighter end, to routine requests for permission to issue a visa at the more tedious extreme.

This may sound pedestrian, but after the Japanese grind it was a welcome relaxation; moreover the atmosphere of the small unit was very appealing. The three-letter alphabetical codebook had, I believe, been 'acquired', and each day there was a different substitution table for the code-groups. Two codebooks were needed: one, arranged under words, to encode, the other, arranged alphabetically under code-groups, to decode. The first corresponds to a telephone directory, and the second to the list which the telephone company uses when it wants to see who has a particular number:

FWT	ايران	Iran
NGA	تهران	Teheran
JPL	كتاب	book (kitab)

SUBSTITUTION TABLE;

	A	B	C	D	E	F	G	H etc
4 July	T	L	J	Z	P	A	Q	Y
5 July	E	P	M	I	S	Y	H	B
6 July	O	C	G	X	U	D	K	F
7 July	V	R	J	N	L	W	A	P

So simple a form of concealment was already naively inadequate by the 1920s, let alone the 1940s. But it is a mistake to assume that alphabetical codes in themselves are somehow less advanced than numerical codes. As there are 26 letters and only ten numerals, a three-letter codebook has 26^3 ($26{\times}26{\times}26$) = 17,576 combinations as against 1,000 for three-digits and only 10,000 even with four digits. Three symbols can be sent faster than four by Morse, especially when the symbols are letters with shorter Morse forms; all this makes for speed and security. The snag is that whereas numbers can be added or subtracted as part of a recipherment, there is no orthodox way of adding two letters to make a third, so that transposition or substitution are the only straightforward forms of concealment.

The Persian code was all the more vulnerable because there were frequent cribs, some from press releases, which I must say no more about, even though these were accidental whereas David Kahn's book gives a beautiful example of a *planted* crib used by the Austrians against the Italians as long ago as 1911 or thereabouts.

Eventually the dispute subsided. Attitudes were struck, views were noted, statements were objected to, compromises were reached – and nothing happened; whereupon it was decided that because of the troubled condition of Nuristan and other parts of Afghanistan close to north-west India, we ought to form an Afghan section; I was appointed not so much to run it as to be it, for it was a one-man job. The fly in the Afghan ointment was the Faqir of Ipi, a celebrated old rogue who, with his forebears, had long played a tune which many tribesmen in the whole Hindu Kush area were happy to dance to. He was again becoming restive and the Pathans were getting excited. A lot of this was simply letting off steam: the rugged local tradition expressed joy at fairs, festivals and weddings, or grief at funerals, by firing rifles into the air. Sometimes things got out of hand, and kidnapping, arson, murder and attacks on local forts (on both sides of the border) led to the risk that any clumsy action by the civil or military administration could produce a dangerous flare-up. Once again the signals traffic reflected little of this, and did not match the strenuous language and anxious overtones of the intelligence summaries which we regularly had from Delhi but to which we were rarely able to contribute much of value.

The penalty of being a one-man section outweighs its grandeur. I had to take every signal from its arrival, fresh from the intercept section over the road, through its substituting, decoding and translating stages to its evaluation, and then pass on to Delhi or to Whitehall anything that seemed of interest. The Afghan crypto material was almost identical in pattern to the Persian, and the whole job became easier when I realised that although they too changed their substitution table each day, it consisted of the same garbled alphabet shunted backwards and forwards, sometimes at random but sometimes in regular order. This diagram shows the result, and you will see that the rising line spells TLJZ just as the start of the first line does:

	A	B	C	D	E	F	G	H etc
4 July	T	L	J	Z	P	A	Q	Y
5 July	B	T	L	J	Z	P	A	Q
6 July	M	B	T	L	J	Z	P	A
7 July	F	M	B	T	L	J	Z	P

Consequently the breaking of the substitution table became necessary only once every 26 days, and the routine contents of most messages meant that this took a short time. I used to wonder whether the Afghan clerk over the frontier was getting there first.

About this time we were visited by 'The Auk', that excellent and often under-rated commander Field-Marshal Sir Claude Auchinleck; a typically brief, shrewd, friendly and unpretentious affair. A lesser though more colourful visit was the arrival outside my office window of a hoopoe, a bird I had read about when translating Aristophanes' *The Birds* at school, but had never seen before. It strutted about and obligingly raised its crest, ran along the ground, said 'Hoo-poo-poo' twice, rose into the air on black-and-white wings, and flew off.

One night my room was burgled while I was sleeping in it. My battledress and great-coat disappeared and so did the cashbox with the mess funds which, as Mess Secretary, it was my responsibility to look after. There had not been much in it but naturally an enquiry had to be held; it was decided that the fault was not only mine, because no better place for the cashbox existed. As usually happens, the risk became obvious after the event and a more secure place was at once found. For a time it was thought that my bearer Said Ghulam might have tipped off the robbers, or that he might have mentioned the cashbox casually to other bearers as they squatted waiting for orders from their lords and masters. The thieves, the money and the clothes were never found: another neat Pathan job, carried out in the certainty that nobody who knew or guessed anything would talk.

A far from neat British job was more shameful because it meant deceit at the other end of the social scale. The Abbottabad NAAFI, best known for its life-saving troops' canteens, had its share of one of the first post-war consignments of Swiss watches, and a quota of six

Leonidas wrist-watches was to be distributed fairly between the hundred or more officers of the Abbottabad and Kakul units, as well as a much larger number for lower ranks. A ballot was arranged and, incredibly, all six were found to have been won by the Commanding Officers, Adjutants and other dignitaries of the Gurkha regiments. The howl of protest that greeted this unbelievable coup was relayed to the GOC Abbottabad Area, General Sixsmith, who ordered an enquiry and a second ballot in which I was lucky enough to get one of the six. It was cheap but reliable. What had enraged us was not so much the result of the first ballot but the cool assumption that we would accept it. No heads rolled, unfortunately. As with the Pathans, nobody talked.

The General also had to call on the Army to stand by in case of civil disorders in the area. These were relatively small affairs which, like the Faqir's, needed to be handled gently yet firmly. With the end of the war the 'Quit India' campaign was gaining strength and there were many points on which Muslims, Hindus and Sikhs could not agree. I recall Pandit Nehru's rueful comment on Mr Jinnah, the leader of the Muslim League, after long but fruitless talks: 'He has a problem for every solution'.

In Abbottabad the demonstrators were usually lorry-loads of children who had been trained which battle-cry to raise on which excursion, and most local people did not take them seriously. But they were a nuisance; they might get out of hand, and if so the Army had to be ready to help the police. All units were therefore told to hold parades at which the officers in turn literally 'read the Riot Act' to all ranks. Our motley crew would not have been very effective at quelling riots if they had occurred; they never did.

The end of the war, the smallness of the unit and the usually placid surroundings produced a more relaxed atmosphere which was enhanced by having several married colleagues who lived in bungalows ranged round the bachelors' quarters. One colleague (whom I may not name 'for security reasons') with his wife and two children were hospitably established only a few hundred yards away, and Pat Gibbon was soon joined by his bride Nirvana. Not far away was an Army unit which trained horses for transport companies after taking them in as unmanageable wild ponies. The children had learnt to ride and the family persuaded me to follow their example. Despite misgivings I had lessons on a very tall charger belonging to the Indian Sergeant-Major. It was impeccably trained and walked, trotted, cantered or galloped precisely as the instructor told it; it was deaf when I gave the word of command, and refused to change gear until the instructor repeated it. The steering was equally remote. This lack of direct control, coupled with the height of the animal, decided me to go no further – it was very like driving a double-decker bus from the upper deck, and there were no stairs.

I broke my vow, however, when the sergeants challenged the officers to a polo match on Christmas Day 1945. I fancy the venerable Colonel Harcourt may have played before, and so perhaps had John Sheppard, but the rest of us had no experience. Our mounts were the half-trained ponies, who knew neither us nor the rules and were suspicious of both. We played with hockey-sticks and a football; the game was not for purists. The pony had to be inched up towards the ball, and the rider then moved as far as he dared up the pony's neck, hoping to reach the ball before his opponent did. When the player tapped the ball the pony took fright. One of the sergeants fell off his horse, and the trainer rushed to his aid and revived him from a medicine chest offering a choice of beer or whisky. The match was abandoned when one capsized pony began to roll on his rider, fortunately without causing damage. I have not played polo since – if indeed I did then.

The Indian wireless operators, who easily outnumbered the rest of us, did a demanding job, in three eight-hour shifts, at a time when their loyalty to the British might well have been in question, for any appeal to their patriotism would have been diluted by the ending of the war. They lived in long barrack huts, very much like those at Shenley Road Military Camp, and were of every religion. It was a tribute to them and to everyone in the unit that their work and our relationship with them went so well. They provided the best batsmen and the fastest bowlers in the WED cricket team, which David Allibone captained, and we frequently surprised the teams of other units, who had expected us to be a group of long-haired incompetents.

I spent a few days' leave at Nathia Gali, a small hill-station nearby. There was little to do but stroll or climb, and to enjoy the fragrant pine-log fires in the evening, and I got to know a delightful Indian family on leave from Calcutta, Mr and Mrs Sen Gupta and their son.

The unmentionable collegue, Pat Gibbon and I decided, on my return, to climb Thandiani, a small mountain not far away. It had to be done within the day, and foolishly we wasted valuable time walking to and from the foot of it, and too much energy tackling its modest slopes against the clock, to have long at the top to enjoy the views of the real mountains nearby: Nanga Parbat, over 26,000 feet, and nearer and lower the Kohistan and Pir Panjal ranges.

Another memorable event was an open-air recital by a string quartet of Italian prisoners-of-war who had volunteered to play to Allied troops in any continent. I think it was there, with the players on a raised platform surrounded by hundreds of silent people, that I first heard the second Borodin quartet.

One morning a baggage-train laden with carpets arrived outside the Mess. They had come from Iran along the traditional route through Afghanistan, and were anxious to do business at Abbottabad. We were, they said smilingly, the first place they had encountered – persuasively forgetting Peshawar – and it brought them good luck to offer extra low prices at the start of their first visit to India since the end of the war. They had not expected a group of Farsi-speakers, delighted to practise the spoken language. They stayed for some days, engaged in a patient round of bargaining: 'Very beautiful, but much too expensive' we said. 'British officers very rich' they countered. 'Nonsense, my friends; American officers very rich, British very poor.' 'We come back tomorrow.' 'Good morning, sahib; today we cut our prices the last time' and so on. After trying the Gurkhas and the gunners they returned, still optimistic, still full of gentle flattery. Meanwhile we had read John Sheppard's book on Persian carpets and each memorised a chapter, and we bought as a team. 'This is not a good Gordes knot'. They threw up their hands in horror; I too was surprised, having always thought of the Gordian knot as a literary myth. They sliced a little more off their prices. Eventually I bought an Afghan prayer-rug, reduced because of an overlap of dyeing which gave the centre a richer stripe, and a used Persian carpet with soft warm colours. The Gibbons, still setting up their first home, fell for an exquisite Tree of Life carpet that filled their living-room floor. Security forbids me to say whether our other colleagues bought a carpet or not.

The Afghan troubles subsided and we wondered how long it would be before our turn came for repatriation and demobilisation. With limited transport available from Asia to Europe, the first priority went to the many who had been in Japanese prison camps. For the rest points were awarded for age, length of service, compassionate grounds or – in reverse – the specialised needs of the services. At this rate I should be the last officer to leave WEC.

About this time, the summer of 1946, we were invited to apply for jobs in the peace-time GCHQ, 'the racket', though it was made clear that this did not constitute the offer of a job. Harcourt, who had come out of retirement, I think, to lead our section, was evidently not interested, but the other three applied and were eventually accepted. I was in a different position; I was greatly tempted but decided against it on two grounds. The first was that I ought to finish my degree, in whatever subject, before committing myself to such a decision; the second, that although it was relatively easy to do a Top Secret job in wartime, when the need for secrecy was obvious and so many people were in the same boat, the thought of doing indefinitely in peacetime a job which I could never discuss, and which would always require some sort of cover story, was unattractive. I was about to take some long-planned leave in Kashmir when I was posted to Singapore. But I was to travel by way of Bangalore so as to pick up 'an important item' which was also bound for Singapore. The unit was to be wound up soon, in any case, and as keepsakes each of us had a pewter mug made – I still have mine – inscribed with all our signatures, as well as those of Eric Wilson, an opthalmic specialist, and Stanley Rogol, an anaesthetist, who belonged to the nearby hospital but shared our mess. The old hands told us that any mess funds still intact when we closed down would be taken care of by the Army financiers, so we spared them that responsibility by arranging several banquets before we departed.

I still play correspondence chess with the friend who must not be named; he always wins.

6

Bangalore, Singapore and Cambridge

The rail journey from Abbottabad to Bangalore took five days, not simply because there were no expresses on that route, nor even because it covers 1,550 miles (London–Sofia) as the crow flies, but because we again stopped at station restaurants for our main meals. It was tedious; the countryside was rarely varied enough to hold the interest, though my eye was caught somewhere near Nagpur where wagons were being shunted, one at a time, by three men who pushed them. Our meal stops marked the passage of time. The further south we went, the stickier it became, and even the punkah-boys had scarcely enough energy to swing the large punkah fan, hung from the ceiling and swung by a string pulled by hand or toe, enough to produce the semblance of a breeze. I was lucky to reach Madras, a notoriously sweltering city, at night, and to catch an early train next morning for the remaining 400 miles to Bangalore – a far more interesting trip, with small hillside stations showing their polysyllabic names in Tamil as well as Roman script.

Bangalore, the capital city of Mysore state, is high enough to be healthy but its surroundings seemed tame after the extreme north, and the Western Wireless Sub-Centre was several miles out in barren country. The title may suggest something puny, but this was an offspring of WEC at Delhi, quite sizeable in its own right, though now free-wheeling with little to do. I was at once warned that the servants were Christian. Warned? Because, I was told, the doctrine of forgiveness has not travelled well. Islam condemns sin, and Hinduism encourages virtue, but Christianity allows you to be wicked *and* be forgiven – so your belongings are not safe from your bearer. My bearer, Lawrence, stole nothing from me during my short stay, but it is true that after this warning I had played safe and kept my belongings locked up.

The 'important item' which I had to collect was a cube-shaped crate, about a metre in each direction, very heavy and very expertly packed, padded, sewn up and sealed, marked TOP SECRET on every face. There were no handles for lifting it. I was told not to let it out of my sight; Singapore needed it urgently. To obey this order precisely meant that I could not sleep for five days or so, I protested. I learned that I should be in charge of a small party of men also bound for Singapore, and 'out of *our* sight' would suffice, as long as it was plain that I was responsible. We trundled down to Madras again, ready to jump on board the ship which was said to be waiting for us.

Shades of Glasgow! The ship was not even in port; not expected to arrive for several days, which we sweated out in Madras. The humidity was high. Each evening I showered about 6.30, when the sun was setting, carefully put on a freshly-starched bush jacket and slacks, and walked to the mess as slowly as I could, leaving the wretched Top Secret crate in my room. By the time I had covered the hundred yards my shirt was soaked through. A pity: Madras looked a fine place with its long sea-front and impressive harbour, its palm trees and its brilliant cotton fabrics, but it was a hellish place at that season.

The ship, a small merchant vessel, at length arrived and we got ourselves and our crate on board. At last we moved off and made a laborious passage to Port Swettenham on the west coast of Malaya, a cheerless spot with its approach through mangrove swamps. A train took us on to Kuala Lumpur, where we spent our first night in Malaya. The people were small, active and friendly: Chinese, Malays and Indians squashed higgledy-piggledy into a maze of tiny streets. We were off early next morning, having had great difficulty in finding space for the infernal crate as well as ourselves.

The train rumbled down through Johore state, and the view from the train was never dull. Tall palm trees overhung the tiny neat houses, never squalid, often thatched with palm leaves themselves. There were banana trees with their wide split leaves, and short nut-brown men hacking great bunches of green bananas down from them. Cycles and rickshaws overloaded with grinning people. Rice-fields at every stage of planting, harvesting and flooding. The little train rattled on and at last slowed down to crawl across the causeway that links Singapore Island to Malaya. We passed some fine green hills in the middle of the island, and at last arrived at the main station.

Everything happened twice as fast as in India. Nobody knew about us but they soon found out. In no time a truck was produced to take us to our destination. On the way we ran through Chinatown, with innumerable miniature shops doing a roaring trade, sampans and small boats of every kind crammed tightly along the coastal moorings and creeks, and everywhere Chinese hats of light bamboo strips, some with straight-sloping sides and others, which I instantly coveted, curving stylishly up to a central point like Fujiyama. Then we turned inland and drove along twisting roads to Yio Chu Kang camp, set among rubber plantations near the centre of the island.

Immediately a familiar face: Robin Gibson, now a Major, commanded the unit and greeted us warmly. In the normal way it would have been called South-East Asia Special Intelligence Company, but nobody cared for the queasy acronym SEASIC, so it became 800 Special Intelligence Company. The mess was in a long bungalow, but we lived in tents, well set out and very comfortable with their walls brailed up in warm weather. We handed over our crate and I insisted on a signed receipt.

There were several days, so flexible as to be almost free, before we were to settle down to our unknown duties, and everyone seemed to be playing cricket. I had never been enthusiastic, and at Abbottabad had joined the team to make up the eleven. Here I suddenly found that I could bowl, medium-pace, to an exact length, and spin the ball as I chose, though I continued to be useless as fielder or batsman. It had never happened before, and it lasted barely a year, from Singapore back to Cambridge, but while it thrived I was pressed into service to destroy rival teams on the island. I cannot account for the phenomenon. We celebrated our victories by visiting the many Chinese restaurants at Tanglin, where the BBC were establishing themselves, and were given expert and patient tuition in the use of chopsticks.

Next week the plans were revealed: we were to learn Russian, another thing I had hardly ever considered. There was good news for me as well: my captaincy came through at last. The days passed happily. Our group of six or eight were well taught by a youngish instructor, who insisted on getting pronunciation exactly right from the start. We worked hard but the evenings were free and further cricket victories followed. The mess had a wind-up gramophone and a few records with the well-known concertos and Palmgren's West Finnish dance as a fill-up. Noel Coward's 'Mad dogs and Englishmen' was played almost constantly, and at the words 'In the Malay States they have hats like plates, which the Britishers won't wear' the large plate-like hat which I had bought was lowered through the open mess window on to Robin Gibson's head.

Next day we had a cable to say that my Class B release had been authorised and I was to fly back to the UK by the first available plane. Sorry as I was to leave both the course and the island, I was delighted by the news, especially as I had heard from my Bedford colleague Hugh Melinsky that he had just got back. I knew that if I could reach Cambridge before the division of term in late October, I could count that term to my credit and that might ultimately make a year's difference to my studies. We telephoned RAF Changi and Robin pulled all the strings he could; in a couple of days I had a seat booked. Many of the others envied me but I felt no guilt because they were all graduates and I was not.

Changi airport, run by the RAF, was my first experience of service transport working smoothly and punctually. They gave us an excellent breakfast while the plane was checked and re-fuelled, and then we climbed on board. It was an Avro York, a civil version of the Lancaster bomber, originally meant, they told us, for the use of VIPs, but now rearranged to carry us in bulk; yet it was no more squashed than the modern jumbo. Originally the five legs of the flight back had been done in pairs, so that the whole trip would take only two and a half days, but after two crashes which were put down to pilot fatigue the five legs were spread over five days.

We flew across the Bay of Bengal to Ceylon, landing at Negombo, set in palm-groves beside the coast just north of Colombo – an idyllic place when the weather is kind. Next across India, most of which was invisible, to Karachi, or rather to Mauripur airport nearby, a desolate place on the edge of the desert. The next leg took us to Iraq and Habbaniyeh airport. Onwards the next day, flying over Tel Aviv to Malta, with fine views of the Grand Harbour. At each stop, unfortunately, we had too little time and energy after landing and having supper to get from the airport to see the town.

The last leg took us right across France, but almost all was hidden by cloud. At one point there was a gap in the cloud sheet; we banked steeply and circled: 'Clermont-Ferrand', the word came back. Near the Channel the sky gradually cleared, and southern England in October looked inviting. We landed at the Air Transport Command base at Lyneham in Wiltshire, and knowing that I should be demobilised next morning I had no hesitation in coming down the gangway in tropical kit plus the giant coolie hat. Next morning we handed in anything belonging to the Army and collected our 'demob clothes': a none-too-hideous baggy suit, a pork-pie hat, brown cardboardy shoes and some oddments. The train journey to London seemed ridiculously short by Far Eastern standards.

A few days later, just in time, I returned to Cambridge. The system in force meant that I had to finish Part I of the Classical Tripos before changing subjects, so I had a rush to prepare for that hurdle and some difficulty in adjusting to Latin, Greek and Ancient History. The examiners were kind.

I had already decided to change subjects after that; to continue in Classics seemed to point only in the direction of teaching, for which I had no ability and no appetite. Persian was an attractive option, and Arberry, whose textbook I had used at Abbottabad, was teaching in Cambridge. Yet somehow the Shahnameh, which I tentatively read during the Long Vacation, did not live up to its first promise, and on learning that Eric Ceadel, one of the two instructors on that remotely distant Bedford course, had just been appointed Lecturer in Japanese, I decided to make that my main subject, with classical Chinese as a subsidiary, together with Far Eastern history.

One of the Japanese set books was *Taketori Monogatari* (The Bamboo-Cutter's Tale), written in the late tenth century; a fairy tale that was naive, fantastic, yet endearingly humorous in parts. We also studied modern colloquial Japanese, of which I knew virtually nothing. The main Chinese prescribed text was by Mencius (Mengtse), one of Confucius' most important followers in the third century BC, and a writer full of human wisdom and gentle precepts: the first advocate of 'humane government'. Far Eastern history was an enormous closed book. The whole course had only tenuous links with my wartime activities, where the Japanese vocabulary had been limited and military in flavour, and in any case it was two years since I had used it, and Farsi, Latin and Greek had come between. At the same time there were some foundations on which I could build. The course promised to be both demanding and rewarding.

PART TWO

JAPANESE PUZZLES

7

Japanese Codes and Ciphers –
What were they like?

In previous chapters I have often referred to the various crypto systems used by the Japanese. What were they like? What did they tell us? How were they sent? How were they intercepted? How were they broken? I shall try to answer these and similar questions in the next chapters.

To understand the volume and the value of the information they gave us – the whole purpose of signals intelligence – we need to remember that by 1942 Japan occupied or controlled an area with an outer radius some 3,000 – 4,000 miles from Tokyo, compared with a German radius, excluding U-boats, usually under 1,000 miles from Berlin. Moreover in Asia and the Pacific overland communications were poor – in some places they scarcely existed – and telephone, cable and telex networks were scanty and unreliable. One telex link, newly installed between WEC Delhi and WWSC Bangalore, ran for twenty seconds and then went on strike for days. A really good radio network was therefore vital, and it carried almost all the countless orders and reports which a country's armed services require.

But whereas Germany used versions of the Enigma cipher machine for nearly all the signals of the army, navy, air force, SS and security services, the Japanese used many totally different crypto systems. The US *Operational History of Japanese Naval Communications, December 1941–August 1945*[17] lists three strategic and administrative, eight tactical, nine attaché and intelligence (i.e. agents), and four extra-naval, making twenty-four in all at any one time. That figure includes the naval air force but excludes various ancillary material such as books of signals (in the older sense), abbreviations, address codes and an array of tables to conceal map references, dates and times, call-signs and the like. The army is likely to have had just as many, again including several for the army air force. Diplomatic and consular traffic, civilian agents working for the Foreign Office, and the commercial transactions of various ministries will account for a few more. We end up with a probable total of 55 or more, 27 of which I refer to below, with the caution that some on my list may represent earlier and later versions of the same system. The evidence is too thinly spread to be sure about this. Some which I have called 'unnamed' may well have JN or JA labels.

A total of over fifty is perfectly possible. The list of German Enigma keys attacked at Bletchley Park between June 1943 and June 1944 gives a similar picture: 21 for the army, 10 for the navy, 16 for the air force, 5 for security services, SS and police units, making 52 Enigma variants plus *Geheimschreiber* and hand-cipher systems.[18]

I had made a rough estimate of the total number of Japanese signals that we intercepted and read each day in 1944, but have been asked to remove it since it might still be a relevant clue, 45 years later, to our present cryptanalytical abilities. Despite my surprise I have naturally complied. Some technical details of certain codes have also been deleted.

In all Japanese military, naval, air and diplomatic traffic, codes heavily out-numbered ciphers, a fact which is often obscured, partly because some writers do not distinguish clearly or correctly between codes and ciphers, partly because the process of further concealing a code-text is called reciphering, and partly because so much public attention has been directed on the Purple cipher machine, simply through its link with the Pearl Harbor episode. Japanese codes were generally based on numerals rather than on letters – though they used both – and were mostly reciphered for extra security. Letter-codes were reserved for lower-grade signals.

Before listing some two dozen crypto systems I must explain several points. Burglarious references to 'breaking and entering' are not to be understood in an exclusive sense: a code shown as 'broken at Delhi' may have been broken about the same time at Arlington, Virginia, since although some clear lines were drawn, dividing responsibility between Britain and the USA, some crypto systems were important or difficult enough to be attacked at both, so that the breaking would be a shared success. Wartime security meant that few people knew the details of Allied cryptanalytical co-operation. Since the war some writers, often without personal experience of the subject, have used language more appropriate to cut-throat competition than to the co-operation which actually existed, especially from middle or late 1943.

Similarly 'read currently' does not necessarily mean 'read immediately'. It means that enough progress had been made to enable most messages to be read without undue delay, though the process may have taken one or two days or even longer. The intercept unit was, after all, assuming the role of all the enemy units to which the whole mass of signals were sent. The delay lessened as the war progressed, and by 1945 a lot of traffic was solved and read at once. But at any moment a stubborn code might at last yield, and release a back-log of signals which had to be examined to assess their importance. Quite often the delay was caused simply by the volume of signals to be dealt with. Every effort was made to deduce from such evidence as the length and address of messages which were most urgent or most important – not always the same thing – and to deal with them first, but there were bound to be miscalculations. Fortunately the tactical messages, which most needed urgent attention, were often sent on lower-grade systems which could be broken more quickly, and some delay was of less consequence in messages of strategic importance. The distinction between tactical and strategic content began to break down, however, as the Japanese gradually lost control of some key areas, especially in the Pacific. Often it had proved impossible for them to distribute the new keys which should have been regularly changed, and recourse had to be had to whatever was thought to be still a secure signals system. This has to be remembered when, in the list, we find a low-grade system described as carrying surprisingly important messages. With these provisos, here is an interim list:[19]

1   *JN 14* (Allied name) Four-digit naval code, usually reciphered, which sometimes revealed not only the movements of coastal vessels but also major fleet movements. Either this code or JN 25 will have been the code which disclosed the details in September 1942 of the Japanese plans for attacking Milne Bay, at the south-eastern tip of New Guinea, where they were heavily defeated by the Australian troops which this information had placed there. By 1944 it was largely phased out and superseded by JN 147; but the garrison on Rota, in the Marianas (the island next to Tinian, the base for the bombers which raided Hiroshima) were cut off and had to continue using JN 14, which gave us a lucky break. Rota's messages were mostly lists of casualties, which Tokyo answered with lists of posthumous promotions while becoming increasingly evasive about the chances of relieving the garrison.

2 *JN 147* (Allied name) Five-digit reciphered naval code replacing

JN 14. There is evidence that JN 147 as well as JN 25 disclosed the whereabouts of a Japanese cruiser which the British sank in 1945, as reported more fully under JN 25. This too seems to have been originally intended for coastal vessels only, with its use widened later.

3 *JN 23* (Allied name) Five-digit reciphered naval code devoted to the construction, launching and completion of new warships, together with delays in construction, expected dates of sea trials and commissioning, and details of the first harbours to be visited.

Three successive versions were used, and were read almost currently. At first the intercepts picked up at Colombo were faint and scrappy, but they were followed next day by clearer intercepts forwarded from Washington. The last version, introduced in late 1944, was compromised when a charred but still partly legible codebook was recovered.

4 *JN 25* (Allied name) Major fleet five-digit reciphered naval code. The British and the Americans had broken earlier versions of this system intermittently from 1939, and successive changes in May and August 1942 had produced only temporary setbacks. It seems from Kahn's account that the codebook was one of those captured in January 1943 when two New Zealand corvettes rammed a Japanese submarine off Guadalcanal and forced it to beach on an outlying reef.[20] It was found to be carrying some 200,000 'codebooks', a word which may include other crypto material, probably for several systems. Despite Japanese attempts to destroy the material, much of it was captured, thus simplifying life for the Americans at Hawaii and the British at Colombo and Kilindini. The Japanese changed some material but left the JN 25 codebook itself unchanged.

It gave advance warning of the big carrier-based raids on Ceylon in March 1942, although the British Eastern Fleet was still so outnumbered that it could do little but slip away and avoid a major fleet confrontation. Later the tables were turned when British carrier-based aircraft raided Japanese naval bases on Sumatra and Java on the strength of JN 25 sigint.

It also revealed the detailed movement of a Japanese naval force in the southern Bay of Bengal in May 1945, and led to the sinking of the Japanese cruiser *Haguro* by British destroyers south-west of Penang on 16 May, and later the torpedoing of its sister ship *Ashigara* by the British submarine *Trenchant* in the Bangka Strait, south of Singapore, on 8 June. *Ashigara* had represented the Japanese Navy at the Royal Fleet Review at Spithead in June 1937.

Both cruisers had been hoping to evacuate Japanese troops cut off in outlying islands after the fall of Rangoon had given Britain control of the Bay of Bengal and much of the sea around Malaya and the East Indies. They had been the last two large enemy warships in the area, and their loss left Singapore with only one destroyer, the *Kamikaze*, and a few auxiliary craft. The British official history describes both sinkings but does not explain how the cruisers were located, because it was published in 1969 when all references to sigint were still banned.

JN 25 also contributed to the shooting-down of Admiral Yamamoto's aircraft. The episode is well known, but I summarise it in Chapter Eight because of its implications for security. The code system used several internal sub-codes to disguise dates, times and map references such as the celebrated 'AF' for Midway Island. A specimen page of the JN 25 codebook is reproduced in Kahn's *The Codebreakers*.[21]

About this code system 'Nigel West' makes the surprising comment that 'European countries had abandoned this type of hand cipher' (*sic*) 'in 1917, so they presented few difficulties for cryptographers at either SIS or, for that matter, GCHQ. However, their decryption had become progressively more difficult during the 1930s as the Japanese experimented with machines to superencipher the texts of messages between Tokyo and certain missions abroad'.[22]

West's terminology and chronology are so unspecific that it is hard to be sure what he is trying to tell us, or whether it is relevant. It is not true that European countries had abandoned hand ciphers either in the accurate sense (Germany continued to use them for some naval traffic throughout the Second World War) or in West's sense as applied to JN 25; the Royal Navy 'ciphers', as they mis-leadingly called reciphered codes when used by officers, were in use up to the middle of 1943, and so were the notoriously leaky merchant shipping codes. He appears also to believe that machines are *in themselves* more secured than numerical keys for reciphering a code-text. The truth is that everything depends on the quality of the key or the machine, the frequency with which the materials are changed, and the procedural reliability of the cipher and radio operators. The penetration of Enigma and Purple hardly strengthens his case for praising machines in themselves.

To add to our difficulties West, the author of *Unreliable Witness* as well as of *GCHQ*, does not distinguish between codes and ciphers, or even keys, either in connection with JN 25 or elsewhere.

In the text he mentions five Japanese systems (JN 19, 25, 36 and 37, and PAK–2) as 'codes' or 'keys' although he lists them under 'ciphers' in the index. This confusion would not matter two hoots in a thriller, but it is remarkable in a book about signals intelligence.

5 *JN 36 and 37* (Allied names) Naval meteorological ciphers, both of which were being read at Bletchley by 1942. At first the Americans were content to solve JN 36, but later they attacked JN 37 as well. It is not clear if the two ciphers were distinct, or formed different versions of the same system, but they appear to have been hand, not machine, ciphers, probably based on a kana text.

6 *JN 40* (Allied name) Merchant shipping code of four-syllable kana groups, used to report attacks on Allied submarines or aircraft, and often revealing the detailed routes of convoys and the identity of some of the vessels in them. The messages usually followed a set pattern, giving latitude and longitude, ship's number, name ('X maru') and cargo.

7 *Unnamed naval code* This flummoxed Bletchley Park for a long while. It was soon recognised as a book code, that is to say one which uses a novel or some other literary work which both sender and receiver possess, from which letters, or more rarely words, are borrowed to spell out the message by quoting page and number. It was only when a merchant vessel was captured with the book intact that it was found to be the Authorised Version of the Bible in English. If the colleague who gave me this information had not shown his credentials by giving other checkable details I should have suspected a leg-pull over this Gilbertian contrivance.

8 *Unnamed naval cipher* A plain Japanese text, written out in kana syllables, each of which was then substituted by another kana syllable on the basis of a table which changed daily. A form of slide-rule was used for reading it, at least at Bletchley Park, which suggests that there was some underlying pattern, moved bodily each day, rather as in the Afghan code which I described in Chapter Five. This must have started as a low-grade affair, though it too carried some important messages towards the end of the war.

9 *CORAL* (US name) Naval attaché machine cipher, broken by the Americans about April 1943. Deavours and Kruh, two of the founder-editors of the very respectable quarterly *Cryptologia*, give useful accounts of this and other members of the Purple family, Red and Jade, in their book *Machine Cryptography and Modern Cryptanalysis*.[23]

10 *Unnamed cipher* used by the naval mission and naval attaché in Berlin. Though we have no details it is clear that this is distinct from CORAL, since it was broken in March 1944, and by GCHQ and the Americans working in collaboration.[24]

11 *Unnamed Army water transport code* The curious title arises from the Army's allocation of merchant ships and troopships for its exclusive use. WEC is credited with having made the first break into this high-grade system, of which no crypto details are available, in March 1943; the internal address code was broken in August 1943.

This is one of four codes referred to by Lewin as having been penetrated by the Allies.[25] He gives no details, and if his dates are right I do not see how they can duplicate other systems on my list. Lewin is a conscientious authority who does not pretend to be a cryptographic expert, and it is unfortunate that his reference cannot be more specific.

12 *KA KA KA* (Japanese name) Army field code, chiefly for use at battalion level in the New Guinea area; read from 1943 or earlier, and probably first broken at Brisbane by Professor Room, who had held the Chair of Mathematics at Sydney University. A three-digit code, with 232 standing for 'ka' and 426 for 'yori', the postposition (the Japanese equivalent of a preposition) meaning 'from'. The code-groups were reciphered with a numerical key which was frequently changed and as frequently broken. It gave very useful information within its limited area of use.

13 *Unnamed army code* with four-digits reciphered with additive key, apparently broken in part by 1943 and read with occasional delays until October 1944, when some material was recovered from a warship sunk off New Guinea, after which it was read currently for a few months. A new codebook was introduced in January 1945 but no copies could be delivered to isolated garrisons, which had to continue using the old one. A copy was captured in February 1945. An unnamed army code 'broken by the British in 1933, but then lost until spring 1943' (Lewin) may be the same as No 13.

14 *Army address code* read at WEC Delhi in 1944–45, in two self-checking forms; one using four digits, the last being the non-carrying sum of the first three, the other having eight digits, the last four checking the first four. These address codes were outside and independent of the messages they directed.

15 *Army's chief administrative code*, of which Lewin tells us only

that 'an entry was apparently made at the turn of the year' (1943–44) and 'In February 1944 a copy of the code itself was captured, as well as some of the mechanical devices employed, making available a tremendous volume of messages dealing with virtually every field of activity in the Japanese Army'. This date almost tallies with Horner's observation that 'in January 1944 a trunk of army code-books was captured'.[26] Lewin's context does not make it clear whether the original break was made by British or American units. The reference to 'mechanical devices', in conjunction with a code-book, is puzzling. Mechanical recipherment is not known to have been used with any other system.

16 *JMA* (Allied name) Military attaché code, broken largely by Tiltman at Bletchley Park in the summer of 1942, after which it was read there and at Colombo and Arlington despite setbacks in May 1944 and the spring of 1945 when materials were changed. At the second of these changes the Japanese cover-name was altered from HNM to PLT, but the full title remained 'Bukan-yō kaeji-hyō' (Military attaché's conversion table).

It was unusual: two-letter groups stood for common words, but the squared table in which the resultant codetext was set out held a surprise, in that certain pairs of letters were written diagonally instead of straight across. The letters stood for themselves, and the original kana syllables were retained, spelt out in their simplest form, i.e. TI and TU instead of CHI and TSU, which give a better phonetic guide. Among the horizontal pairs AB stood for 'sei' (west), NV for 'kekka' (result) and NW for 'ron' (discussion). A typical series written in diagonal pairs ran AK, BL, CM ... JT, standing for the numerals 1, 2, 3 ... 0. GG opened and closed kana transcriptions of foreign words, but JL opened and closed such words when the foreign spelling was retained. DD showed where the text began, and AV meant 'tsuzuku': 'message continued'.

The military attaché in Berlin disclosed the details of the Normandy beach defences after he had been shown painstakingly round them and signalled the results to Tokyo; I give a fuller account in Chapter Eight. A further message came at the end of the war from the Embassy in Berne to say that Yamamoto, the military attaché, had committed suicide on hearing of the Emperor's order to surrender. As early as 14 May, three months before, his superior Kase, the Minister in Berne, had sent a long and thoughtful message suggesting that it was time to sue for peace – soon after the German surrender and the fall of Rangoon.

17 *J 19* (Allied name) Medium-grade consular reciphered code, introduced in August 1941 to replace J 18. Read fairly currently by Australians, Dutch, British and Americans; the latter sometimes read theirs late because of the priority given to Purple. A simpler version, Gaimusho LA, was usually readable but rarely fruitful.

18 *PURPLE* (US name) Machine cipher used for high-grade diplomatic traffic, and famous for having been broken by Friedman and his team well before Pearl Harbor. Conspiracy theories abound for this episode and for the bombing of Coventry; both are totally wrong-headed. Nor was Purple derived from Enigma; it used stepping-switches instead of rotors, and it was used only for high-grade diplomatic traffic. Its use by Ōshima, the Ambassador in Berlin, inadvertently revealed a vast amount of information on Germany's plans and technical developments, some examples of which I mention in Chapter Eight.

19 *GEAM* (Allied name) Greater East Asia Ministry, a sort of Colonial Office for Japan's newly-acquired territories; used originally for routine messages about rice purchases and the like, but later containing news of political or military interest. The kana syllables were represented by letters from the European alphabet and were written out horizontally on a grid of ten squares by ten,

73

with blank squares in asymmetrical positions which were frequently changed: 'a lopsided crossword puzzle' as a colleague astutely called it. When the text was complete, it was reciphered by transmitting it in vertical columns, so that a message enciphered as BAJME NSWLP ZUGFF etc would appear, and be transmitted, as BLTJK NOAFU XBIPT, etc. (See diagram.)

20 *Unnamed diplomatic code* possibly used only for espionage. This was used at least between the Foreign Office in Tokyo and the Japanese Embassy in Kabul, where a good deal of Axis intelligence work in the Far East was organised. It had a codebook of some two-letter and some four-letter groups, e.g. KT ship, KY German(y), LI report, MNEQ Singapore, NP troops, OPQV embassy, PG submarine, VL towards, VO sighted. This code-text was written out horizontally in the lop-sided crossword fashion of the preceding GEAM code, and reciphered by being transmitted vertically, but this time with the columns in a garbled order. Imagine that those columns are numbered not as 1234567890 but as 7458061392; then the column called '1' is sent first, followed by '2', and so on; the signal now reads:

NYCKM SRWLQ ITNJG etc.

A greatly simplified version of this code was to have been used by two Gurkhas who had been captured at the fall of Singapore and induced to volunteer to be dropped into Nepal as Japanese spies. After six months' training they were mistakenly dropped into India and captured. When interrogated they fell over themselves in their eagerness to explain how the code worked, but became hopelessly confused. The mind boggles at the havoc their signals would have wrought in Tokyo.

The Japanese could be careless over details. In the same Tokyo – Kabul traffic they twice sent the names and addresses of two of their agents in India, one of whom used the cover-name 'Bengal Tiger'. Both the messages and the agents were picked up.

21 *Unamed naval air code* Read at Brisbane, sometimes currently, otherwise without great delay. It used groups of two or four kana syllables for each word or phrase and was not reciphered. Most of its messages were between transport or reconnaissance aircraft and their bases, revealing air and sea movements, convoy escort duties and local weather reports. Although a low-grade system, it sometimes mentioned journeys by VIPs. The code was broken by Captain Nave, Royal Australian Navy, and his team at Melbourne in 1943 or earlier.

22 *Unnamed air force meteorological code* This used some three-digit code-groups as well as uncoded numerals which were self-summing: e.g. 0930 hours would appear as 099 303 (the third digit checking the sum of the other two) and 088 would stand for '8' in 'eight-tenths cloud'. It is, of course, an inadequate check; if the third figure is not the sum of the other two, which of the three is wrong? It gave daily forecasts which were invaluable for Allied airmen and air planning staff over a vast area; probably broken at Bangalore.

23 *Unnamed army air force 'main code system'* According to Lewin this was broken in the spring of 1944, probably by the British. He gives no further details by which to identify it.

24 *ABC* (British name) Army air force system, probably low-grade, used for weather reports, 'enemy aircraft spotted' reports, estimated times of arrival and similar tactical messages. Broken quite easily, and may have developed into or made way for BULBUL (No 25) later, though it has one cryptographical feature in common with No 22. Three-digit code reciphered with a key, the starting-place of which was indicated by a self-summing group: if the key was to start at group 52, this was shown by 527, hence the name ABC, meaning A+B=C. The key was usually added to the code-text but sometimes subtracted from it.

25 *BULBUL* (British, later Allied name) Army air force three-digit reciphered code, read until the end of December 1944 when it was replaced by a four-digit code which was never broken. The reason for this change may be possible to guess at: a colleague of mine recalls hearing some unsuspecting fighter pilots 'who marvelled at the boffins who presented them with so many sitting targets'. They of course knew nothing of sigint, and assumed that improved radar or some other electronic wizardry was at work. So ironically it may have been their success which led to the drying-up of BULBUL sigint. This was also a period when other units in Burma tightened up their signals security. It certainly seems clear that it was the source which enabled the RAF to shoot down over 100 enemy aircraft over Burma during a critical period in late 1944.

It is tempting to connect this code system also with intelligence about the movements of Japanese aircraft which were being ferried into Burma and nearby bases in Thailand. These reinforcements were adjudged important enough for the presence at WEC of a section concentrating on the Japanese 'kōkūrobu' (Air Route Departments whose function was 'to despatch, control, service

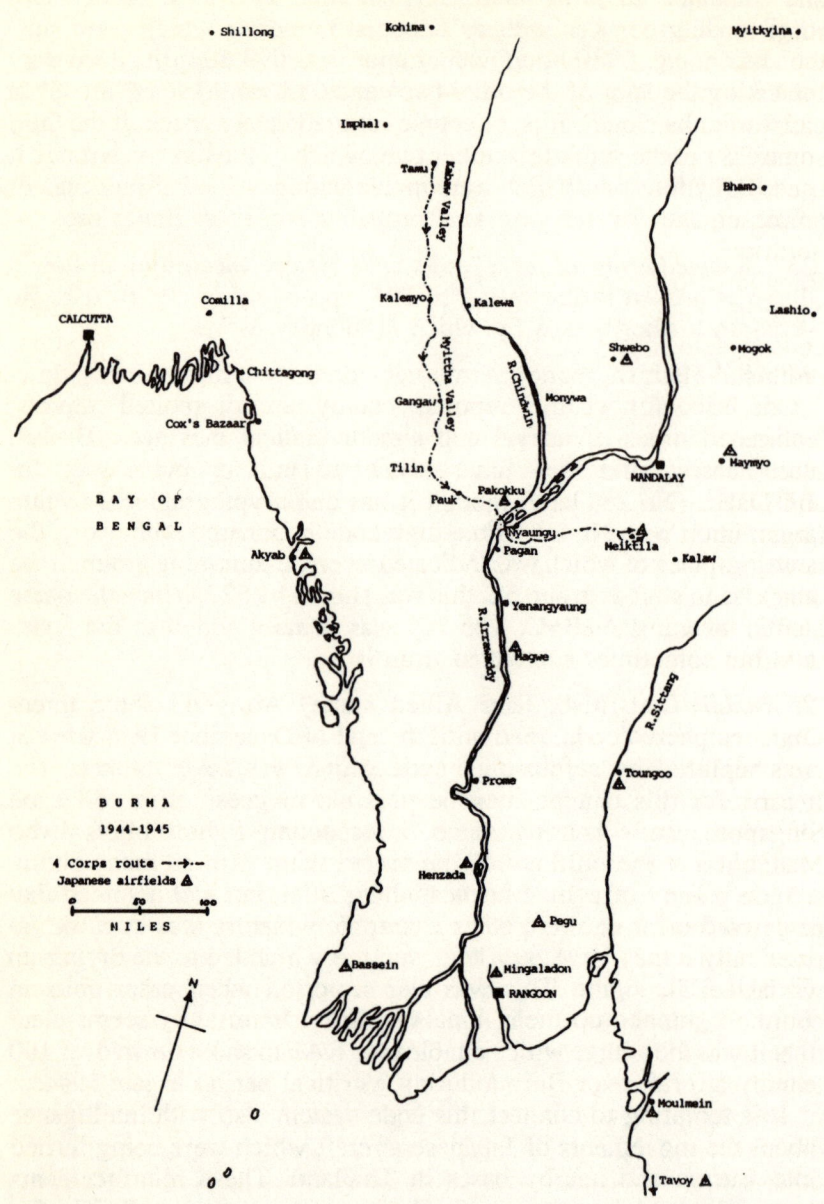

Map of Burma, 1944–45

and maintain aircraft, and supervise their crews, whilst en route to each Air Army area'. An important aspect of this job was the ferrying of replacement aircraft, particularly as Japanese losses mounted just when other units were being transferred eastwards.[27] Ferried aircraft entered the BULBUL area at Tavoy, some 250 miles south-east of Rangoon, and other airfields which used BULBUL included at least twelve which would have provided ample choice for ferrying to forward units. From south-east to north-west and north, these were Moulmein, Mingaladon (the Rangoon airfield), Pegu, Bassein, Henzada, Toungoo, Magwe, Meiktila, Pakokku, Maymyo, Akyab and Shwebo. No doubt other code systems also contributed to the tally of up-to-date information on this subject.

One BULBUL message announced a projected bombing raid on a place designated by an unbroken group in the alphabetical code of place-names, falling between two that had been broken: Chittagong and Dacca. The intercept unit at Comilla assumed they were the target, but it proved to be Cox's Bazaar – whereupon they added a new group to the codebook. Yet another concerned an imminent attack on a Dakota. The intercept unit, 368 Wireless Unit, alerted a Hurricane squadron, which 'jumped the Japanese' but unfortunately after they had shot down the Dakota.

26 *Unnamed army air force or army four-digit code*, captured on Okinawa, probably in May or June 1945. No cryptographic details are available, but it appears to have been widely used in every sense. It carried not only reports between major centres such as Saigon, Singapore and Tokyo on B29 reconnaissance flights over Manchuria, Force 136 (SOE) landings on the Kra isthmus, and a suicide poem from the Commander-in-Chief, but also more trivial news of footrot among troops trying to escape across the Sittang river, or of a sack of rice stolen from under a sentry's head while he was asleep – some sentry. This blurring of distinctions is a feature common to many systems from late 1944 onwards: the niceties had to be ignored. It also reported the move of a crack Japanese division from further north to the area provisionally selected for the invasion of western Malaya, Operation Zipper, which caused a flutter in the dovecots at headquarters. We shall see in Chapter Sixteen what other self-inflicted problems Zipper encountered.

27 *6633* (Japanese name) Army air force four-digit reciphered code, mostly for squadrons and above, interlocking well with BULBUL in producing intelligence about the Burma area and

disclosing orders (not usually tactical), squadron movements, reports of Allied air attacks, serviceable and damaged aircraft, aircrew fit for duty, fuel and ammunition stocks, and reinforcements expected. The codebook had been almost entirely broken, at least at Bletchley, before the end of 1943 – possibly as early as the middle of 1942 – and when a copy was captured in the Solomons it confirmed all the large part that had been broken, and filled in the gaps for code-groups that had rarely or never been used. Nevertheless changes in its other layers meant that it could not always be read currently, and in late 1944 there were hints of the impending introduction of a new codebook. Fortunately this did not happen.

I have explained the detailed working of this system, unusual in using not a key but a substitution table, in Chapter Nine. It was used over a very wide area from Imperial HQ in Tokyo to the Philippines, New Guinea, the East Indies and south-east Asia, including Burma. In the latter area it dealt with signals within the area of 3 Air Army (Kōkūgun), first at Singapore and later moving to Saigon to accompany its partner Southern Army HQ. 3 Air Army commanded units in Malaya, Java, Sumatra, north Borneo, Thailand and Indo-China as well as Burma; the six Air Regiments (Hikōsentai) were controlled by 5 Air Division (Hikōshidan) with its headquarters at Rangoon, linked with Burma Area Army (Biruma Hōmengun, which Slim curiously calls Burma Army Area) and an advanced HQ at Kalaw until the fighting drew near.

6633 was particularly illuminating during the enveloping moves which Slim was planning in central Burma in late 1944 and early 1945, when the exact plans of the Japanese Army were difficult to fathom. Troops operate *progressively* over a combat area, pushing forward or falling back as tactics permit or demand, and their signals frequently consist of a miscellany of localised orders and reports. In contrast, aircraft can operate from only a few airfields, particularly in a country of swamps, jungles and mountains like Burma. Every time a squadron was ordered to move its base from X to Y it gave a strong pointer to enemy intentions. Such a move was the pulling back of one of the Air Regiments, nominally of 48 fighters but by then of barely half that strength, in late 1944 – a crucial early hint, detected by 6633, that Kimura's defensive plan differed from that of Kawabe, and that he intended to fight from behind the Irrawaddy, not in front of it. This was an essential wisp of information, small in itself but clearly showing which way the wind was blowing, that influenced Slim in re-casting Operation Capital into

Extended Capital – a more drastic change of strategy than the slight variation of name suggests, and one which effectively won him the campaign.

6633 also carried one of the first Japanese reports of the second Chindit operation, under Wingate, in March 1944. This deep penetration, which landed nine thousand airborne troops hundreds of miles into Japanese-held territory, and within a few days had anti-aircraft guns and even Spitfires established there to defend them – an ambitious enterprise quite without precedent in the area, whatever place it ultimately occupies in the strategic balance-sheet – provoked a signal which a colleague remembers as showing 'an offended punched-in-solar-plexus anguish'.

The most striking thing about this batch of over two dozen codes and ciphers (21 codes and six ciphers) is their dazzling variety. Few people would have expected any one country, let alone one noted for its methodical approach to and experience of war over a long period, to devise so motley a collection. It should now be clear that there can be no simple answer to Kamaga's question 'Why were the Japanese army codes not broken?' First: several of them were. Second: there were probably as many as twenty.

8

What did they tell us?

Signals intelligence, like all intelligence, is most fruitful and most reliable when it is carefully co-ordinated, so that the products of several crypto systems are interwoven and matched with information coming in from other sources such as captured documents, prisoner interrogation and aerial reconnaissance. But I shall start by giving typical messages from single crypto systems.[28]

Notice that the phrase 'X groups lost' means that an error has crept in at some stage between the initial encoding and reciphering of the message and its final breaking and translating by the intercept and codebreaking unit. Sometimes the nature of the error may be obvious; then the codebreaker's emendation will be shown, but in brackets, to stress that it is conjectural. Similarly remarks like 'strong indications Mandalay' or 'fair indications Meiktila' will be found when the text has been mangled, or when the message hints at something not explicitly stated, which the person collating and evaluating the message, rather than the cryptographer-translator, wishes to add for the benefit of the intelligence staff at headquarters. It is not the codebreaker's job to make such conjectures on the basis of what he believes to be operational probability although he will naturally have that in mind when he casts up possible restorations of the text.

1 (Prome – Rangoon) 'On 16 September (1944) enemy fighter-bomber aircraft, probably of type HARIKEN (Hurricane) attacked river transport on the Irrawaddy 10 km south of here. Some of them were carrying stores and ammunition for this unit. Out of seven vessels three were sunk, one was set on fire, and one was badly damaged and had to be beached. The survivors of the native crews abandoned ship and escaped into the countryside. It is becoming increasingly difficult to recruit men for this job. One enemy aircraft is thought to have been damaged by anti-aircraft fire and may have crashed.'

Comment: All our Hurribombers returned safely. Their claims tallied closely with the Japanese account.

2 (Bassein–Rangoon, 7 December 1944) '50 Air Regiment (Hikō-sentai) statement of aircraft: 33 aircraft (one group lost: serviceable?) of which 15 Type 42 (Oscar), 18 Type 84 (Frank). One undergoing large-scale repairs, one awaiting parts ordered last month ...'
Comment: The usual complement of aircraft in a fighter-bomber unit such as this was 48, not 33, plus two out of action. Both aircraft referred to by the Japanese and US code-names were Nakajima-built fighter-bombers.

These were typical messages sent on the 6633 system, No 27 in Chapter Seven. Signals on this and other systems could contain surprises:

3 Madang (New Guinea) – Tokyo, 25 February 1944: 'The quality of the new Australian Army' (i.e. militia, not regular army troops) 'now facing us is far inferior.' On the other hand four days later Rabaul (New Britain) reported: 'The American Army in this area, compared with the Australian Army, is far inferior; when subjected to a sudden attack of fierce fighting they scream and run away'.[29]

A further long signal of 28 February 1944, sent to Tokyo and other HQs from Motozan (New Guinea) describes recent ground fighting and gives valuable details of Japanese units, their movements and their immediate plans:

4 'The withdrawal of the NAKANO group and MO unit has now been completed. The grace of Heaven and the most pertinent strategy employed by the NAKAI Detachment are directly responsible for the success ... Changes are now being made in the disposition of our forces to ambush the enemy forces in the Madang and Hansa areas on 22nd ... 3 Battalion of 102 Infantry Regiment ... has advanced to the Buna-Buna area on 27th. 20 Division (next 7 groups garbled) Madang by 25th ... The purpose of our plan to complete the concentration of 41 Division in Madang area by the end of February is to prepare defensive positions. At this moment 41 Division is in the area betwen the Gogol river and Mugil. Exclusive of anti-aircraft guns, 70 guns consisting of battalion guns, rapid-firing guns and so forth are at hand ... 51 Infantry Group is at Wewak. 6 South Seas Detachment is scheduled to be moved to Wewak upon the arrival of 20 Division in Hansa ...' and so on, with this all too voluble account.[30]

When intelligence from crypto and other sources was brought together it was possible to see a very detailed picture of the Japanese

81

forces in any area. On 29 May 1944 the 'Magic' summary began by reminding its readers that most previous reports of enemy army air force flying personnel had been 'fragmentary and scattered' but that they could now provide 'a complete return of pilot strength for the Fifth Air Army on 16 March.[31] This formation consisted of nine air regiments and one independent air squadron with a strength of some 150 aircraft, based in south China; its nominal strength should have been close to 400 aircraft. It is one of the ironies of war that at the same time Fifth Air Army was monitoring radio traffic between US aircraft and airfields not far away in order to predict when American bombers were likely to attack Japan.

From May 1944 regular editions of a book giving details of all major army units were being published, and by March 1945 the whole wartime history as well as the current order-of-battle of the army air force was available, together with the names of most of the commanding officers. One typical entry reads:

5 '75 *Hikōsentai (Air Regiment)*
Aircraft 'Lily' (Kawasaki Type 48–II light bomber)
Operational Code No 2379, Manshū 301
Home Depot Unit: 4 Kyōiku Hikōtai-Chūbu 94, Yokaichi, Honshū
Commanding Officer: Lt-Col DŌI Tsutomu
(The capitals for DŌI are a reminder that the surname comes first)
Organised June 1939. Stationed at Malang, Java, June-December 1943. Moved to New Guinea under command of 8 Hikōdan (Air Brigade) February 1944 and set up advanced base at Hollandia and rear base at Amahai, Ceram (Molucca Islands). Patrolled New Guinea coast and attacked US airfields and ships until its strength fell from 30 to 8 serviceable planes in April 1944. Withdrew to Amahai in April and to Ambesia, Celebes, in August, but was still staged forward for bombing attacks from Ambon and Ceram under 7 Hikōshidan (Air Division) and 3 Air Brigade. Attacked US landings on Morotai in September. Had strength of 22 Lilys in mid-October. Shifted to operations in Philippines in late October, where it appears at one time to have controlled 3 Hikōsentai in Leyte attacks. By early December 1944 strength was reduced to 3 planes, and on 28 December it was ordered to go temporarily to Hokoda, Honshū, for re-equipping. On 10 February ordered transferred from 7 Hikōshidan to 5 Kōkūgun (Air Army). However, unit was still at Hokoda in mid-March'.[32]

By April 1944 the standard of accuracy in reporting the movement of new aircraft from Japan to outlying islands was so high that there was serious Allied discussion whether they should be shown on the strength of their new units when they left Tokyo or when they arrived at their destination. 'After all, the books had to balance.'[33] It seems likely that during the closing stages of the war the Allies had a clearer and more up-to-date picture of Japanese unit strengths and detailed dispositions in the outer islands than Imperial General Headquarters in Tokyo.

These circumstantial assessments contrast sharply with Japanese staff appreciations of Allied plans, drawn with a broad brush and relying heavily on newspaper reports and bland generalisations from obvious facts:[34]

6 'By virtue of the new allocation of personnel of the Australian Air Force, Squadrons 450 to 459 which have been stationed in Britain are now on their way back to Australia by aircraft-carrier. British Sunderland flying-boats are shortly to be flown to Australia and it is expected that they will be used by the Australian Air Force. [Statement by Australian Air (Minister?)] Britain has despatched a fleet of 3 battleships, 3 aircraft carriers, 8 cruisers, 3 destroyers, ... 8 submarines for operations in the Pacific.' (23 February 1944)

7 'General Staff Tokyo appreciate the present war situation as follows:
(i) As the Allied operations in the Philippines progress, the greatest effort will be made by the Allies to develop bases in the Marianas and Philippines for offensive operations against Japan.
(ii) Bases will be advanced to the coast of Asia and to the islands near Japan.
(iii) An attempted invasion of Japan is envisaged in mid-1945.
(iv) Allied task forces may possibly operate in Imperial (Japanese) waters in March or April of this year.
(v) In the spring of 1945 Russia is expected to abrogate the neutrality pact with Japan and to enter the war against Japan during the latter part of 1945, if the European situation allows.' (13 February 1945)

A typical summary prepared by Allied Land Forces, South-West Pacific Area (MacArthur's HQ) interpreting the results of collating and assessing all available intelligence, runs:

8 *Movements of Japanese forces* (13 February 1945)

Further evidence has come to light of the westward movement of 5, 46 and 48 Division, though lack of shipping may delay the move. It now appears that three battalions of 48 Division from Timor will move to Malaya instead of a portion of 5 Division. 46 Division from the Lesser Sundas is also to move to Malaya. Special security measures are to be carried out in conjunction with all these moves. *Comment*: It was originally intended that part of 5 Division should move from the Arafura Sea area to Malaya, but now part of 48 Division from Timor is to move instead.' (This sentence seems to be for the benefit of those who had not read the two previous short sentences.) 'This re-arrangement is undoubtedly due to the acute shortage of shipping and the difficulty, therefore, of moving 5 Division elements over a longer distance ... The net result is that ... 5 Division is to spread over the whole area previously occupied by these three Divisions.'[35]

Similar predictions had successful outcomes:

(i) The complete plan for a Japanese attack on Bougainville Island, including the exact date; this enabled the Americans to repel the attack with serious Japanese losses;

(ii) The complete plan for an attack on Aitape in New Guinea was discovered a month before D-Day;

(iii) It was discovered before an American landing at Hollandia, New Guinea, that it was defended only by service troops and that no Japanese reinforcements had arrived;

(iv) The orthodox intelligence estimate of Japanese strength on Biak Island was 3,000. Sigint showed that this was nearer 7,000, and this figure was confirmed after the landings, which fortunately had been on a much larger scale than at first proposed.

(v) The location of almost every formation, down to division level, outside Japan and Manchuria, was regularly reported;

(vi) Long before the attempted invasion of India, early in 1944, the movement of four Japanese divisions into Burma was revealed, together with other evidence of the impending attack.[36]

Separate reports based on sigint gave explicit details of shipping movements which would be passed on to Allied aircraft and submarines. There had been particularly close co–operation between air and sea forces in the western Pacific in November 1944, when a code message from the Transport HQ at Moji, on Kyushu, asked for air escorts for two convoys, HI–81 and MI–27, leaving Japan on 15 November and carrying troops to reinforce the Philippines. This message gave expected positions at noon on each day from 15 to 22 November. At least one of the convoys was sighted by an American aircraft, and American submarines, given full details of the ships' course, sank two ships and disabled two others.

From the start of the war merchant shipping had been Japan's

Achilles' heel. Only two-thirds of its imports were being carried in its own vessels in 1941, and since many of these would be called on to transport and maintain its troops over an immense area, it was evident that the merchant fleet was inadequate. Yet nothing was done to increase the output of the shipyards until much later, and by mid-1944 Japan's losses far exceeded its new launchings.

The raw material most affected was oil, more than half of which had been imported in foreign tankers before the war. It seems probable that the oil shortage, aggravated by the freezing of its assets by Britain, the USA and the Netherlands in July 1941, and exacerbated by the knowledge that the longer it waited, the smaller its reserves would be, played a large part in Japan's decision to attack Britain and the USA in December 1941, and in the priority given to acquiring the oil refineries of the Netherlands East Indies. New tanker construction, and the seizure of the oilfields in Sumatra, Java and Borneo held the position stable until late 1943, but as the American offensive in the Pacific gained momentum their submarines could operate closer to the main tanker routes. In purely naval actions in early 1944, off Truk and Palau, the US fast carrier fleet sank a third of the tankers attached to the Japanese combined fleet, and in February 1944 a message from Tokyo to Manila reported 'the present position is that most of the tankers returning to Japan' (i.e. fully laden) 'are being lost'.[37] During the rest of the war these losses continued to rise.

By June 1945 the shortage of shipping in the East Indies area was so acute that the Japanese had decided to use a hospital ship, the *Tachibana Maru* 'for purposes other than those prescribed by the Geneva Convention'.[38] The ship was renamed the *Hirose Maru* and bore floodlit red crosses twenty feet high. It was to carry 1500 troops and 150 tons of stores and munitions from Tual in the Kri Islands to Surabay in Java. In case the vessel was stopped and searched, the troops were issued with hospital clothing, daily sickness reports were kept, and the regimental colours were sent by air so as not to give the game away.

The messages arranging this deception, sent in May, were read, and the vessel was intercepted by two destroyers north of Timor. The search party found that cases marked 'medical supplies' contained ammunition, and the only wound among the patients was confessed to being the result of a packing-case being dropped on a thumb. In order to conceal the source of the information leading to the interception of the ship, its sighting had to be attributed to air reconnaissance, and – as always in such instances – a flight was especially arranged so that the enemy would not become suspicious.

The best-known single message of the war was probably that which led to the death of Admiral Yamamoto on 18 April 1943. The JN 25 code carried a message on 13 April, giving details of his impending visit to naval air bases in the Solomon Islands. (Kahn gives an excellent account of the whole affair.)[39] The detailed timetable gave all units time to prepare for the occasion – Yamamoto was a stickler for precision – and it soon emerged that his aircraft would come within the extreme range of US combat aircraft.

The Americans weighed the risk that to use this information would be to blow the gaff and perhaps gain them the assassination of one man for the loss of great quantities of tactical and strategic intelligence. The heavy personal item in their balance-sheet was that they could not forgive him for the totally unexpected, unprovoked and devastating attack on Pearl Harbor, which was known to be his personal idea. It was also reckoned that his loss would depress Japanese morale, and that he was a ruthlessly efficient naval commander whom it would be hard to replace adequately.

The opposing case was that the area he was inspecting was some 360 miles from the nearest US air base, and the best place to intercept him, so as to avoid the defences at his destination, was 40 miles further on. Clearly there was only an outside chance that American fighters would be operating by pure chance at the extreme limit of their range exactly at the place and time which coincided with Yamamoto's arrival. The plan proved irresistible, the attack went ahead, Yamamoto's plane was shot down, and he was killed.

Why was the JN 25 code not altered? Probably not because of the lame cover story which sought to suggest another source for the information, but because no country cares to think objectively about the possibility that its codes may be penetrable – however well it breaks enemy codes. Even when rumours arose in the USA, just as they had after the Midway leak, the Japanese chose to ignore them.

The enormous Pacific area affords a great many spectacular examples of the successful use of sigint; what is more surprising is that the breaking of a Japanese machine cipher could also reveal important details of what was going on in Germany and its occupied territories in Europe.

The central figure was Ōshima, who had been military attaché in Berlin from 1934, and Ambassador, while still an Army Lieutenant-General, since 1938. He had met Hitler as early as 1935, and from then until 1945 he remained in close touch with all the Nazi leaders, who as Axis partners frequently confided secret information to him. He predicted the German attack on the Soviet Union and sent regular reports on the German assessment, and above all Hitler's assessment, of Russia's ability to survive. In 1942 he passed on details of the German blockade-runners carrying strategically important materials between Germany and Japan. By March 1943 so many of them had been lost that Germany inaugurated a submarine transport service to carry rubber and other scarce materials from Asia to Europe. It was Ōshima who broke this news to Tokyo, and thus to the Allies. The machine ciphers used by Ōshima and his military and naval attachés were routinely read with only occasional setbacks, and they yielded an abundance of material.

The extent of U-boat activity in the Indian Ocean was something which the Admiralty was perhaps reluctant to recognise, and it is still largely overshadowed by the Battle of the Atlantic. It began in reverse: in the summer of 1942, after taking part in an attack on British shipping in a Madagascan port, the Japanese submarine I-30 proceeded round the Cape of Good Hope and through the Atlantic to the Bay of Biscay, finally docking at Lorient in early August. In October the first of the German U-boats of the new class IXD_2 arrived in the Indian Ocean, and 'by the end of the year five U-boats had sunk over 170,000 tons of Allied shipping there. More were sent in 1943, some of them operating out of Penang. By the end of the war 57 U-boats had been in operation in the Indian Ocean, and had sunk at least 151 ships, totalling some 935,000 tons'.[40]

Ōshima's reports in early 1942 not only gave some warning of that unwelcome threat but also alerted us to the coming offensive in North Africa. On 17 March Ribbentrop emphasised that 'Germany would eagerly welcome a Japanese invasion into the Indian Ocean whereby contact between Europe and Asia might be achieved'. Hitler was 'about to start a new blitzkrieg to give an all-out blow to Russia, and intended to attack through the eastern Mediterranean, Africa and the Caucasus, and to fight through to the Indian Ocean'. Ōshima mentioned that Ribbentrop had read this from a written document, so as to make the German position very clear. Later he reported that the Germans intended to destroy not only London but the whole of Britain with their V-weapons.[41]

For his part the head of the Japanese Naval Mission in Berlin and the naval attaché visited Admiral Doenitz in April 1944 and were given first a pep talk and then full details of two new types of high-speed U-boats: their size, tonnage, armament, speed, endurance and ability to evade radar and depth-charge attack. Four months later they visited Danzig to inspect the large-scale production of the larger 1,600-ton U-boat, and reported on the speed of construction, assembly methods, numbers and performance.[42] These reports both corroborated and were corroborated by aerial reconnaissance, captured documents and reports from agents: the classic formula for bringing several channels of intelligence to flow together.

A more comforting discovery, through an Ōshima report of early July 1943 was that the Germans were now less suspicious than they had been earlier that U-boat Enigma was being broken. When U-boats were withdrawn from the north Atlantic in May that year, the German naval command had been uncertain whether the Allies' ability to divert convoys and locate U-boats was the result of penetrating Enigma, technical wizardry or treachery. Increasingly Allied radar was perceived to be the explanation, the more so when the introduction of the fourth wheel for the Enigma machine failed to reduce the effectiveness of attacks on U-boats. They were not to know that, against all the odds, Bletchley Park had succeeded in solving the problems posed by the extra wheel with little delay. Subsequent German efforts to improve their defence against airborne radar were constantly watched through Enigma.[43]

In July 1944 the Japanese naval attaché announced that although the German Air Force had only 100 jet aircraft it would have 300 by September and would be receiving them at the rate of 1,000 a month by January 1945. By December he blamed the relative failure to build the jet-propelled Messerschmitt 163 on Germany's inability to produce more than a tenth of one of the components of the aircraft's special fuel, and this reason was later confirmed. Finally in October 1944 he sent a lengthy account of the Arado 234 jet aircraft.[44]

The military attaché in Berlin, Colonel Ito, was no less communicative.[45] After touring the Atlantic coastal defences in autumn 1943 he sent Tokyo full details of the fortifications near towns like Boulogne, Dieppe, Le Havre and Cherbourg: for example 'tank-ditches, in three rows of two mines each for every three square metres ... in La Rochelle district four 200mm naval guns, Le Havre four 300mm guns, Cherbourg four 380mm heavy field guns' and so on. I need not stress the value of this minutely detailed information in planning the invasion of Normandy.

This summary does no more than lift the veil from some corners of a large and intricate picture, yet it should demonstrate how wide and how detailed an understanding sigint gave of every aspect of Japan's – and occasionally Germany's – activities, capabilities, problems and plans.

9

How were they sent?

Let us follow a typical message from start to finish, remembering that the finish may be a dead heat, or at least a close-run thing, between friend and foe. The details will vary from one system to the next; I have chosen to illustrate the pattern by the reciphered code which was my daily or nightly bread-and-butter for several years.

1. Lt-Col ETO Toyoki, commanding 64 Air Regiment at the Army Air Force station at Meiktila in central Burma, writes out his plain-text message to HQ 5 Air Division at Rangoon, and sends his orderly to the signals office with it. It begins:

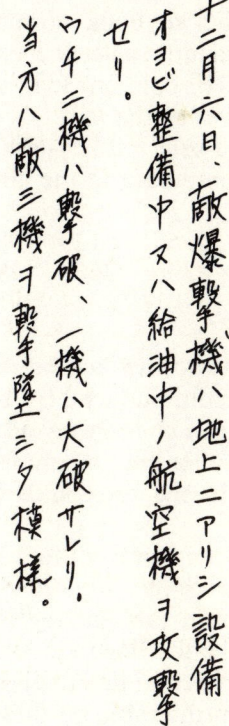

2. It reads 'On December 6th enemy aircraft attacked our ground installations and aircraft which were being refuelled. Two of our aircraft were destroyed and one was badly damaged. We believe that three enemy aircraft were brought down'.

3. The contents, security grading and identity of sender of the message will normally determine the crypto system to be used.[46] This is a fairly important Army Air Force message, so it will go by 6633 (see Chapter Seven, No 27). The cipher clerk selects Volume One for encoding, and looks up each of the words, numerals and phrases in turn, writing down the four-digit groups as he goes, thus forming the code-text:

juni-gatsu	'December' (literally 12th-month)	is 2671
roku-hi	'6th'	8453
teki	'enemy'	6967
bakugeki-ki	'bombers'	5129
wa	(indicates subject of verb)	0813

giving 2671 8453 6967 5129 0813 etc

4. Next he picks up the keybook currently in use, opens it at random, and equally at random selects a starting-point on that page. If the start is on page 16, column 3, row 7, he writes down the indicator 1637 at the head of the text.

5. He now writes out the selected key-text under the original code-text, group by group, continuing to the end of the message:

| | 2671 | 8453 | 6967 | 5129 | 0813 | etc | (code-text) |
| (1637) | 9814 | 5205 | 7348 | 3682 | 4987 | etc | (key-text) |

6. If this were a normal additive key he would simply add the two lines together and the result, prefaced by 1637, would be the signal text. Notice that this is *non-carrying* addition, which is normal cryptographic practice. After all, you are working from left to right, and are not interested in the total as a useful statistic; it is not ordinary arithmetic.

7. But 6633 uses a different procedure, a square substitution table consisting of 100 random digits. The cipher clerk takes each pair of upper and lower figures in turn, disregarding the indicator 1637, using the first figure of the top line to give the column of the square, and the first figure of the second line to give the row, and then writes down the figure given in the table by these co-ordinates:

Columns shown by code-text

Rows shown by key-text

	0	1	2	3	4	5	6	7	8	9
0	4	7	3	0	5	9	2	6	1	8
1	9	5	1	8	3	0	6	2	7	4
2	5	0	7	4	2	1	8	6	9	3
3	3	9	2	7	4	6	0	1	8	5
4	2	3	8	0	9	7	0	4	1	5
5	7	2	0	1	3	5	9	8	4	6
6	0	1	9	3	8	4	7	6	5	2
7	1	8	6	4	2	7	5	0	9	3
8	6	1	9	5	7	2	3	8	0	4
9	8	4	7	2	6	3	1	5	7	0

which gives:

	2671	8453	6967	5129	0813	etc	(columns)
	9814	5205	7348	3682	4987	etc	(rows)
(1637)	7323	4291	5508	6193	2714	etc	(signal text)

This is not a Latin square, in which no number is repeated in the same row or column; this one has been rather carelessly compiled. Sometimes such a signal will be prefaced by the discriminant 6633 to show which system it uses.

8. The cipher clerk passes this signal text to the signals staff. The unit address, if it is outside the text, is disguised by using an address codebook. The place of origin, Meiktila, and the destination, Rangoon, may be similarly disguised, and the signal is ready for transmission, prefaced by such clerical details as the reference number of the signals office, the number of groups in the signal, and the date and time at which the message was filed.

9. The Meiktila operator contacts the Rangoon operator as soon as his schedule permits, checks signal strength and clarity, and transmits the signal, using the international Morse letters to represent the

numbers (a system introduced about 1937 to replace a very cumbersome kana transcription):

```
0 1 2 3 4 5 6 7 8 9
O N Z S M A T R W V
```

10. The Rangoon operator, working at 1 Kōkū tsūshin rentai (Air Signals Regiment) receives the signal as letters but transcribes them back to a numerical text. He passes it to the cipher clerk, who puts it through the successive stages in reverse order. The indicator shows him where the key-text starts, and he uses the square by seeing in which column figure 7 stands in the 9th row (answer 2) and so on. That is where the snags of a non-Latin square appear: he can find it in columns 2 and 8, so that the original text may have either of these. A properly constructed square will eliminate this uncertainty. Once the process is complete he passes the text of the message to HQ 5 Air Division for action.

10

How were they intercepted?

WEC at Delhi was part of a comprehensive array of Allied sigint units, large and small, which co-operated to ensure good coverage and exchanged news when progress was made. Furthest back were the very large units at Bletchley Park and Arlington Hall, Virginia, formerly a spacious girls school. Both of them tackled the really intractable problems of high-grade crypto systems that had never yet been broken, and fundamentally new materials which had lost us the ability to read a hitherto broken system. At a halfway stage came the large American and British units at Delhi, the former called 'US 8', the latter WEC with its two main out-stations: Western Wireless Sub-Centre at Bangalore in south India and Eastern Wireless Sub-Centre at Barrackpore near Calcutta. These were concerned with Japanese Army and Army Air traffic.

There was also a large naval sigint unit at Anderson, near Colombo, and smaller ones at Kilindini near Mombasa and on Mauritius. They worked closely with US naval stations at Guam, Leyte and elsewhere, and acted as longstop for signals, travelling 4,000 miles or more, which through the vagaries of short-wave transmission, had evaded the main chain of intercept stations. These, quite apart from the huge US network in the Pacific, ran in a great arc from Melbourne, Canberra, Brisbane and Darwin through Ceylon to Calcutta and south China.

Further forward were smaller units, many of them semi-mobile in the sense that their men and equipment could be carried by truck to a new site where they could unload and settle down to work in tents and bashas – the local thatched huts. They were generally attached to Army or Corps headquarters and their RAF equivalents, and later to Divisional HQs also. In Burma they included the Army 115 and 202 Special Wireless Companies and the RAF 355, 367 and 368 Wireless Units, as well as 33 Corps SWC and 14 Army Special Wireless Group. Some names were changed as the campaign developed: the SWC at Monywa became 300 Indian Special Wireless Section. They worked mainly on lower-grade traffic with more immediate tactical significance, some of it too low-powered to be intercepted further back, and on various forms of traffic analysis: wireless-telegraphy, radio-telephony and direction-finding; much of the 'low-grade' traffic yielded intelligence of great tactical value, and as the Japanese found their communications under increasing strain the boundaries between grades of sigint became blurred. They also intercepted and sent back to their parent units some higher-grade signals, and were thus co-ordinated within the wider inter-service arrangements for the region.

These units moved forward from Bengal and Assam into Burma as the 1944 campaign got under way: Comilla, Cox's Bazaar and Akyab, Imphal and Monywa, with remoter sites at Shillong and Bhamo. Similarly in other theatres units moved up into the Philippines, New Guinea and the Cocos-Keeling Islands, strategically placed south-west of Java and halfway between Ceylon and Australia, regularly reconnoitred but never occupied by the Japanese; the cable station continued relaying traffic throughout the war. Enemy signals in and around Sumatra and Java were monitored by vessels taking part in offensive operations east and south-east of Ceylon, an enormous tract of water which was particularly hard to cover by normal intercept arrangements.

Sending the text of intercept from the Far East back to Bletchley Park was an arduous business. Presumably because it was considered vital to avoid even the tiny risk that the Japanese might in turn intercept this traffic and recognise it as their own, every numeral or letter was enciphered by one-time pad or later by Typex, and transmitted in that form. I have no figure for the Far East, but in the Middle East the RAF by itself set a record in June 1943 by transmitting 104,764 five-figure groups of Luftwaffe traffic to Britain *in one day*.[47] It speaks eloquently for the dedication of the cipher and signals clerks and the operators at each end of this 'nonsense' traffic that it travelled so well – though since they would certainly not have been told its nature it was actually no more nonsensical than any other enciphered text. As we shall see in Chapter Twelve, the summarised information derived from these signals was handled at least as securely when it was sent out to the overseas commanders.

Almost all this network had been set up in a hurry, reacting to disasters as they occurred. Practically the only pre-war British intercept unit in the whole area concerned with Japanese signal and other intelligence had been the Far East Combined Bureau (FECB), set up at Hong Kong in 1934, and later perforce evacuated first to Singapore and then to Ceylon. This out-station of GC&CS included a small Australian contingent from 1937, and early in 1940 the Australian General Staff established their own sigint section, recruiting four academics, who later joined forces with a group at Melbourne headed by Commander Nave. Most of Australia's sigint personnel were in the Middle East, but intercept stations were built at Melbourne, Canberra, Brisbane and Darwin, and the group co-operated with FECB at Hong Kong and the Dutch in Java.[48]

Nave had trained with the British China Fleet as a Japanese linguist in 1925 and had worked in London, on the China station and at FECB before returning to Australia. He was a pioneer in Japanese sigint, like Tiltman, and his team is said to have broken JN 25 and decoded the preliminary 'West wind clear' signal sent out on 19 November 1941 in J 19 to the Japanese mission in Australia, warning them to stand by for a further message that relations with Britain were in imminent danger, meaning an imminent attack.

James Rusbridger, whose book on Nave, *Cryptographer Extraordinary*, is expected shortly, wrote in *Encounter* of January 1986 that FECB broke the first 'Winds' message and sent it to Washington before the US had broken it, and the Dutch team broke the 'Winds *Execute*' message of 4 December and gave it to the US Consul-General in Java, who replied, 'I attach little or no importance to it, and view it with some suspicion. Such reports have been common since 1936'. Nave's unit also broke the signal of 4 December ordering the mission to burn most of its codes and ciphers, and the 'Execute' signal. Unfortunately breaking and transmission took too long for it to reach the Australian Defence Department until the day after Pearl Harbor.[49]

The Australians were, however, unable to extend these first promising results, and when the Japanese carried out a crippling raid on Darwin in February 1942, using nearly 250 aircraft, they had been unable to give even the most general warning; the impression had been that the enemy were about to assault Java.[50] The unexpected ferocity of this attack, and Australia's apparent inability to do much to prevent it, led to fears that the Japanese would soon be mounting an invasion, probably on the long and vulnerable coastline of northern Queensland, and there were demands for troops to be brought back from north Africa to defend the homeland, especially after the initial Japanese successes in New Guinea, which was seen as a stepping-stone in a 'Drang nach Süden'. In the event, it has become clear that although the Japanese Navy would have favoured this, the Army felt that other areas had a higher priority in its plans. Soon after this Australia was incorporated into MacArthur's South-West Pacific Area.

The Dutch had set up a three-man army cryptographic unit, Room 14, as part of the General Staff at Bandung as early as 1933, and in 1934 they added a two-man navy team at Batavia, now Jakarta.[51] Although their linguistic qualifications were slender they made a fairly deep initial penetration into a narrow section of Japanese signals traffic; like us, they were surprised by the variety of ciphers used and the difficulty of applying the understanding of one system to help in breaking another. Nevertheless the tiny naval team were able to continue reading a fleet code despite the sweeping changes made when the Japanese armed services were partially mobilised after the 'Marco Polo bridge incident' of July 1937; later they passed on the text of Purple intercepts to GCHQ, and co-operated with Britain, Australia and the USA. Both teams were strengthened as the long-term intentions of the Axis powers became clearer, but it was impossible for the Dutch sigint staff to keep up with the ever-tighter security introduced into Japanese signals over the next four years, just as it had been for the Poles with Enigma. We must bear in mind the demoralising effect on the Netherlands East Indies of the Dutch capitulation in May 1940 following the German invasion. But one of the intercept stations was safely evacuated when the Japanese invaded Java shortly afterwards, and the staff finished up in Darwin and Arlington. Nigel West calls this a 'clandestine station'; I cannot understand his choice of words.[52] The station was of course moved before the Japanese occupation of Java was completed.

Canada too formed a part of the intercept network. Earlier their main commitment had been to the Battle of the Atlantic, but as well as the Royal Canadian Navy tracking room at Ottawa and an intercept station in Nova Scotia there were two units in the west: one at Victoria on Vancouver Island and another further north on the British Columbia coast. These had an important role in extending the coverage of the large area round the Alaska peninsula and the Aleutian Islands, especially during the Japanese operations there from mid-1942, and their occupation of two islands. It is tempting to speculate whether modern history would have evolved very differently if Imperial Russia had not sold Alaska to the United States in 1867 for some seven million dollars – the first step in American expansion.

Canada had had problems in 1941 when it ill-advisedly decided to employ Yardley to oversee their cryptanalytical team. Yardley had been a brilliant codebreaker during the 1914–18 war, but when his department had been closed down in the late 1920s he had written an autobiography which embarrassed the susceptibilities of the US government. He later decided to offer his services where they might be better appreciated – including the Nationalist Chinese government of Chiang Kai-Shek – and GCHQ believed that he was too much of a rolling stone to be a good security risk. He was removed from his post at Ottawa at Britain's urgent request.

Britain's main partner in sigint, at least after Pearl Harbor, was now the United States, and the relationship grew closer as the Americans saw how urgent it was to set their house in order after the Pearl Harbor disaster, which better internal organisation could have prevented, or at least minimised. Their potential manpower and resources were incomparably large, and the problem was to mobilise them in the most effective way possible. At first the reorganisation was held up by shortages of appropriately-trained personnel, aggravated by the failure of the Civil Service commission to understand what was at issue. By April 1943 these obstacles were being overcome, and Colonels McCormack and Telford Taylor visited Bletchley Park to see what their opposite numbers were doing. They were accompanied by William Friedman, one of the most distinguished of American cryptanalysts.

Before then there had of course been co-operation, and some crypto ideas had been exchanged, but that was all. It was not until this visit, nearly eighteen months after Pearl Harbor, that real progress was made, presumably because it was not expected that Britain would be able to offer much more than a begging bowl, but also because the Americans were doubtful about the efficacy and security of another British intelligence organisation, MI6, in comparison with their own ISS.

When the Americans arrived they learnt for the first time – although there had been a few Americans working at Bletchley Park since the middle of 1942 – how very successful the British had been in penetrating and exploiting German high-grade military traffic sent by the Enigma machine, and how useful this traffic would be to them. They were also particularly struck by the systems used for giving sigint wide circulation to those who needed it, while maintaining a very high standard of security. Finally they agreed that it was essential to accept a sensible division of labour over the great volume of Japanese traffic to be dealt with.

This important visit laid the foundations for close co-operation of a sort that had hardly been dreamed of before in so sensitive a field of activity. The formal BRUSA (British–US Agreement) provided for much more than fraternal goodwill and friendly exchange visits. Very close practical integration of the sigint services was sought, and wherever possible techniques, practices and vocabulary were to be standardised in order to avoid misunderstandings. Of course there were hiccups. From time to time each side trespassed on ground allocated to the other, and overseas heads of units did not always see eye to eye over their terms of co-operation, or accept that the other party was sticking to the agreement. Nevertheless it was a remarkable achievement and it reaped a rich harvest.

I never had occasion to visit the enormous American unit at Delhi, not far from WEC, which worked closely with us. Rumours abounded: that every officer had his own jeep; that genial black Master-Sergeants addressed colonels as 'Bud'; that to save time generals travelled along the interminable corridors by scooter; that research projects were devoted to subjects more rarefied than the most abstruse PhD thesis yet conceived; that groups of well-groomed majors sat trying to prove the identity of a code-group only once encountered, and even then suspect – and so on. I sometimes wonder if this rumour-laden unit really existed. *'Rumor'*, like *amor*, *'volat undique'*. Most of it was probably eyewash, fed on envy; but it is true that they were far more generously staffed and provided than we were.

As in other branches of intelligence work, Britain was often the poor relation. General Slim mentions the occasion when he was invited to pose for a photograph while he was visiting Stilwell's US troops and airmen, and said, 'I should like to have it taken shaking hands with an American private soldier'. A long search ensued, in which 'sure enough, they were all sergeants; the nearest was a two-striper but never a simple private'.[53] A typical British non-commissioned officer with several years' service (for example a 'sergeant, 1st class, clerk, special intelligence duties') would be amused to find that his opposite number was a raw US lieutenant with a roomful of staff and a chestful of medals. An American Private, First Class, was paid more than a British lieutenant. The Americans were often embarrassed by this material gulf, but both parties learned to live with it.

The Americans' impression was that the British had 'a horror of precise planning and a preference for inspired muddling-through'.[54] They had several advantages: though the Japanese entry into the war in December 1941 caught them unawares they were able to make some use of the experience we had gained, after an equally unpromising start, in two and a quarter years of modern warfare.

Their mainland was never seriously threatened, let alone attacked. They enjoyed a far more generous supply of personnel and equipment for signals intelligence, which enabled them to maintain a higher intercept standard by double-banking operators and sets on each assigned frequency and on 'search' tasks. They were also able to use, in this and other branches of intelligence, many very bright 'Nisei' personnel – second-generation American-born Japanese – and to spare a lavish number of men and women on the intensive Japanese language courses, which lasted almost twice as long as the Bedford series.

It is true that their research into minor oddities of signals traffic was sometimes over-indulgent and even 'ivory-tower', but this was offset by their characteristic flair for 'playing their hunches'. The discrepancies were minor: once they had got over their initial surprise that we were doing what they thought they were doing on their own, and could teach them a thing or two in return, we could work closely together and produce excellent results.

11

How were they broken?

The message which we left at the end of Chapter Nine has been picked up not only by the Rangoon operator for whom it was intended but also by one of the intercept stations described in Chapter Ten. The Allied operator has been standing by for the scheduled transmissions on the Meiktila-Rangoon frequencies which he has been assigned to cover, and he intercepts the signal. It now acquires further clerical prefixes, showing the frequencies, call-signs, day and time of interception, quality and strength of signal, and so forth, and is passed to the codebreaking unit.

Here I have to watch my step. The British authorities naturally do not wish to reveal detailed codebreaking techniques that might enable potential enemies to break our codes, or to alert them to ways of tightening their crypto security so as to stop us breaking theirs. The question is how far the methods used between 1939 and 1945 are relevant to the days of the one-time pad and the powerful 'number-cruncher' computer. In the words of Sir Stuart Milner-Barry, who succeeded Gordon Welchman as head of Hut Six at Bletchley Park, the methods of 1939–45 'must seem to present-day cryptanalysts rather like fighting with bows and arrows'.[55]

I have no intention of tweaking the noses of those in authority, and shall therefore give some examples from the eighteenth and nineteenth centuries, and closer to our time will confine myself to what has already been widely written about since 1974, when Winterbotham let the Enigma cat out of the Ultra bag. Many of these principles were already known to readers of the Biggles or even the Beau Geste era; others have been compendiously explained in David Kahn's important book *The Codebreakers*, published in 1967.[56] Most of them are familiar to, or immediately guessable by, solvers of any respectable crossword puzzle.

Let us be unorthodox and start with the hardest case. It is common knowledge that if properly used the one-time pad (OTP) is unbreakable. Yet if an air force HQ regularly sends orders by radio, using an OTP, in a set pattern, so that a 13-group signal frequently precedes an attack on point X, and a 17-group signal on point Y, then it is not necessary to break the signal to deduce something significant about its contents – and to act accordingly by warning those at either point to stand by, to alert the defences, and so on. That is not codebreaking but common sense. It will not be dependable: if the first message has four groups added to specify the scale or urgency of an attack, or to identify a target in greater detail, it will be misleading; perhaps we should alert both places. We have taken the first steps in attacking a crypto system, but we shall get no further with an OTP apart from learning what we can about the background to the signal: where was it sent from, and to whom, and what do we know from other sources about the units that may be at each end of that signal link?

Commonsense similarly shows the next state. One of the commonest signals, even in the 1914–18 war, was 'Your message indecipherable; please repeat', and one of the most smugly comfortable moments for a codebreaker is to know that he had no difficulty in reading it. If, therefore, a message is intercepted which is repeated soon afterwards, it is a fair guess that the short intervening message, sent in the opposite direction, is a request for repeat.

The over-use of regular preambles, stereotyped address patterns or predictable 'pro-forma' styles of messages has been widely condemned as bad security for at least seventy years, yet it did not prevent all parties in the 1939–45 war from succumbing to the same deadly sin. The Japanese regularly ended messages with 'owari' (end), and when they were long enough to require sending in two parts they used 'tsuzuku' (continued) in the middle. A celebrated Enigma example was provided by the German officer commanding a small patrol in the Qattara Depression in North Africa, who sent daily reports saying 'Nothing to report', which helped to reveal the daily key-settings. It was important to leave him there undisturbed.

There is a fundamental psychological problem here. The orthodox military mind, like the proverbial Civil Service mind, is noted more for conforming to established precedent and using hackneyed official phrases than for eccentricity of outlook or originality of language. Of course there have been honourable exceptions. It is no accident that their scholastic background has been partly conditioned by the phrase 'It's not done'. Nor is it an accident that Lord Dacre wrote of the 'apparent anarchy' at Bletchley. He was not suggesting that we were a bunch of red-hot revolutionaries but that we were free-thinkers, and that this flexibility of approach paid dividends. Signals security means avoiding uniform practices and deliberately keeping messages short and clear and their expression varied. This certainly entails following instructions, and it is to be hoped that they emphasise this principle. Kahn points out that the Allies were quicker to recognise this: their 'instructions for cipher clerks on how to set up their machines and how to encipher sometimes explained that certain procedures should not be used because they would help the enemy solve the messages. The German instructions never motivated like that'.[57]

To train the officer who drafts the message, the cipher clerk who turns it into a signal, and the operator who transmits it, to follow the principle of constant variation is not easy. The stronger the military machine, the harder it becomes — it is almost a self-contradiction. They feel safer if they follow the 'regular' procedure and don't 'step out of line'. Even the words are comforting.

Yet this is precisely what lets the enemy in. In Aileen Clayton's words, 'Repetition is a God-send to the codebreaker'.[58] Patterns of signals procedure emerge clearly, whether within one formation or across a dozen. If you can work out the position of a new signals HQ, by direction-finding, and the type of formation to which it is attached, by combining all branches of intelligence, you can deduce the probable subject-matter of many of their incoming and outgoing messages even before they are sent.

Sometimes the codebreakers can provoke a message: the RAF were asked to mine certain clearly-defined channels so that the German minesweepers could be instructed to sweep them, thus providing a crib since their message would specify the known co-ordinates of the area to be cleared, and this would give the new key: this process was known as 'gardening', not because the message was planted but by the accident that the RAF's contribution was randomly called 'Operation Garden'.[59] I instance another ingenious planted crib by the Austrians in Chapter Twelve; but the device must not be over-used or even the dullest enemy will notice.

Aileen Clayton describes the complex interplay of friendly and enemy signals very well: 'It was a case of our listening to German messages about them listening to us', and she describes an RAF reconnaissance aircraft which sent a signal back to its base in Malta with details of an Axis convoy that it had spotted. The signal was intercepted by the German *Horchdienst*, the equivalent of our Y Service, concerned with plain-language or low-grade cipher messages, and they reported it to their HQ. 'Malta Y Service, of course, intercepted the German signal, and since they knew exactly the contents of the original reconnaissance message, they were then able to break the code for the day.' If the Germans seemed to have missed the message 'Malta would re-transmit the original RAF message at high power, ostensibly to the Navy in Alexandria, thereby presenting the enemy with another opportunity to give us a lead into the current code'.[60]

If much of a message has been broken but several gaps remain, common sense will often suggest what the missing letters, numbers or groups may have been; sometimes it is merely that two numbers have been transposed – whether by the enemy operator or by your own intercept operator. You may even have copied them wrongly yourself. Intercept operators generally have a harder time than their opposite numbers; they are further away from the transmitter, the signal strength may be lower, and the interference from static will be more of a nuisance. Some groups may be missed, or the signal may straddle the groups, so that what appears to read:

8704 2108 7365 9423 0651 3967   etc   should really be
8   7042 1087 3659 4230 6513 9674   etc

The operator may cover this error by adding random figures at the end to make it look tidy; then you have no hint that the signal has side-slipped earlier.

The embryonic codebreaker will cut his teeth on such messages; the filling of gaps and the correcting of errors are the first steps towards practical codebreaking.

A cipher text reveals itself as soon as the cipher-breaker penetrates far enough. Letters, syllables, words and phrases are always just below the surface, revealed by the frequency and pattern of their appearance. Japanese and other non-alphabetic languages are not exempt. In signals they have to use some form of transcription which exposes these characteristic features just as ruthlessly as the European alphabet does. Therefore everything depends on the capacity of the cipher to break up these patterns in a way which is as nearly random as possible; the OTP, or the high-grade cipher-machine which avoids the technical and procedural limitations of Enigma, can achieve that. So can a numerical key, provided it is used so sensibly and changed so often that it becomes virtually 'one-time'.

If it is an alphabetical cipher, the numerals must be spelt out. They will show all too readily even in a cipher text, because they are built up on repetitive units: the twenty-two words for the numbers one to twenty, hundred and thousand recur with terrible clarity when messages discuss the identification numbers of formations, the totals of men, guns, tanks, aircraft or drums of fuel available or the distance between points. Some of these routine reports are from army commanders, effectively giving an order-of-battle of the formations under their command, and their areas of responsibility – but for the moment we are concerned more with their cryptographic significance than with the strategic value of their contents. Most ciphers do not follow the excellent pattern of semaphore, in using a symbol which converts the letters A–K into the numerals 0–9, and then another symbol which returns them to letters. As Noel Currer-Briggs has shown, the lack of this simple device compelled German message-drafters to spell out numerals *in full*.[61] Instead of a string of figures for their daily fuel returns, or the like, which might have read simply:

1 15, 2 5, 3 20, 4 0, 5 736, 6 1240, 7 0, 8 0 ...

they had to send, with 'e' to denote the *umlaut*

Eins fuenfzehn, zwo fuenf, drei zwanzig, vier null, fuenf siebenhundertsechsunddreissig, sechs eintausendzwohundertvierzig ...

making 124 letters in all, instead of twenty-three numerals; over five times as long to transmit, harder to absorb, and needing transcription into numerals before they can appear on a sheet of totals. This is not a peculiarity of German; the same phenomenon occurs in all languages.

Codes do not rely on this flimsy screen. Each code group can stand for anything which the compiler of the codebook specifies: sentences, phrases, letters, numerals, geographical names, military formations, units and ranks, service abbreviations and so on. It is normal practice to provide alternatives for common words and for punctuations, and cipher staff are trained to use these randomly. A convenient device is to divide information between two groups; to take an example from the ill-fated merchant shipping codebook, one group stands for 'Buoy(s) formerly situated in [next group] is/ are no longer there'.[62]

Even unreciphered code provides immediate disguise, but frequent use can expose the commonest groups of a code as readily as the commonest letters or numbers of a cipher. A reciphered code, however, has great security, and if protected by an OTP is essentially unbreakable. But codebooks, one for encoding and one for decoding, are cumbersome affairs and laborious to change, given that all the units using them must change simultaneously if they are not to give a crib into the new material. If a signals office is threatened with capture, a cipher table can be destroyed quickly, but a codebook takes a long time.

During the Second World War both routine and emergency changes were made to Japanese crypto material, and sometimes changes which were overdue could not be made because of severe distribution problems. I think it is self-evident that the longer any part of the system is used, the likelier it is to be penetrated. It is probably safe to reveal that an Admiralty order, instructing the commanders of Royal Navy vessels operating in dangerous waters in the English Channel and the North Sea to use one set of recognition signals on even days of the month, and another set on odd, was issued as far back as 1782.[63]

All this presupposes that you are attacking a code or cipher text and no more; if it has been reciphered the difficulties are at once multiplied. In the 1914–18 war some of the additive keys were so short that they repeated frequently, but those easy-going days have gone. This is the point at which teamwork is called for; some will be attacking the codebook while others, working closely with them, are tackling the key. The time-honoured way of breaking the key is to 'build up a depth', where the same section of key has been used to recipher more than one message. Kahn's book reminds us of the principle which, far from being a recent and secret technique, was first expounded by the Frenchman Kerckhoffs in 1883 in *La Cryptographie Militaire*,[64] but it is essentially little different from solving a crossword puzzle. There the letters have to make sense in two or more crossing lines; in key-breaking the numbers have to make sense in two or more parallel lines. The process is like that of filling gaps in a single message, except that here we have corroborative evidence. The more messages there are in the 'depth' (or 'superimposition') the more convincing the result: a key that produces sense in even two messages can hardly be wrong.[65]

I must admit that in 6633 the process was harder. Whereas an additive or subtractive key always uses arithmetic which never changes, each new substitution table for 6633 provided an entirely new arithmetic. To make it worse, whereas six plus three or three plus six both equal nine, in a table the figure in column six and row three will hardly ever be the same as that in column three and row six.

The 'breaking and entering' of wartime machine ciphers, of

which I can speak only as an onlooker, was the same in principle but its application was very different. More mathematicians and electronics specialists – a science still then in its infancy – were called for, yet the linguists were still needed, and the ability to organise the breaking process became a skill in itself. The first break-in will be far more difficult and that difficulty may prove insuperable; but once a break-in is made, it is often easier to follow successive changes in the various mechanical processes. The machine retains certain characteristics which it cannot lose, and in this sense it is less versatile than other cipher or code systems, in which some material can be basically altered without disturbing the rest. Yet the cipher machine can only provide the framework; capturing the machine will show what sort of internal devices it contains, but without them one is facing a blank page.

Geoff Jukes has recently pointed out that the surrender at Stalingrad, early in 1943, of twenty German divisions, five corps and one army HQ – in other terms one field-marshal, 24 generals and over 90,000 prisoners – will have entailed also the capture of at least two dozen Enigma machines.[66] Probably most but not all of the lists of key, ring and plug settings would have been destroyed, and many of the wheels themselves might have been buried. Even if some were recovered, the various keys would have been changed as soon as it was realised that the material was hopelessly compromised. This would have left the Russians still at the beginning of the long process of breaking the vital and constantly-changing inner permutations of keys. (This leaves unasked and unanswered the question whether they had made progress on Enigma like ours, between mid-1941 and early 1943).

The fact that German Enigma and Japanese Purple were broken, while British Typex and American Sigaba were not, is not only a compliment to British and American cryptanalysts. It also shows that the machine-cipher principle was carried further and that tighter drafting and, above all, operating procedures were followed. It might so easily have happened the other way round – in which case, dear reader, I should not be writing this book and you would not be reading it.

I have referred already to random matching of code-groups to the words or phrases that they represent, and to random keys. This may be the point at which to ask: who produces all these random numbers, and how random are they? Until 1945 most of this detestable job was done by hand, with occasional checks – at least in theory – to ensure that no obvious patterns or favourite numbers were discernible. It is very difficult to avoid this, above all if the stuff has to be churned out hour after hour, day after day. A sceptical colleague of mine tried it once, and rattled off line after line. When we looked at the result we found no fours and hardly any sevens. Similar exercises with students have given the same result.

In his book *The Hut Six Story*, describing the breaking of Enigma, Welchman reveals that one German official, whose job was to create new random material for Enigma ring settings, key settings and the like, must have thrown up the sponge after several boring years. He started re-using old ones, though in new combinations. Unfortunately someone at Bletchley had on his own initiative been keeping a record of all these variables, as fast as they were broken, and at this point his patience was rewarded: when he checked the 'new' sets they were instantly recognised, and Bletchley was saved a great deal of work. On one occasion they knew in advance all the daily keys that Rommel would use in north Africa for a whole month.[67]

Peter Calvocoressi has a more macabre example: another German cryptographic clerk believed that he could use the daily returns from the concentration camps which showed the number of new prisoners brought in, the number killed and the number still alive. Surely these should have been random enough? They were conveniently transmitted in a medium-grade cipher, and he simply copied them for his Enigma settings each day. Alas for Enigma security: the medium-grade cipher was also being read at Bletchley, and again someone saw the figures were the same.[68]

There are no reliable short cuts for human beings. Machines can now be used to produce numbers at random (allegedly so, in the case of 'Ernie') at least in the sense that if there is any pattern it is on so infinitely remote a plane that it can never be expected to help any cryptanalyst. It resembles the theoretical proposition that if an infinitely large number of monkeys type at random for an infinitely long time, eventually they will produce all the works of Shakespeare. Unfortunately we do not have an infinity of time to avoid losing a war.

Nigel West asserts that the ultimate machine, the modern computer 'can discern a pattern in any series of numbers ... chosen by human intellect. In other words, unless a one-time pad has been constructed by a machine process, it will ultimately be susceptible to a machine'.[69] There are practical objections to this statement, even if it is theoretically correct. Is 'ultimately' the same as 'after an infinitely long time'? At the other extreme of time, many messages enciphered on an OTP will be so short that there is no pattern long enough to exist, let alone to recognise. Another is that – to put it naively – the OTP should never be used more than once, so no gain can accrue from deducing a pattern; that was the whole point of its invention, as a logical step towards randomness, in the USA in 1917–18 (in tape form) and in Germany in 1921–23. If an OTP is re-used it is not the pad but the procedure that is the weak link. We move closer to reality if we bear in mind all the time that faulty procedures are the bane of even the finest cryptographic material.

12

What is so special about signals intelligence?

Why this great emphasis on sigint? What is so special about it? What about the other ways of finding out what the enemy, 'the man over the hill', to use the Duke of Wellington's words, is up to? Surely spies, captured documents and the interrogation of prisoners are all tried and tested methods, joined more recently by aerial photography and, even nearer to our own times, satellite surveillance? The answer is that all of these have their value, and intelligence is at its best when it draws together the results of all reliable probings, both to complement and to check each other. But most of the other methods have inbuilt limitations which hardly apply to sigint.

Spies can go over to the enemy, be captured, be fed false information or be completely turned and 'played back'. Once abroad they are out of reach, out of control, out of protection. These are not just whimsical arguments. Although some spies did useful work on both sides during the Second World War, the example of the German spies sent to Britain affords a salutory lesson. They were easily the most productive and important spies used by either side in Europe – but the side they served so well was the British, to whose victory they made a useful though largely involuntary contribution.

They were rounded up as they arrived and offered the choice of execution – the fate of any captured spy throughout the centuries – or collaboration. Almost all chose the latter. For the rest of the war they sent back to Germany, under the close direction of Masterman's XX (Double-Cross) Committee, carefully-selected and well-orchestrated false information which was accepted at its face value at the highest level in Germany. Its acceptance could be judiciously monitored by Ultra (material derived from Enigma decrypts) to see how it was being swallowed, where and how it could be improved, when the bait was taken reluctantly and when it needed to be better flavoured to suit the consumer's taste.

To give two examples, both well-known: it played its part in reducing casualties and damage during the flying-bomb campaign by passing misleading reports on the point of impact and the need to correct the range. The V-1s were tending to fall a little short of the centre of London, and when the agents were asked by their controllers in Germany to say where they were exploding, instead of advising them to lengthen the range the agents were ordered by their British controllers to do the opposite, admittedly making life hotter for those in the south-eastern suburbs but reducing casualties in the most thickly-populated areas of central London.[76]

Above all the agents contributed to the German High Command's mistaken view about the decisive landings in Operation 'Overlord', the invasion of France in June 1944, by conjuring up a wholly bogus army group which was allegedly planning to land in the Pas de Calais, not in Normandy. The need was obvious: there were nearly sixty German divisions in France, against seven Allied divisions in the initial assault in Normandy. As late as a week before D-Day the German intelligence staff were convinced that there were nearly ninety divisions in Britain; in reality there were less than fifty. Even after the landings in Normandy Hitler was so mesmerised by one double-agent's signal, seeking to persuade him that the Normandy landings were mere diversions, intended to deflect German attention and troops from 'the main assault in the Pas de Calais', that he intervened to prevent two Panzer divisions, already on their way to Normandy, from continuing their journey. He ordered them back to the Calais area. It was not until 25 July that he authorised the moving of some of the units still held in reserve into the area where they were needed. That was *seven weeks* too late.

But the agents' messages were only the icing on the cake, which contained ingredients from other branches of intelligence, as well as deception. It was the wholly imaginary FUSAG (First US Army Group) in which, as Ultra revealed, the Germans had shown particular interest; once they had learned that General Patton had arrived in Britain they were ready to accept the fiction, which they believed they had discovered despite our best efforts, that Patton was to command FUSAG. They were steadfast in their certainty that FUSAG was in south-east England specifically for the impending assault on the Pas de Calais, and Ultra soon revealed that German direction-finding on FUSAG's bogus signals network had confirmed the agents' reports and the German High Command's own deductions. This may be taken almost as a test case of the efficacy of agents between 1939 and 1945, and the evidence it supplies is unequivocally damning: in the words of Masterman, 'we actively ran and controlled the German espionage system in this country'. Moreover, it was Ultra which showed which of their false information was most readily swallowed, and which needed to be spiced up, and it was the overall deception scheme 'Fortitude South' which converted these titbits from being simply attractive in their own right and made them part of a well-planned feast.[71] There are narrow limits to the credibility or veracity of spies, and Field-Marshal Alexander's verdict is apt: 'Espionage can never play anything but the most minor role in military intelligence'.

Captured documents have a long history of revealing secrets, but they too have seen better days. The documents washed up on the Spanish coast with 'the man who never was' in Operation Mincemeat strengthened the Germans in a view which they were known, again through Ultra, to favour and which they were given other inducements to take as gospel: that the eastern Mediterranean, rather than Sicily, was the Allied target next on the list after the German surrender in north Africa. Such documents can be ingeniously fabricated and convincingly 'lost', and provided that they fit in with other plausible information they can be mistaken for the genuine article. But the methods of delivery are limited, and the classic examples are so famous internationally, from Meinerzhagen's original 'lost haversack ruse' of 1917 to the various 'lost maps' of both world wars, that they come close to being counter-productive. The success of Mincemeat was that it was a novelty; no future body washed ashore is likely to hold water – if I may be forgiven the phrase – for long. And the principle is risky in itself. The evidence presented must be absolute, one way or the other; if it is not genuine, then it must be a plant. Once seen to be a plant, it concentrates the enemy's mind powerfully on the very target which it is intended to remove from his gaze. A further practical limitation is that documents are more often captured by an advancing army than by one in retreat, yet it is the retreating army which needs help most urgently.

All this suggests that planted documents are likely to be used more rarely and viewed more sceptically in future, and if the tide runs far in that direction the genuine captured or lost document may come back into its own. The problem is that there are fewer actual documents about. Paper is being replaced by radio and by the visual display. Parallel with this runs the tendency to place less emphasis on the acquisition of, or reliance on, the printed word. Even during the Burma campaign, for reasons which are far from clear, it seems that the enemy simply did not notice the documents that we so artistically provided to mislead them.

The last traditional option is the interrogation of prisoners of war. The Allied armies told their men 'If captured, give your name, rank and number; never more'. A similar tradition held good in the *Wehrmacht*. In the Far East the position was totally different. The Japanese were not accustomed to defeat, even initial defeat followed by a long grind towards victory, as has become the pattern for Britain in both world wars. Because of the Bushido tradition that death was preferable to capture, very few Japanese were captured until the later stages of the Burma campaign, and no officer above the rank of Major was taken prisoner there until its closing days. [72] But there was a surprising *volte-face*. They had assumed that our treatment of prisoners would be as brutal as theirs, and that they might well be executed at once. When they found that they were still alive, and quite reasonably treated, they had no guide-lines to follow. Capture was supposed to mean disgrace or death, and when neither ensued they had to improvise. This took the unexpected form of being remarkably talkative.

General Slim commented:' For the first week all tried to commit suicide. After that they gave up and worked docilely for their captors. They did not reconcile this with their patriotism; they simply chucked their hand in'.[73] They even became willing to talk about military secrets. I shall return to this subject in the next chapter.

If the Japanese, whom one might have expected to be tight-lipped in the extreme, were as garrulous as I have suggested, perhaps it is less surprising that in Europe and north Africa prisoners could be so careless in what they said. Their gossip rarely produced jewels of great value, but it did provide countless small clues which could be fitted usefully into the general intelligence picture. In general, officers were less loquacious than other ranks, but they could all too easily be stung into words if it was suggested that they were keeping quiet because they had too little responsibility, were too lowly-placed, to have much to be worth talking about. Then their pride was touched and out came interesting titbits which they knew, on reflection, were best kept dark.

It is hard to find or to imagine examples of prisoners being briefed to give false information. There are few volunteers, and in any case it is hardly necessary:

You cannot hope to bribe or twist,
Thank God, the British journalist;
But seeing what the man will do
Unbribed, there's no occasion to.[74]

When prisoners from the same unit are captured they do not usually tell the same story, if indeed they have much to tell. Often they have little idea what larger formation their regiment belongs to, or what their unit commander's plans are; they are marching, or crawling, for some nearby objective which their sergeant knows about.[75] Senior officers are rarer birds to find in the cage, and they are the least likely to let slip anything of importance. Some of the most useful facts learnt in the Second World War came from bugging the rooms in which senior German officer prisoners met. It is unlikely that this would succeed nowadays.

With each of these channels of intelligence the critical question to be asked is its reliability: is it genuine, not fabricated? Even if we are sure that it is given in good faith, is it accurate or not?

There is a further reservation. Captured documents, spies' reports and prisoners' interrogations, like front-line identifications of enemy troops, are potentially valuable for local news, but they rarely throw much light on enemy dispositions or movements outside their immediate area. It is even rarer for them to reveal the enemy's tactical or strategic intentions. Often they are already out of date. In stark contrast an American analyst, admittedly exaggerating, states 'After the development of Ultra material every movement of a Japanese division was discovered either while it was still in transit or very shortly after it had reached its destination'.[76] The exaggeration concerns the word 'every', but he errs on the side of understatement over the time-scale, for often one can trace in German or Japanese sigint the earliest thought being given to the despatch of a division, together with probable date and destination. Often one can read the enemy commander - Rommel, for instance – demanding reinforcements and equipment and fuel if he is not to face rapid defeat, and, just as eloquently, one can learn to recognise when this is actually necessary and when it is part of his policy of demanding more than he hopes to get.

The strength of signals intelligence is that it comes from right inside the enemy's organisation, without his knowledge, and at every level from the top downwards. It is eavesdropping, not on local tittle-tattle but on the inner secrets. It is like listening to the enemy commander talking to his superiors, to his colleagues, to his

113

troops and above all to himself. Moreover it is often available in profusion and in fair continuity, so that a message that has developed a fault at any stage, let alone an attempted plant, sticks out like a sore thumb. Moreover, to quote Calvocoressi again, 'It could be unbeatably prompt. In the nature of things a wireless message is intercepted the moment it is transmitted'.[77] It is so dependable that a comprehensive order-of-battle for the enemy's army, navy and air force can be built up and kept up to date.

There are few examples of its being used to mislead. Messages in plain language or in low-grade code which the enemy is thought to have penetrated have been used to mislead, but a little reflection will prompt the question why, if the information is important, it is not better protected. The logic of bogus messages is tangled. Everything depends on having good reason to believe that the enemy is currently reading the crypto system used to carry the bogus message – but what about all the genuine messages sent by that same system that are meanwhile being sacrificed? If all the rest are stopped, the bogus one stands exposed. If the bogus message is recognised as a plant, then the whole system is blown, and the enemy will have nothing more to do with it, except that it turns a spotlight on items which he is being invited to misunderstand. That in turn will prompt him to wonder why is being misled, and what the true explanation is. We end up poorer than we started. How far along this tortuous and speculative path is it wise to go? The results of bluff and triple bluff are the same.

A bogus message can carry conviction only if it supports or is supported by other evidence. It must form a plausible part of a larger credible idea which can be sold to the enemy without much sales resistance. But there are two exceptional examples which come under the heading of freaks, and I am indebted to David Kahn for both.

The first shows a planted crib, not so much bogus as artificially inseminated into another country's code. Before the 1914–18 war the Austrians had tried hard to break an Italian code, but had made little headway. They placed a tempting morsel of military information in an Italian-language newspaper published in Constantinople, as it then was. The Italian military attaché noticed the paragraph and transmitted it to Rome in the code, thus giving the Austrians a perfect crib and a comfortable break-in.[78]

The second is an example of a bogus message which completely hoaxed the enemy, when all that mattered was the immediate result – and hang the consequences. When Yugoslavia attempted to invade Italian-held Albania in 1941 its two divisions posed an acute threat to the Italian occupation forces. The Italian signals intelligence section drafted signals, using the Yugoslav Army cipher and radio procedures and purporting to come from Yugoslavia GHQ, ordering both divisions to halt the offensive and retreat. By the time the ruse was discovered it was too late. The Yugoslavs realised that their cipher was being read and that it was impossible to transmit orders by other methods in time to restore the situation.[79] The logic was clear: the Italians knew that if they could not immediately neutralise the Yugoslav attack, they would be beaten. If they could, they were bound to win, since the Germans were pressing Yugoslavia from the north. Their coup blew the gaff, but that was of no consequence.

It is unusual to risk the loss of sigint for a temporary gain; only a commander facing imminent defeat or scenting immediate victory is likely to gamble on such stakes. Slim faced a lesser dilemma when he decided, in the closing stages of the Burma campaign, to order the RAF to destroy all the forward Japanese signals units they could find. He calculated that the wholesale disorganisation that this would cause outweighed the loss of some sigint. This could be called a classic case of killing the goose that lays the golden eggs. The time-honoured motto seems to be that a commander should never put himself in that position, because 'the best is yet to come'. There must be occasions towards the end of a successful campaign when that ceases to be true, and when the bird in the hand is what matters. In Slim's case that was plainly relevant: it was of great importance to clinch the campaign before the monsoon arrived and threatened to prolong the war for a further year. It paid off, since he won it with two days at most to spare.

An international conference was held in Germany in 1978 to assess the impact on the Second World War of the German Enigma sigint, Ultra. It was attended by representatives of the armed services and intelligence communities of both sides, and included sceptics as well as devotees. It reached the conclusion that Ultra had played a vital and perhaps decisive role in winning the war, and that it had first enabled Britain to avoid defeat between 1940 and 1942. When one speaker was asked why, if Ultra was so important, the war did not end sooner, he answered, 'It did end sooner'.[80] Professor Sir Harry Hinsley, the official historian of British intelligence in the Second World War, and not a man given to exaggerated speculation, has hazarded a guess that it shortened the war by three years.[81] Clearly the actual figure is of less significance than the order of magnitude; if we can contemplate a three-year difference in a war which lasted for six, we are speaking of a factor of enormous importance.

An unexpected rider to the verdict must be that by shortening the war it thereby saved millions of lives on both sides, and untold suffering and destruction; the military casualties alone (in round figures USSR 13.5 million, China 6.4, Germany 4, Japan 1.2, USA and UK .3 million each) come to over 25 million, with more than that figure for civilian casualties. It may seem gruesome to apply simple arithmetic to statistics of so horrific a kind, yet the implication is inescapable. Equally it may be thought casuistical to claim this as a humanitarian benefit, since this was not its purpose, yet beside the argument that the atomic bombs 'humanely' shortened the war it has some merit and fewer obvious defects.

Three important factors, apart from technical comparisons, contributed to the success of Allied intelligence in general and signals intelligence in particular. The first was that the people who produced it generally had no hand in its operational application. Their job was to obtain clear, reliable and prompt information which was collated and evaluated by others. The process did not include making suggestions for action. That was the job of the commander and his staff, and the division of responsibility freed intelligence personnel from the temptation to warp their findings so as to flatter his preconceptions. This was no frivolous bugaboo. A dominating or even domineering commander – MacArthur, Montgomery and Stilwell come to mind, and perhaps we should add Hitler at a different level – could easily convert his subordinates into sycophants, thereby bewitching them into slanting or suppressing the evidence. One of MacArthur's intelligence officers wrote that 'More than one intelligence officer's career was blighted by writing accurate but unpalatable reports'.[82] It seems likely that Stilwell too was over-protected from worrying news by having members of his own family as members of his staff. The risk of bending the facts is lessened if the intelligence-producers are out of a commander's immediate reach. They cannot in any case make his decisions for him; his grasp of his and the enemy's logistics in men and materials and morale will be the ultimate criterion.

The second factor was the integration of the crypto resources of all three British services, and later their fertile intermarriage with the Americans, despite their earlier separation. Here the Americans had a lot to learn before they followed our example. The US Army and Navy had long maintained separate sigint organisation, and co-operation between them was at first poor or simply non-existent; the early history of the Pacific War was bedevilled by suspicion or rivalry. It took a long time for them to make the fullest use of their massive resources by eliminating these corrosive inter-service jealousies. One American military historian has written: 'The reader may be pardoned for concluding that American commanders and their staffs spent almost as much energy battling each other over the control and exploitation of Ultra as they did battling the Japanese'.[83] Under General Marshall's direction this dichotomy gave way to an integrated system.

The third and last factor was that Ultra and all high-grade sigint was protected with extreme care. ('Ultra' describes not the actual decrypts but the intelligence summaries based on them.) It was transmitted from Bletchley Park, Arlington and similar units at first by OTP and later by the British Typex and American Sigaba cipher machines. These were faster to use than OTPs, and though they worked on the same basic principles as Enigma they were never broken. At the far end it was passed to specified commanders and their immediate staff officers only. The Special Liaison Unit officers who personally delivered British Ultra to Army and RAF commanders in the field were men who, despite their modest rank, had the specific duty and right to insist that the origin, significance and nature of Ultra could be revealed only to those commanders and staff who were authorised to receive it. The Navy required a separate distribution system because, unlike the War Office or the Air Ministry, the Admiralty was an operational centre directly commanding ships at sea. Moreover, it took longer for naval Enigma to become significantly useful.

With the Army and the RAF, 'The SLU officer was responsible for personally delivering the Ultra message to the commander or to a member of his staff designated to receive it. All messages were to be recovered by the SLU officer as soon as they were read and understood. They were then destroyed. No Ultra user was allowed to transmit or repeat an Ultra signal'.[84] The slender personal authority of the SLU officers carrying this responsibility was backed by the commanders having been individually briefed by Group-Captain Winterbotham, whose scheme it was, before becoming authorised recipients; by the Chiefs of Staff, and ultimately by Churchill.

These SLUs were quickly recognised by the Americans as something they should copy so as to improve their distribution of signals without jeopardising it. Because of the US Army's allegedly lax security, the US Navy had refused either to let them have its own naval sigint although it was going to the British, or to let the British send them relevant naval sigint. The official history of the Special Branch of the US Military Intelligence Service says explicitly that they learned how 'the British had developed security principles and methods well beyond the point reached by the US Army' and that 'it was only through [their] adoption that the US Army was able to get full access to the results of the British signals intelligence operations; adherence to [them] had a great deal to do with persuading the US Navy to make available in full the traffic it turned out' − that is, instead of deciding for themselves what to pass on to the Army.[85]

General Marshall insisted on the adoption of the British system, renaming the SLU personnel 'Special Security Officers' and later 'Special Security Representatives. By late 1943 they had largely set up the new organisation. MacArthur characteristically was the most stubborn in wanting to vary the procedures in his area so as to meet his personal ambitions. He was over-ruled by Marshall. It was not until 1944, just in time for the Normandy invasion, that the whole Allied signals intelligence system was fully effective.[86]

Having grappled with their distribution problems the Americans now faced, as the British had earlier, the question how to protect this important material while disseminating it to all those who needed it. The procedure was already in force in several commands where British or Australian formations were operating alongside American troops, for example in the China-Burma-India Theatre ('Vinegar Joe' Stilwell) or the South-West Pacific Area (MacArthur). The details varied from one Command to the next though the principles stayed intact. The orders laying down the rules ran to some five, six or seven Top Secret foolscap sheets, depending on the Command, and would be tedious to reproduce in full, but some salient points, taken from the C-B-I and SWPA versions, show how seriously the subject was taken.[87] First the preamble defines what is at issue:

> SPECIAL INTELLIGENCE is the designated term for highly secret information obtained by intercepting and reading enemy messages which have been enciphered in cryptographic systems of a high security classification. The extreme importance of Special Intelligence as a source of reliable information concerning enemy activities and intentions has been repeatedly proved. Preservation of this source requires that the

enemy be given no reason to suspect that his communications are being read. If from any document which might fall into his hands, from any message he might intercept, from any word revealed from a prisoner of war, or from any ill-considered action taken upon the basis of such knowledge, the enemy were given cause to believe that his communications are not adequately safeguarded against interception which he knows to be employed against him, he would effect changes which would deprive us of knowledge of his operations on all fronts. Extreme secrecy is therefore required, and these regulations are to be strictly observed.

All messages or other documents transmitting Special Intelligence information based thereon, or any direct or indirect reference thereto, will contain the codeword ULTRA to indicate the source. [ULTRA DEXTER, ULTRA CORRAL, ULTRA RABID and other terms were substituted for ULTRA by US sigint units until May 1944, when General Marshall's agreement with the British to use ULTRA for all high-grade sigint deprived local commanders of the luxury of inventing their own brand-names.] When transmitted by wire or radio the word ULTRA will be buried within the body of the message near the beginning, and cryptographed as part of the text.

Some detailed regulations were:

1. In each Command authorised to receive Ultra, only the following officers were to see it: the Commander and his deputy, the Chief of Staff and his deputy, Senior Intelligence and Operations Staff Officers, and, at certain Commands, Senior Planning, Signals and Signals Intelligence Officers, together with their RAF equivalents at all levels. No officer was entitled to see Ultra solely by reason of his rank; i.e. Corps and Divisional commanders were excluded. In the C-B-I Theatre 'each recipient will be furnished with a yellow card, $1\frac{1}{2}$ by 2 inches, with the letter "U", one inch high, on both sides in red. At any conference where ULTRA DEXTER is to be discussed, all persons present shall be required to show these cards, and any unauthorised persons shall be excluded from the conference before such discussion begins.'
2. All authorised recipients were carefully briefed, and signed a document stating that they had read and understood the regulations and would observe them.
3. No recipient or former recipient of Ultra was to be exposed to

119

any risk of capture by the enemy; if Ultra material was carried by air (by courier or by bag) the route must be completely secure and must not cross enemy, enemy-held or even neutral territory.

4. Any operational action based on Ultra must be so camouflaged that the action itself could not lead the enemy to the conclusion that it was based on Ultra. Momentary tactical advantage was not sufficient ground for taking any risk of compromising the source. Pilots whose briefing for an operation was based on Ultra were to have only such details as might have been obtained, for example, by aerial reconnaissance. Orders must be so given that their inspiration could not be traced to Ultra, and must never contain the precise date, time or place of an enemy operation, or the name of any ship or tactical unit revealed only by Ultra.

5. All possible precautions were to be taken to prevent any know-ledge even of the existence of this class of intelligence. The meaning of the word Ultra must not be disclosed to a non-recipient. Infor-mation from Ultra sources was never to be included in journals, logs or war diaries.

One of the most awkward conditions to satisfy was the fourth: action taken on the basis of Ultra must always be so designed as to avoid the slightest risk of compromising it. The risk had occurred earlier when Ultra disclosed the sailings of enemy naval or merchant vessels in the Mediterranean. They were not to be attacked without having been sighted by RAF reconnaissance aircraft, even when these were sent out solely on the strength of the very Ultra evidence which they were now to disguise. This was a nuisance, but well justified. On various occasions the Axis powers soberly considered whether some breach of their signals security could alone explain setbacks that they had suffered. On each occasion they were able to persuade themselves that other explanations sufficed, and thus Ultra was able to continue without interruption.

13

Loose ends

a *Traffic analysis*

This modest term changed its meaning during the war and it can hardly be surprising that it continues to be ambiguous. By late 1943 it should have meant only the exploitation of plain-language conversations, low-grade codes and ciphers, direction-finding and enemy procedures in signals networks, frequencies, call-signs, operators' transmitting characteristics and even radar warning systems. For most people these activities lack the glamour that sometimes attaches to sigint, but they were responsible for a formidable volume of useful intelligence. Aileen Clayton's book *The Enemy is Listening* gives an excellent picture of what was involved, particularly in air operations in Europe and the Mediterranean.

The interception and study of signals in plain language relies not only on the conversations themselves but also on careless operator chat before and after transmissions. These can help to identify units, both by overt descriptions and by such subtler methods as TINA, the recognition of individual radio-operators, and the identification of different types of radio set by RFP. This information in turn can pinpoint the move of a unit from one area to another, which may well betray a significant feature of the enemy's plans. If operator X, with his idiosyncratic 'fist' (or 'signature' or 'handwriting') was originally in the LEMUR signals net and has now turned up in LEOPARD, what can that tell us about units common to both nets? The answer will suggest how one further piece should fit into the jigsaw puzzle of the enemy's order-of-battle.

Both the British and the Americans took a remarkably long time to realise how vulnerable plain language conversations could be. This naive innocence may spring from the arrogantly insular view that no Englishman, or perhaps nobody whose mother tongue is English, need acquire a foreign language; all that is necessary is to speak a little louder to the foreigner – and conversely one need not take too seriously the notion that any foreigner will understand English, unless one actually wants something from him. The attitude was a common fault of those in rear wireless nets who believed themselves safe, in any case, from enemy eavesdropping, and it occurred widely even in forward areas where the risks should have been more obvious.

John Ferris gives a graphic illustration of the vulnerability of such conversations, conducted in clear language. 'Two brigade commanders in north Africa were talking on the air. One asked the other, "Can you do anything about closing the 3,000 yard gap between your left and my right flank?"

The second replied "No, I can't. Can you?"

"No, I can't either."

Twelve hours later the Germans did something about it.'[88]

Two points call for comment. This event took place after some two years of war, when the risks should have become apparent even if they were not in September 1939; and these were senior officers, who might have been expected to rise above the level of feeble-mindedness that the episode suggests.

Radio-telephone talk can be picked up over great distances, even though it may be more prone than Morse to interference from static. Japanese airmen, like their British and American counterparts, often gave themselves away in the exchange of messages, with or without wisecracks, between aircraft and control-tower even before take-off. At Cox's Bazaar, in Bengal, the RAF 367 Wireless Unit could overhear conversations from aircraft over Sumatra, about 1,200 miles away,[89] and a colleague who was on a training course at Newbold Revell, near Rugby, heard German tank crews chatting to each other by radio in the Ukraine, some 1,500 miles distant.[90]

I must also emphasise that 'low-grade' codes and ciphers often carried messages of a surprising importance; the term refers to the security which the crypto system is supposed to provide, rather than to its normal contents.

b *The index*

The comprehensive indexing of all information was vitally important, and not just a clerical chore. It showed personalities, units and formations as they were mentioned, without waiting for them to be more fully identified – a process in which it helped. Was Army Air Force Captain Miyazawa, now revealed as flying from

Singapore to Rangoon, with no further details given, the same as A.A.F. Lieutenant Miyazawa who was mentioned in an earlier message from Manila as an expert on aerial photography? If so, why was he going to Rangoon? Was a unit forming there for him to command? Was there a course on the subject at Manila; if so, who else went on it, and where did they go afterwards? The Japanese had relatively few units carrying out this special task, so this could be a significant pointer. The same message might provide a provisional identification for an unbroken code-group possibly meaning 'high-altitude camera' which will fill gaps in other messages – again a powerful argument for close liaison between sections.

c *Interrogation*

From time to time some of us at WEC Delhi were called in to help with interrogation. This job was usually done by the experts in spoken Japanese who had attended the SOAS courses in London which I describe a few pages further on, but when specialists were taken prisoner their questioning often required a more specialised vocabulary, just as their English equivalents 'discriminant', 'substitution table' and 'key indicator' would have done. After initial questioning immediately after capture, they were brought back to Delhi, to the CSDIC (Combined Services Detailed Interrogation Centre) housed in part of the Red Fort., They were kept in the former elephant stables; if this sounds squalid it is misleading, for they were as clean and cheerful as many army barrack-blocks.[91] Moreover, although the word 'interrogation' has harsh overtones, suggesting head-banging and worse, I came across no indication whatever that this happened, and quite apart from moral objections it was generally thought that it would have been counter-productive.

Whenever I was brought in to help question a prisoner who had been serving in a signals or, above all, a cryptographic section, he spoke willingly. They were surprised to be alive; they were astounded that we knew their secrets and understood their allegedly unbreakable codes. Slim's remarks, quoted in the previous chapter, were as true of these men as of the ordinary regimental officers and their men. They therefore regarded us almost as colleagues, and that was how we treated them. After a casual conversation about their codes we would innocently ask 'Let me see; was that when we' (not 'you') 'began enciphering the indicator group?' – and they would obligingly agree or put us right. The veil of secrecy which was so familiar to them within their own army, as it was to us in ours, seemed to have been withdrawn in the transition from one side of the battle to the other, and the move from the constant strain of the Burma campaign to the relatively calm routine of the Red Fort, even if it was not a high-class hotel, doubtless supplied another factor in the transformation of attitudes.

An important feature in this questioning was the gaining of the prisoner's confidence. Few of them had expected to be questioned in Japanese; they could hardly believe that foreigners could cope with it. The same phenomenon persists today and is not confined to Japanese. Most Chinese, similarly, may hear a foreigner speaking their tongue but instead of taking the experience at its face value they react: 'It is almost as if that man were speaking Chinese, though of course it is impossible. ... It must be a mirage.'

Patience is needed for a further reason: most Asians regard politeness so highly that they consider it natural to answer a question in the way they hope will most please the questioner. Even now 'Is the museum open today?' may well be answered 'Yes' whether it is or not, because 'No' is thought impolite.

The interrogator tried to conduct the conversation so as to follow the direction in which the prisoner was happiest to talk, steering it only gently. He matched his approach to the prisoner's brightness, his perception, his family and educational background, his apparent candour. This gentle approach was far more fruitful than the snap question or the implied threat, which would simply have met a brick wall.

CSDIC compiled the BOOB or Burma Order of Battle, based not only on the interrogation of prisoners but also on their pay books, identity tags, savings books and unit or personal diaries – many written in soldier slang. Later CSDIC became SEATIC, South-East Asia Translation and Interrogation Centre, when it moved to Singapore to deal with the enormous number of prisoners, especially senior officers whom it was thought worth questioning, some of them because they were suspected of atrocities.

It was notable that practically no senior officers were captured during the Burma campaign, and those who were not there may assume, wrongly, that this was because they were comfortably far back, away from danger. Nothing could be further from the truth. When suicidal and usually pointless attacks were launched they were usually headed by the more senior officers and NCOs. Louis Allen mentions a Punjabi unit which was ferociously attacked by the Japanese. The battalion commander and some NCOs had penetrated their defences, junior officers and one first-class private were behind, and second-class privates further back still.[92] The grading corresponded approximately, but not exclusively, to the length of service and the 'regular soldier' attitude which the men had acquired.

Equally the *bushido* tradition, which required a man to take his own life if the alternative was to face the disgrace of being captured, was held in differing degrees. Robin Gibson met one signals Major at CSDIC 'who was made of sterner stuff and did not spill the beans till I met him again at Singapore'.[93] By then not only the campaign but the war had ended, and there was no point in continuing to withhold information from an enemy who already knew so much.

d *Japanese cryptographic security*

The Japanese attitude to crypto security was varied and often surprisingly lax. Having devised a formidable system of codes and a few ciphers they assumed that they were impregnable, and some still maintained after the war, just as did a few in Germany, that they had never been broken. Some separate formations in Burma, like some in Germany, had doubts about this in 1944 and 1945, but the central cryptographic authorities in both countries were unwavering in their convictions. They never hit upon specific instances where the evidence seemed incontrovertible that we had broken them; the Germans suspected 'treachery' but later settled for technical wizardry to explain their U-boat losses, and the Japanese, whatever they suspected, took no concerted and decisive action. By then even the routine distribution of new crypto material was difficult enough: to attempt to introduce sweeping changes presented an impossible task, and there was always the risk by then that a unit would be cut off, would have to continue to use the old material, and would thus scupper their plans by providing a crib into new materials. But some units in Burma at least tightened up their procedures.

In all this they were slower than the British and the Americans, who entered the war with poor signals and worse signals discipline but improved fairly quickly. Like all the countries that fought in the war, they faced any specific suggestion that their own codes had been compromised with disbelief. It was not until Bletchley Park produced unassailable evidence that the German B-Dienst were reading them that the Admiralty at last condescended to change the naval and merchant shipping codes whose inferiority had caused the loss of frightening numbers of men and ships. That evidence came from Ultra. There are two lessons to be learnt, or morals to be drawn. The first and more cynical is supplied by the Navy's reaction, in the face of these appalling losses and casualties, to repeated warnings from Bletchley Park about German penetration of these maritime codes: 'Don't believe your own side; wait until the enemy confirms what they have been saying, and then believe him'. The other must be Bletchley Park's message for the German Navy and the B-Dienst: 'Do as the Americans did and copy our distribution system for Ultra, noting particularly the section about not allowing any hint of this Top Secret source to appear in your ciphers'. For what finally convinced the Admiralty was that the German naval Enigma messages did not just order their U-boats to appropriate positions or specific tasks; they did this in a way which revealed too close an adherence to the naval and mercantile code signals that they had broken. If they had avoided that habit, it is possible that the Admiralty would have continued to believe that their signals were secure, and then there is strong reason to believe that we might have lost the Battle of the Atlantic and possibly the war.

The incident mentioned in Chapter Seven, in which submarine I–1 was lost off Guadalcanal with a cargo of some 200,000 codebooks, is another example of a serious event which the Japanese treated coolly, even complacently. It could not be reported until the survivors reached their base at Rabaul about a month later. Orders were then given to 'dig them out' (from the sandy beach) 'and destroy them', but 'one or two of the numerous places where the documents were buried could not be located' (hardly surprising, since many, if not all, had been recovered by the Americans); moreover, as many had been left in the submarine, it was both bombed and torpedoed but 'complete destruction was not confirmed'. The curious feature of this episode is that it was written as if no Americans had been around, and as if the New Zealand corvettes which had rammed the submarine and forced it to beach could not have been relied upon to report its position, since any enemy vessel which can be examined always is.

The countermeasures were blandly summarised:

1 Emergency measures were taken and new codebooks were used.
2 The additive table [key] of the wartime codebook was immediately revised and the encoding procedure was altered.
3 The original of the strategic codebook was not changed.[94]

But patently the submarine would not have been sent on this hazardous mission if new codebooks had not been urgently needed? It is curious that the higher-grade strategic codebook was left in use while the others were changed, presumably because the 'encoding' procedure was changed; 'encoding' is probably a mistranslation for 'reciphering' (we have already seen how readily confusion arises even within our own language) and this may be another instance where an additive key becomes a subtractive key in an emergency. But even so, the loss of as many as 200,000 codebooks surely suggests, however many were bound for other destinations, that many systems, and not only naval systems, were jeopardised.

The Japanese were also casual in their assessment of 'enemy' codebreaking abilities. They concluded that if they read any messages it was only with the aid of cribs from outpost units which still used old codebooks; not very flattering, and not at all accurate. They would not be able to break their codes since these had at least the key revised 'about every month'. There might also have been some leakage from 'the diplomatic relations' code.

These conclusions, reached after the war by Japanese officers, make a further categorical statement which must cause some raised eyebrows: 'The Americans reported that the disaster to Admiral Yamamoto at Buin, Bougainville, was due to cryptanalaysis.'[95] Who told them, and when? The report was published by the American Army Department, although it concerns the Japanese Navy's communications, in 1953, far too early for any general revelations about such matters. It is unlikely that they confided this information to their late enemies before then. It is known that rumours about the source of Yamamoto's movements had spread. 'Much of official Washington was whispering at cocktail parties and dinners'. But this rumour, unlike the Midway Island story which had carelessly been allowed to reach the *Chicago Tribune*, did not appear in the press.

The report goes on to say: 'However this' (the report that Yamamoto's death had come about through US cryptanalysis) 'was impossible, as his movement was never despatched in the Navy code. Furthermore, from the success in the Kiska withdrawal operations and others, it was concluded that the main codebook had not been broken.'[96]

Kahn's conclusion, on whatever evidence, seems more credible than the Japanese. He plumps for the fleet code JN 25, and it is difficult to suggest what other they would have used. It seems that this may be yet another case of sheer obstinacy – an international disease where a nation's own codes are in question – obliterating the logical explanation.

e *The Japanese as codebreakers*

The surprisingly perfunctory view which the Japanese took of their own crypto material and its possible penetration by the Allies may stem from their own poor showing as cryptanalysts, who may have believed the British and the Americans to be as unsuccessful as themselves. They had begun intercepting foreign signals before 1920 and had exchanged crytographic information with Germany and Italy from the 1930s, even though Germany was at the same time reading some Japanese diplomatic traffic and went on to bug the Japanese Embassy in Berlin in 1942.[97] There were three separate sigint organisations: the Chūo Tokushu Jōhō Bu (Central Special Intelligence Department) of the Army, the Tokumu Han (Special Service Section) of the Navy, and the Angō Kenkyū Han (Cryptographic Research Section) of the Foreign Office.[98] These seem to have co-operated only on an 'ad hoc' basis in Tokyo, with the CTJB undertaking some monitoring of foreign diplomatic traffic from Canton, and with the Burma Area Army receiving intelligence derived from traffic analysis by the Navy. In Burma there was a naval sigint unit based at Rangoon, where there was probably an Army Air Special Signals Unit (Kōkū Tokushu Tsūshintai) as well. One of the larger Special Air Radio Units is known to have been concerned with Soviet radio interception.

How successful were they? Every indication is that they enjoyed some success with Chinese military and air traffic in the 1930s which gave them a firm foundation on which to continue breaking this and the signals of the USAAF in China. Chinese crypto security was far from inscrutable, and this lax discipline opened the door into low-grade army, diplomatic and military attaché signals, which were read with fair accuracy. Sometimes this opened further doors into the signals of other Allied formations in the area, for example the British 36 Division, which was in the American-Chinese Northern Combat Area Command. They seem also to have made some headway with the code used by Mountbatten when communicating with Chungking, the V Force code used by Allies fighting patrols gathering intelligence close behind enemy positions in Burma, and the Indian meteorological code.[99]

Otherwise they had little to show. The BAMS codebook, already notoriously leaky, had been captured by a German raider and the

Japanese had been given a copy, yet they seem to have made heavy weather of the relatively easy matter of stripping the key and thus securing valuable information about the position and course of Allied merchant shipping in the Pacific. Their complaint, 'By the time the code message was decoded, the ship was no longer in the original area', sounds naive and pathetic in contrast to the speed and accuracy both of the B-Dienst's verdicts and predictions based on the same code, and of the Admiralty's Operational Intelligence Centre in combatting the results of the B-Dienst's information once it had been passed on to the U-boats.[100]

Here too the same pattern emerges that we have seen before. The side with the better sigint is not just the winner by that margin of superiority. Its penetration of the enemy's codes warns it of any shortcomings in its own; it is a form of what is now being called 'a force multiplier'. We knew a good deal about their sigint from our intercepts. Whenever we broke a 'special Intelligence' signal, as often as not reporting the text – often fragmentary – of a signal sent by the Chinese Air Force, it was put on one side and one man looked after all that traffic. Similarly as the British and Americans built up a more and more detailed order-of-battle, the various special-intelligence units were identified and located. The O/B of April 1945 for the Army Air Force alone lists seven of them, from Manchuria to Singapore and Manila.[101]

The Japanese also knew about the possibilities of radio deception through bogus radio traffic, and had used it to conceal major changes in its volume which might otherwise have revealed troop movements, so they were clearly in a position to suspect our use of the same device. But they seem to have been completely taken in by the radio part of the deception scheme Cloak which I describe in Chapter Seventeen. They went about the whole business of code-breaking in a half-hearted way, assuming from the start that their only hope lay in attacking low-grade signals, and even in this their approach was scrappy and unmethodical. It rested more on signals procedures than on the signals themselves: call-signs, frequencies, volume of traffic, careless air-to-ground conversations, direction-finding and weather reports. Even at this level many messages were only partly broken.

It is also significant that they seem never to have contemplated using their sigint to cut their teeth on trying to break their own messages – not through any fear that they were being read, since they refused to think that possible, but as a preparatory exercise to give them greater confidence. Probably the intelligence service was

129

too rigidly subdivided and too monolithic in outlook for this to happen. Moreover the aggressor does not need first-class intelligence so desperately as the defender; Japan had been a notably successful aggressor since the middle 1930s.

Several countries have set their sigint people to attack their own codes and ciphers, but generally on specific occasions, not as a continuous or surprise check. The assumption seems to be that such practices are a waste of time and money. The very opposite is true. In other aspects of intelligence one country stands out as promoting self-examination. Following the failure of its intelligence service to give warning of the Yom Kippur war in October 1973, Israel established a unique unit within its Intelligence Branch, responsible for scrutinising official intelligence analysis and estimates and trying to prove, from the same data-base, the possibility of a different conclusion. This greater openness has helped the analysts to develop a much higher sensitivity to possible mistakes in their evaluations.[102] It is interesting to note that in this 'Devil's Advocate' process even the most junior member of the intelligence community is permitted to dissent from the views of his superiors and is given 'as much space as those whose views he challenges.[103] But to institutionalise independent thought by creating posts and processes for it is only half the battle: an act of faith without any guarantee of success. What also matters is the atmosphere in which independent thought can flourish, so that the Devil's Advocate is accepted as a vital force and not just a part of the constitution, let alone a safety-valve. It may be impossible to re-create the Bletchley Park phenomenon in peacetime; it requires a deft and imaginative policy on the part of any government even to try to provide it.

What a breath of fresh air and overdue self-criticism, or at least self-examination, this would send through certain offices – not only in intelligence – where false assumptions can go unquestioned for years and where any slight tendency to oversteer can eventually take their judgements further and further away from reality. Japan was an extreme case. It is true that the fire-eaters in the Army and at the centre of power in the government held views on strategy which were not fully shared in the Navy, but inter-service rivalry is no substitute for open discussion on such matters. In their intelligence departments the lack of integration, their reliance on relatively poorly-qualified staff, and their curiously half-hearted approach both explain and are explained by Brigadier Dudley Clarke's telling phrase 'the Japanese innate distrust of their own intelligence service'.

f *The Japanese language*

Japanese is not just a difficult language; it is totally different in form from most European languages. It has postpositions instead of prepositions, so that 'from Tokyo' is 'Tokyo-yori'. It suffers from being largely written in Chinese characters despite the difference between the two languages. Chinese is monosyllabic, tonal, and has a flexible word-order; the words themselves have no terminations: Pidgin English gives some impression of the way it works. Japanese is polysyllabic, without tones, but with a clear-cut sentence-structure. The verb, at the end of the sentence, has a welter of terminations to express tense, probability, politeness and so on.

Originally it had no script, so Japanese scholars, who had been influenced by Chinese civilisation from the fourth century onwards, began to write Japanese words with borrowed Chinese characters having the same meaning, now called the 'kun' readings or pronunciations. Later they borrowed further characters to write down new ideas, pronouncing them in rough imitation of their Chinese sounds: the 'on' readings. So now the Japanese word for 'east' is either the native 'kun' reading 'higashi' or the 'on' reading 'tō', derived from 'tung' in Chinese. Both are readings of the same character, which was 'the picture of an idea' in its Chinese origins.

It follows that when you see a 'Japanese' character for the first time you have no guidance as to what it means or how it is pronounced. Each character has to be learnt separately, and this entails memorising:

1. How the written character is formed and in what order the separate strokes are written – otherwise one cannot write or read the more cursive and simplified forms in which it often appears, for example in rapid handwriting.
2. How it is pronounced; there are generally both 'on' and 'kun' readings, and sometimes more than one 'kun' reading.
3. What it means; again there may be several meanings. For example, the second syllable of 'Nippon' is a common five-stroke character which can be read ('on') as HON (meaning book, main, this, real, or an auxilary numeral for counting long cylindrical objects) *or* ('kun') as MOTO, meaning origin, foot or base.

There is one advantage: because of their pictorial or representational origins the characters can be understood by people who pronounce them differently – with slight variants from dialect, or in radically different ways as between China and Japan. The language comes close to being an international system for communicating, like written numerals or traffic signs.

The student also has to learn the 214 radicals in their traditional order, under which characters are grouped in a dictionary – there being no equivalent of 'alphabetical' order – and how to count the strokes, since that determines the position within each group possessing a common radical. He has to learn two syllabaries, each of 51 basic sounds, which can be used as a phonetic system for writing verb-endings or for spelling imported words. Finally he must get used to reading and writing characters in vertical lines, each running downwards and starting 'on the back page' at the top right-hand corner, and to the fact that the Japanese and Chinese regard calligraphy as an art form. Even a hurried scribble should have some artistic merit. In Lu Chi's words, 'In a sheet of paper is contained the Infinite'.

Our main reference books on the Bedford course were the *Beginners' Dictionary of Chinese-Japanese Characters* by Arthur Rose-Innes (I still possess my battered and much-travelled copy) and the tubby red Kenkyusha Japanese dictionary. But the real tool for learning characters was the card. We made these ourselves, carefully drawing the characters and listing the readings – which in itself was a valuable start to learning them – kept them in cigarette boxes and carried them about with us, shuffling them to make sure that none was forgotten, or picking out real brutes to study more intently.

I forget how many we learnt in those six months, but a colleague thinks about twelve hundred, and that seems very plausible. There are under five thousand in Rose-Innes. We learned the meaning and pronunciation of many others which we would have had difficulty in writing correctly, or perhaps of pronouncing if we encountered them for the first time: the equivalent of many people to know the sound and meaning of 'physiotherapy' or 'psychology' but cannot spell either confidently. I doubt if I was the only member of the course who had to have spectacles made; the tiny detailed characters, printed on poor yellowish wartime paper by early and slightly fuzzy photo-reproduction, were difficult to read for long without eye-strain.

Let us take two characters as examples. The first is BU meaning part, section or department, or more narrowly a copy or volume of a book. The second is TAI meaning party, squad or crew; a body of men. BU forms the first component of several pairs of characters: BUKA a subordinate, BUBUN a part or section, BUIN staff. We also encounter it as the last component in JŌHŌBU, intelligence section. Similarly TAI can be the first component in TAICHŌ, leader, commander, or TAIGO, rank or line; equally it can come after another character, as in RENTAI, regiment, TSŪSHINTAI, signals unit. If put together to form the word BUTAI, they mean unit in the military sense. This tendency to use two syllables where we might expect one to suffice is a feature which is accentuated by the need to avoid ambiguity; there are several other words pronounced BU or TAI, but only two common compounds BUTAI: 'unit' or 'stage' and the context will usually show which is meant. 'Take a bough' will separate itself from 'Take a bow', as will 'Where is the quay?' from 'Where is the key?'; site/sight, die/dye and maid/made are other pairs which are theoretically as confusing as pairs in Japanese.

Let me explain how the characters appear in printed and hand-written form. Learning the order and direction of strokes is an integral part of the process of learning to write characters, and the result is shown here first in printed form, or as they might be written by brush for particular clarity, then in 'exploded' form to show stroke-order, then in two more cursive forms, showing how the main elements remain recognisable. Where the context allows, they can be abbreviated still further without ambiguity. I hope that the last example gives some idea of the way the two characters appeared in a captured document, written at great speed, in which BUTAI occurred frequently.

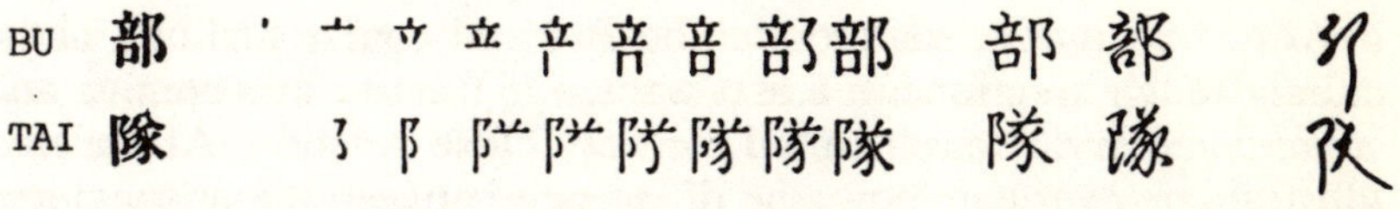

BU　部　　'　亠　亠　立　产　咅　咅　部3　部　　部　部　　　𢿥

TAI　隊　　　�　阝　阝⺌　阝⺌　阝⺌　隊　隊　隊　　隊　隊　　　隊

The 'box' in the bottom left-hand corner of BU, and an element found in many characters, is written with three strokes only:

1. Down the left side;
2. Across the top and down the right side, in one stroke including the angle;
3. Across the bottom from left to right. This order is invariable.

Nearly all vertical strokes are written downwards, and nearly all horizontal stokes from left to right. To find BU in a dictionary we have to know under which radical it is classified. Most characters have their radical on the left, but BU happens to have it on the right; it is radical number 163 out of the total of 214, in an abbreviated form. In that section of the dictionary allotted to each radical are listed, first, all the characters with one stroke added to the radical, then two, until we find ours in the section with eight added strokes. These can be as many as twenty added strokes, or even more.

Some twenty or thirty of the radicals are particularly common as a basis for more complex characters, and the student soon learns their number and can start looking in the right place in the dictionary. Sometimes the radical forms the top or bottom half, instead of one side; some form a vertical backbone, and others wrap part or all of the way round the outside.

All these characters are referred to as 'kanji'. In contrast there are two syllabaries, each containing 50 syllables plus the final consonant 'n', the only sound without an accompanying vowel. There are a further 25 syllables which the Japanese treat as modifications of the main set, as well as many odd or rare readings.

Katakana, the simpler and more angular syllabary, is more often used for writing words borrowed from European languages. Hiragana, the more cursive form, shows verb-endings and particles which show the subject and object of the verb or the equivalent of a possessive form. Nouns and the stems of verbs are almost always written in kanji.

Traditionally Japanese, like Chinese, is written in vertical columns, but European influence, and the need for horizontal captions under photographs and illustrations, mean that today we may encounter either, especially in newspapers and magazines.

After four and a half months the Bedford course had one particularly tough assignment: a text written in a hurry in a cursive and abbreviated style which called for very close scrutiny. As the two illustrations overleaf show, the difference between the original and the 'text-book copy', elegantly written with a brush by Hugh Melinsky, one of my colleagues on the course, is striking. This was a despatch printed in the *Yomiuri Shimbun* of 23 October 1941, from its correspondent in London. The text, which starts in the top right corner, begins:

ROUTES TO RUSSIA

Reports that items of American aid to Russia will in future be sent by the Boston-Archangel route are even here arousing a not inconsiderable interest; many questions have been raised concerning the reason for making this decision now, when we are approaching winter and the usefulness of Archangel is declining, and speculation of all kinds is rife. In some quarters they are taking it as a friendly gesture by the USA to Japan, but British Government circles consider it is the shortest route to the place where Russia thinks maximum aid necessary, and has no connection at all with the Far Eastern situation. There is also the explanation that as a result of the tenseness of the Pacific situation the USA has ordered US shipping to withdraw from the Far East area and has taken measures to avoid sending her ships to the most dangerous zones, and her avoidance of the Vladivostok route is based on the same reasoning.

The smaller signs between the characters are hiragana, the more cursive of the two forms of the kana syllabary.

g *The Chinese Telegraphic Code*

This accessory is often misunderstood. The Chinese Telegraphic Code (CTC, or MING as the Americans cover-named it) is not a code in the cryptographic sense, but a way of identifying and recognising characters. It is basically a commercial code, widely used in the areas of China and Japan, which indicates which character is meant, when several are pronounced in the same way. It was therefore useful to anyone who drafted a signal and wished to use a character which was not in the military codebook. The European method, to spell the word so that it can be looked up in a dictionary, cannot work for a language which has no spelling. Even showing it in kana would leave it uncertain which KAN or SEN, for example, of several KANs and SENs, was intended.

The CTC book, as the illustration on page 138 shows, contains 10,000 characters, each listed under its radical in the traditional way, with a code number or, in reserve for those preferring an alphabetical reference, a three-letter group. The reference is then placed and followed by code-groups for 'open CTC' and 'close CTC', which rapidly become familiar.

The seven small characters shown vertically outside the top left of the frame are the radicals under which the characters on that page are grouped, and with a little patience the reader can trace the affinity between them.

135

The difference between a text written in a hurry (above) and a 'fair copy' (right)

米國の對露援助品は今後との報道は當地でも少からぬ注意を喚起して居り冬期に近づきの利用價値が減少する今日何故かゝる決定をなしたかに就て多大の疑問起し各種の臆測が行はれて居る一部では米國の對日友好的 Gesture だとなして居るも英官邊筋では露西亞が最大の援助を必要とする地點えの最短路であつてのに極東情勢とは何等關係ないものとなして居り更に第三説として太平洋情勢逼迫の結果米國は極東方面の米國船引揚を命じ、なるたけ危險地域に自國船を送らぬやう取計つて居るが 航路を避ける事も同樣の理由に基くものであらうとの解釋もある外交消息通は恐以上の三つても考慮に入れられて居ると見伺籠

との報道は當地でも少からぬ注意を喚起して居り冬期に近づき Boston Archangel の航路によつて送られることになる

Archangel

03 ALO—APJ

Code	Letter	Code	Letter	Code	Letter	Code	Letter	Code	Letter	Code	Letter	Code	Letter	Code	Letter	Code	Letter	Code	Letter
0300	ALO	0301	ALP	0302	ALQ	0303	ALR	0304	ALS	0305	ALT	0306	ALU	0307	ALV	0308	ALW	0309	ALX
0310	ALY	0311	ALZ	0312	AMA	0313	AMB	0314	AMC	0315	AMD	0316	AME	0317	AMF	0318	AMG	0319	AMH
0320	AMI	0321	AMJ	0322	AMK	0323	AML	0324	AMM	0325	AMN	0326	AMO	0327	AMP	0328	AMQ	0329	AMR
0330	AMS	0331	AMT	0332	AMU	0333	AMV	0334	AMW	0335	AMX	0336	AMY	0337	AMZ	0338	ANA	0339	ANB
0340	ANC	0341	AND	0342	ANE	0343	ANF	0344	ANG	0345	ANH	0346	ANI	0347	ANJ	0348	ANK	0349	ANL
0350	ANM	0351	ANN	0352	ANO	0353	ANP	0354	ANQ	0355	ANR	0356	ANS	0357	ANT	0358	ANU	0359	ANV
0360	ANW	0361	ANX	0362	ANY	0363	ANZ	0364	AOA	0365	AOB	0366	AOC	0367	AOD	0368	AOE	0369	AOF
0370	AOG	0371	AOH	0372	AOI	0373	AOJ	0374	AOK	0375	AOL	0376	AOM	0377	AON	0378	AOO	0379	AOP
0380	AOQ	0381	AOR	0382	AOS	0383	AOT	0384	AOU	0385	AOV	0386	AOW	0387	AOX	0388	AOY	0389	AOZ
0390	APA	0391	APB	0392	APC	0393	APD	0394	APE	0395	APF	0396	APG	0397	APH	0398	API	0399	APJ

Explanatory Notes

1. The Standard Code Book contains code expressions in groups of four figures, each representing a Chinese character.

2. The code expressions are arranged horizontally from left to right, 100 to a page, e.g., Page 1 from 0000 to 0099, Page 2 from 0100 to 0199, and so on.

3. To code a telegram for transmission, first ascertain the radical of the character and the index of the radical, then look for the codeword of the relevant character. For instance, the radical for the character "中" is "|", whose index is "00", and a short search on page 1 will yield the code expression "0022" for "中."

4. Characters and marks not available in the Standard Code Book proper may be found in one of the appendices named below:

1) For simplified characters, refer to "Code for Simplified Chinese Characters";

Chinese Telegraphic Code Book, with a specimen page showing the affinity between the radicals (0354, 0360, etc) and the characters following them

h *Japanese language courses*

The Bedford courses in Japanese were not, as one might have expected, 'born out of long years of planning by intelligence staff nor established under the professional auspices of a university department'. Almost the opposite was true. Like most British preparations for the European or the Japanese war, they were improvised after the starting signal.[104]

Colonel John Tiltman, whom I have mentioned earlier for his unconventional dress, had been working at Bletchley Park since 1939 and was an expert codebreaker in his own right. He taught himself at least the rudiments of Japanese well enough to be the key figure in breaking the Japanese military attaché code in the summer of 1942. Immediately after Pearl Harbor he was asked to recruit men who knew written Japanese. Most of those who already did were captured in Hong Kong and Singapore, and the dozen or so who were in England were at SOAS, the School of Oriental and African Studies, in London – often known as 'The School of 'orrible Studies'.

'Tiltman went there, explained that he had gained a working knowledge of written Japanese within six months, and said that he wanted them to organise a course, to start as soon as possible, which might teach selected undergraduates the same kind of Japanese in the same amount of time.' SOAS were sceptical about this; they pointed out that it took five years in peacetime to train diplomats to a reasonable standard, and that they might be able to do what Tiltman wanted in two years. Faced with this lack of enthusiasm Tiltman turned to a retired naval officer, Captain Tuck.

Tuck was a remarkable man. He had left school at fifteen, had not gone to university but joined the Royal Navy, served on the China Station, studied Japanese in his own time and on his own initiative, against a good deal of prejudice, and obtained shore leave to improve it. 'Once on the mainland he set up house in Tokyo, studied with a local teacher and kept a diary in Japanese. His persistence paid off, and he was given the job of translating the secret Japanese history of the recent Russo-Japanese war. Eventually he was appointed assistant to the naval attaché and found himself at the centre of Tokyo diplomatic and service life.'

During the 1914–18 war he worked for naval intelligence, and later became head of the Admiralty's Historical Section. In the Second World War he worked with Arthur Waley, the distinguished

Sino-Japanese scholar, as a press censor, blue-pencilling reports from Japanese journalists for their newspapers.

It was Tuck whom Tiltman consulted after his rebuff at SOAS. On 21 December 1941, a fortnight after Pearl Harbor, they met at the Admiralty and Tiltman explained his ideas, suggesting that Tuck should teach the first course; the aim was to teach young students to read Japanese within six months. Tuck's diary records that 'the idea sounded impossible but was worth trying'. He thereupon embarked on a new career at the age of sixty-five.

The first course met over the Bedford gas showroom, in a small room designed for cookery demonstrations, on 2 February 1942, less than two months after Pearl Harbor, 'under the paternal eye of Captain Tuck and the curious gaze of Mr Therm, the Gas Company's advertising logo'. It consisted of twenty-two men and one woman, in their late teens or early twenties, all but three of whom were classical scholars straight from a first year at Oxford or Cambridge. Rightly or wrongly the Classical Sixth, followed by an Oxbridge scholarship in Classics, was regarded as attracting outstanding students. The preference for a classical training was part of the GCHQ tradition, not because of any linguistic qualification but because it was thought that it enabled a student to tackle almost anything. The word was passed round Masters, Deans and Tutors of colleges, and eventually 'a very bright lot' was chosen for interview and rigorously selected for the course. They now include at least three professors and several other academics; three more were appointed to teach at either the later Bedford courses or at those which SOAS agreed to arrange. One of the three older students was the mountaineer Wilfrid Noyce.

The teaching methods were flexible, and no orthodox system could be followed for lack of textbooks. Precisely five books were available for twenty-three students, and all were Tuck's personal property: 'One copy of Chamberlain's grammar, one of Isemonger's Japanese characters, and three different Japanese-English dictionaries.'

There was even a shortage of writing-paper. These basic difficulties seem to have stimulated teacher and student alike, and the spirit of desperate improvisation forced them to depend on their memories – a vital part of the intricate process of learning written Japanese. Moreover even the five books available used colloquial Japanese, whereas the students needed to study the formal language of the military and civil services. One student remembers that he left after six months knowing the word for 'submarine' but not for 'I' and 'you', which do not occur in official communications. I think that was true of our course as well.

Tuck was a born teacher. On the first day 'he talked about the past participle and gave the students a number of words from which they were to make up sentences, which they then read out'. The whole class then joined in a discussion about the sentences. One such sentence which read 'On the subject of the bad relations between Japan and the USA Mr Churchill made a long speech in Parliament' was, according to Tuck, 'just as a correspondent would have written it, and in perfect Japanese, by a fellow who yesterday morning knew nothing of the language'.

In mid-July 1942 a conference was held in London to decide if further courses should be started up elsewhere in addition to the Bedford courses. Two men from Tuck's course, which still had one month out of the six to run, were present, as well as Army and RAF intelligence staff representatives and five teachers from SOAS. The SOAS team, clearly chafing at having placed themselves in an invidious position, challenged the two students, without warning, to translate a Japanese press agency bulletin. The students retired to another room and returned fifteen minutes later having translated all the first page. One of the two, Robin Gibson, continued to translate at sight; the other was Eric Ceadel, who subsequently joined Tuck as teacher on later Bedford courses.

The challenge, delivered slightly below the belt, produced the opposite effect from what SOAS had intended, and they were officially induced to set up parallel courses. There were differences. The Bedford failure rate was 4 per cent; at SOAS an examination was given after one month, and those who failed, amounting to 25 per cent, were at once removed from the rest of the course. This seems to be a comment on selection procedures rather than on teaching, but as late as June 1944 Naval Intelligence considered that the Bedford students were of a higher standard than those from SOAS. This is all the more striking in view of the amateur improvisation that had gone into the Bedford course, compared with the professional expertise of a department of London University, and of the breadth of background which balanced the language teaching at Bedford: talks on Japanese poetry, volcanoes, the work of destroyers in the Atlantic, and mountain-climbing in Nepal. Students were encouraged to give informal talks to the whole group, and a debating society met regularly. Tuck commented after bidding farewell to the first course: 'As I quite honestly told them, I think my work with them has been the happiest in my life'.

Later Ceadel returned to share the teaching with him, and later still they were helped by David Hawkes and Frank Winston. By then the course had settled at 52 De Parys Avenue, and it remained there until the eleventh and last course ended in late 1945.

Despite their reluctant start SOAS ran many valuable courses, ranging in length from six to twelve months or longer. They were more clearly differentiated in purpose, and a student was intended from the start to be either a translator or an interrogator, until the services were persuaded to abolish this division, which had proved wasteful, unpopular and irrational. It had been overtaken by events. SOAS pointed out that 'the rigid separation of functions had broken down in the field ... many of the earlier "literate" interrogators have taught themselves to read after arrival in India, and a number of the "dumb" translators have undertaken interrogation or acted as interpreters'. After the war SOAS produced a report on the courses, which comments on ways in which theirs differed from those held in the USA but makes no mention of Bedford.

Relatively few of the SOAS students went to Bletchley Park; more went on other courses on radio techniques before going on to WEC at Delhi, to forward units in Burma, or to CSDIC and other interrogation centres. Most Bedford students went either to GCHQ at Bletchley or to the largish units in India and Australia; twice as many into the Army as into the Navy, and only one or two from each course to the RAF or the small Foreign Office establishment at Berkeley Street. There were never enough Japanese linguists for British intelligence units. A sympathetic American expert visiting Calcutta in early 1945 found that 'the British sources appear to have dried up' and described a crash course put on at the Intelligence School there, designed to give 'just enough knowledge of colloquial Japanese and just enough practice with recordings of actual transmissions for the trainee to handle the sort of radio-telephone signals used in Japanese Air Force communications'.[105]

The American courses existed on quite a different footing. There was never the same need for improvisation, because every year from 1925 onwards a few service officers had been seconded for a thorough grounding in Japanese. Perhaps because of this more methodical and leisurely tradition they, like SOAS, were sceptical about the value of shorter courses, even after Pearl Harbor. Moreover several experienced pre-war students were at once available to augment the teaching staff and produce new linguists in quantity. They had two further assets. One was the wealth of Nisei (second-generation American-born) Japanese able to work in intelligence and to train others in the language. The other was both practical and psychological: for them the Japanese attacks represented the start of war, not simply One More War arriving two-and-a-quarter years after the first. Perhaps, too, they were able to profit a little from our successes and failures.

The US Army ran courses at Fort Snelling and at the University of Michigan. The US Navy had a famous eleven-month course at Boulder, Colorado. After Pearl Harbor students 'worked 12-14 hours a day for six days a week, used only Japanese in class as far as possible, and were required to speak only Japanese at one meal a day'. The selection was rigorous, only one applicant in eight being accepted and one in eight failing to graduate. There were weekly examinations, taking up some 250 hours in all.

The students and the Navy agreed that the finished product was at worst perfectly adequate and at best excellent. The students' only reservations were that too much time was spent on writing Japanese from dictation, a skill rarely needed except for secretaries, reporters and radio monitors, and that the texts from the Naganuma readers, used also at the Embassy School in Tokyo, which had to be learnt parrot fashion, dominated the syllabus and the oral examination, so that good memory came to be valued more highly than actual linguistic ability. Other criticisms were that most of the dictionaries were obsolete and that the sheer drive and intensity did not produce commensurate results.

Fortunately the '12-14 hours a day' were less daunting than the figures suggest, since they included only four hours' classwork, short daily broadcasts in Japanese and occasional oral examinations in addition to the regular weekly tests; the rest was used for private study which included the use of gramophone records for ear training, and preparation for the Naganuma texts on the following day.

The course aimed to produce students who could read and write 2,000 Japanese characters and have a spoken vocabulary of 8,000 words, so that a graduate from the course could 'read a Japanese newspaper, converse adequately, understand broadcasts and translate documents'. One student commented: 'The course is undoubtedly very arduous and the heavy examination schedule imposes a strain which would be excessive if the subject-matter covered by each examination were not limited. Students are also assisted by the ideal studying conditions at Boulder, such as the perfect climate, delightful surroundings and lack of artificial diversions.'

Perhaps it is surprising that by 1943 the Americans, who had met several former Bedford students at Washington, were clamouring for details of the Bedford teaching methods. One Bedford student who worked in the USA wrote later that although he had always felt himself overshadowed by the brilliance of other people on his course: over there where 'the top people in his section were not so outstanding he found himself doing good and useful work, and often in larger quantities than the Americans'.

The two people who emerge covered in glory for the success of the Bedford courses must be Tiltman, whose imagination and faith led him to entrust them to an untrained 65-year-old when the university department whose speciality it was had turned him down, and Tuck, who by his patient, unassuming and kindly expertise had directed some of the most successful crash courses in educational history at one of the most crucial moments in recent British history. A final comment came from Australia, firmly under MacArthur's control, only a fortnight before Hiroshima. They asked for as many more Bedford students as possible: 'Could you indicate a possible figure and I shall initiate an official request. Your Bedford-trained translators most highly esteemed and would like as many as we may have; we can never have enough.'

i *Glossary of technical terms*

CIPHER A method of substituting letters or numbers for the letters of a message, one at a time, or of transposing their order: hence 'substitution' and 'transposition' ciphers. Also used for a numerical key. Note that the Royal Navy had its own definition; for them a cipher was used by officers and a code by ratings, even when they were similar in form. 'Cypher' is an older form.

CIPHER-TEXT An enciphered message.

CLEAR In ordinary language, not in cryptographic form. The French *en clair* is also used.

CODE A method of substituting groups of two or more letters or numbers for the words, phrases or sentences of a message. They can also stand for numbers, punctuation, personal or place names, foreign words or any selected symbols.

CODEBOOK Usually in two volumes: one for encoding, arranged in alphabetical or other logical order of words, meaning, etc; the other in alphabetical or numerical order of code-groups.

CODEBREAKER Someone who reconstructs enemy crypto messages; the term usually includes cipher-breaking. The staff of a codebreaking unit will often be intercepting, translating, key-stripping, key-breaking, book-breaking and so forth, and many people move between jobs as required; others will be collating and assessing the information obtained, and passing it in summarised form to HQs.

CODE GROUP A group of two or more letters or numbers assigned for a specific meaning; see CODE.

COLOSSUS See MACHINE, 3, and Chapter Two.

COMINT Communications intelligence; a recent near-synonym for SIGINT. No connection with Comintern.

COVER-NAME A word, often chosen at random, to disguise an agent, an operation, a crypto system or anything else that needs to be kept secret. See next section.

CRIB A text or other evidence which, by suggesting parallels of subject-matter or expression, provides helpful clues for breaking a crypto signal.

CRYPTANALYSIS, CRYPTANALYST etc The technique or profession of breaking codes and ciphers; a codebreaker.

CRYPTO An abbreviation which I have used freely to save space, for the last and next entries.

CRYPTOGRAM, CRYPTOGRAPHER, etc A code or cipher message; one who deals with such messages.

CRYPTOLOGY The subject or study of codes and ciphers, their use and their penetration.

CTC Chinese Telegraphic Code; see Chapter Thirteen, section g, page 135.

DECIPHER Transform a cipher signal into plain language; used whether the job is done by friend or enemy. Also: a deciphered signal.

DECODE Transform a code signal into plain language, whether friend or foe does it. Also: a decoded signal.

DECRYPT Transform a cipher or code signal into plain language. Also: a decrypted signal.

DEPTH To 'build up a depth' is to try to reconstruct a short section of key which has not been broken but has reconstructed key on each side, by bringing together several signals, all apparently reciphered on the same section of key, which straddle the gap. A conjectural key which makes sense even of two signals is unlikely to be wrong; see Chapter Eleven. Sometimes called 'superimposition'. See Kahn, *The Codebreakers*, pages 236–7, and elsewhere.

DISCRIMINANT A group of letters or numbers showing which crypto system has been used for a signal.

ENCIPHER Transform a plain-language text into a cipher-text; sometimes misleadingly used for RECIPHER.

ENCODE Transform a plain-language text into a code-text.

ENCRYPT Transform a plain-language text into a crypto (code or cipher) text. Also: a code or cipher text.

ENIGMA The cipher machine used for most German army, navy, air force, security services and SS signals.

GEHEIMSCHREIBER German ten-wheel cipher machine for on-line non-Morse signals sent by radio or land-line.

GC & CS Government Code and Cypher School: the establishment later called GCHQ

GCHQ Government Communications Headquarters: the establishment originally at Bletchley Park, now at Cheltenham. Wartime cover-names included Station X, War Station Room 47, Mousetrap and HMS Pembroke.

HAND CIPHER A cipher (e.g. Playfair or Double Playfair) worked out by hand, not by machine.

HATTED Arranged at random.

HIGH-GRADE, LOW-GRADE The level of security which a code or cipher system has been designed to provide, rather than the importance of the message it carries.

HOLLERITH A British punched-card machine; see MACHINE, 2.

INDICATOR A group of letters or numbers showing where a KEY, used to recipher a crypto text, starts.

KANA A method of writing Japanese syllables phonetically, as distinct from using the borrowed Chinese characters (KANJI). Two forms existed: hiragana (cursive) and katakana (angular); see section f of this chapter.

KANJI The borrowed Chinese characters used to write Japanese; see KANA above.

KEY A random numerical text, sometimes called a cipher, which has no meaning of its own but is used as a second stage to disguise further a crypto text by non-carrying addition, non-borrowing subtraction, substitution table or other methods; hence an 'additive' or 'subtractor' key. 'Long additives' might run to hundreds or thousands of key groups before repeating.

KEY-BREAKING See DEPTH.

KEY-STRIPPING Removing the key which conceals a crypto text: the reverse of RECIPHERING. Generally refers to enemy crypto material.

MACHINE
1. A cipher machine (German ENIGMA, Japanese PURPLE, British TYPEX, American SIGABA, etc) which automatically enciphers a plain-language text letter by letter.
2. A punched-card machine (Hollerith in Britain, IBM, Remington-Rand, etc in USA) which rapidly and automatically extracts cards which have a specified pattern in common from the rest of the pack.
3. A computer used for breaking crypto material. Although this is now common practice, the only such machine used for this purpose in the 1939–45 war was the COLOSSUS at Bletchley Park; see Chapter Four.

MAGIC An American cover-name roughly equivalent to ULTRA and meaning high-grade Japanese SIGINT, but variously used to denote only PURPLE, or to include ULTRA, depending on the author now or the commanding general and his staff then; see next section.

MESSAGE Generally an original text in clear language; but 'code-message', etc, obviously modifies this.

M.I. Military Intelligence. I give the following rough guide to the wartime War Office departments not for its relevance to this book, but because the information appears to rarely. Note that higher numbers were added for new tasks or for existing tasks which had outgrown their original departments; the whole series has now been replaced. The Royal Navy and the RAF had various separate departments, but MI5, 6 and 8 were inter-service. Note that the usual designation of MI5 for counter-espionage, and MI6 for espionage, is misleading. The approximate duties were:

MI1   Administration, personnel, training etc.
MI2   Middle East, India, USSR, Northern and Eastern Europe, Scandinavia, and USA (until 1941).
MI3   Western Europe (including Germany till May 1940, when it became MI14).
MI4   Maps; later operations.
MI5   (Security Service) Intelligence operations in Britain; hence mostly counter-espionage.
MI6   (Secret Intelligence Service) British intelligence-gathering abroad, and counter-intelligence abroad.
MI7   Press and propaganda; later to Ministry of Information.
MI8   Signals intelligence.
MI9   Enemy and Allied prisoners-of-war; the former became MI19
      in 1941, and MI9 also helped in escape and evasion.
MI10 Technical intelligence.
MI11 Military security; Field Security branch of Intelligence Corps.
MI12 Post and telegraph security; later to Ministry of Information.
MI13 (Unlucky)
MI14 German intelligence, after May 1940.
MI15 Aerial photo-reconnaissance; later enemy anti-aircraft defences.
MI16 Scientific intelligence.
MI17 Co-ordinating of intelligence.
MI18 (Not known)
MI19 Enemy prisoners-of-war, after 1941; Combined Services Detailed Interrogation Centres.
MIL   Liaison with military attachés of Allied countries.
MIL(R) Liaison with USSR.
MIR   Special forces, until formation of SOE, Special Operations Executive.
MIX   Recruitment for Intelligence Corps.

ONE-TIME PAD (OTP) A key which cannot normally be employed more than once because as each page, or part-page, is used, it is torn off and destroyed. If used in this way, and not captured, it is unbreakable, since a DEPTH cannot be built up. The principle was first applied in the USA in 1917–19 (in tape form), in Germany in 1921–23, in the USSR from 1927 and in Japan from the mid-1930s, but no country seems to have exploited it methodically until the Second World War.

PURPLE American cover-name for the cipher-machine used for Japanese high-grade diplomatic traffic. Its Japanese name '97-shiki ōbun injiki' meant that it was designed in 1937 (2597 in the Japanese traditional calendar) and 'ōbun injiki' (alphabetical typewriter) describes its use of the European alphabet instead of the kana syllabary. This machine was not copied or modified from ENIGMA, although a much earlier machine, cover-named GREEN, was.

RECIPHER Disguise a signal which is already in cipher or code form, by modifying it by means of a KEY. RE-ENCIPHER and SUPER-ENCIPHER are longer ways of saying the same thing.

SIGABA The standard American cipher-machine, never broken during the 1939–45 war; it later, as SIGTOT, incorporated a teleprinter.

SIGINT Signals intelligence: information gained from breaking enemy codes and ciphers, from traffic analysis, etc. SIGINT generally refers to digests and summaries of intelligence derived from decrypted signals, rather than the broken crypto texts themselves.

SIGNAL A text transmitted by radio, teleprinter, etc, whether in clear or crypto form.

STRIPPING See KEY-STRIPPING.

SUBSTITUTION TABLE A method of reciphering a crypto text by using the upper and lower numbers in each pair not for addition or subtraction but as co-ordinates in a grid of numbers in rows and columns; see Chapter Nine.

SUPERENCIPHER See RECIPHER.

SUPERIMPOSITION See DEPTH.

SYSTEM The complete array of crypto material assembled for a particular type or series of signals; sometimes designated by a DISCRIMINANT, and also known by the enemy under a COVER-NAME.

TINA A procedure for recognising radio-operators by their distinctive habits and idiosyncracies of transmitting. RFP stood for the identification of different types of radio set.

TRAFFIC A quantity of signals transmitted, or at least intercepted.

TRAFFIC ANALYSIS The interception and study of signals in plain language or in low-grade codes or ciphers, of frequencies, and of call-signs, together with TINA and direction-finding, etc. See Chapter Thirteen, Section a.

TYPEX The standard British cipher-machine, incorporating a teleprinter and not broken during the 1939–45 war.

ULTRA Originally a British cover-name, from June 1941, to describe all high-grade sigint, including that derived not only from the Enigma machine cipher but also from German hand-ciphers and Italian and Japanese codes and ciphers. Later adopted by the Americans, who often used the terms ULTRA and MAGIC interchangeably, though MAGIC had at first meant only high-grade Japanese sigint. See Chapter Twelve and the following section in this chapter.

Y SERVICE Originally covered signals interception, traffic analysis and the breaking of low-grade signals. From October 1943 it covered only interception and direction-finding, like the American RI: Radio Intelligence service, but was still often used as a form of cover-name for recruiting, language courses and the like.

NOTES

1. This list is meant to help with actual usage from 1939 to 1945, and sometimes later. It is not always logical, since it reflects the quirks and changes in the British and American usage. A balance has to be struck between the accurate and the concise, and I have tried to include the commoner variants without taking sides.
2. Several terms are ambiguous. 'British codebreaking' means 'work by British codebreakers', not 'breaking British codes'. 'Japanese cryptanalysis' usually means 'work against Japanese codes and ciphers', at least to British and American readers, but to a Japanese reader it could well mean work by Japanese cryptanalysts.

j Cover-names

Cover-names were widely used in the Second World War, and sometimes misused then and since. Many are already well known:

SEALION (Seelöwe) German cover-name for the planned invasion of Britain;
BARBAROSSA for the German invasion of the USSR;
OVERLORD for the Allied invasion of France;
FORTITUDE for the deception operation concealing the true area of the Allied landings in France.

All have a certain heroic ring; but when Churchill and his staff referred to the SEALION operation they called it SMITH, so that if German sigint or espionage detected any reference to the plan and our counter-measures, they would not immediately know that we had learned of it from our Enigma sigint.

At the other extreme are the frivolous names of the FLEA, GIGGLE and SWEETY-PIE variety, that Churchill objected to as trivialising operations in which many lives might be lost.

All too often cover-names were chosen which revealed the pattern and even the purpose of what they were intended to conceal. WOTAN, the single-eyed leader of the Teutonic gods, was the single-beam navigational aid which replaced a twin-beam system. A detection and interception device which followed was FREYA, his mistress. The names of the X-Gerät stations which guided German bombers to targets in Britain were all rivers, which made it all too easy to deduce what ELBE meant in an otherwise uninformative message. Solve one, and you are well-placed to solve the rest.

The same was true of alphabetical jingles. German night-fighter control zones based at HAMSTER for Hamstede, KOLIBRI (humming-bird) for Köln (Cologne), TIGER for Terschelling and ZANDER for Zandvoort were paralleled by the names which British radio-operators used to denote the German stations from which they intercepted signals: BERTIE for Berlin, HARRY for Hamburg and WILLIE for Wiesbaden.[106]

Obviously much depends on whether there is any risk of interception. Bletchley Park and its out-stations were probably safe with BERTIE and the rest, because no such details were included in the Ultra summaries of Enigma sigint which were sent out to commanders in the field. One can always be wrong about the inviolability of one's codes, but if the details are not contained in them, there is no risk from that source.

Bletchley certainly used a great many series in their cover-names for the successive Enigma keys which they attacked on different German systems. They were called after colours, insects, flowers, animals, birds and fishes, and many rare species had to be brought in towards the end of the war. Even without sub-divisions such as KESTREL I-IV, or oddities like BOUNCE, RAILWAY and BLUNDERBUSS, they reached a total of over 160. Other fields of activity yield a wider vocabulary. Clandestine operations in southeast Asia appeared as ACROBAT, BADGER, CAIRNGORM, DILWYN, ELEPHANT, FERRET and the like; blander titles such as BRISK, EVIDENCE and FUNNEL could not be relied upon to guarantee a less hair-raising mission.

It is easy, with hindsight, to become confused by some names which gave no trouble at the time. Some of the earliest Enigma keys attacked were RED, BLUE and PURPLE. RED and PURPLE were also names for Japanese cipher-machines and their output, yet very few people would have worked on or known about both, so no ambiguity arose then. Other Enigma keys were YAK and LEOPARD, which also designated Japanese signals networks, and the periods over which Japanese keys were used were shown by the same range of colours and tints, verging on the fanciful, which GCHQ used for Enigma.

The Japanese crypto systems themselves were labelled methodically by the Americans from the 1930s when they began intercepting them, whether they could read them or not: J for diplomatic and consular, JA for army and JN for navy (each including its own air force), JMA and JNA for military and naval attachés. All were followed by numbers to show separate systems under these headings. But whereas various stages of JN 23 became JN 23a, b and c, the sequel to JN 14 was JN 147.

The greatest scope for ambiguity and error, however, lies in the security gradings given to enemy systems, and the commonest of these are so well known to the media that they have been stirred into wilder disarray still. It is clear that ULTRA began life as a name covering *all* high-grade sigint, whether German, Italian or Japanese, and was thus used 'in British circles and at inter-Allied and US centres in Europe'.[107] MAGIC seems to have been restricted at first to high-grade Japanese sigint, but the Americans soon used it as a near-synonym for ULTRA, and it is not surprising that writers have used it idiosyncratically since. Hinsley shows that the usage varied, and Kahn refers to 'MAGIC, or ULTRA, as it was sometimes called'.[108]

The lower gradings are in a worse tangle. The US Army and Navy used different terms at different times for the same grade. West tries to discern a pattern: 'Three lesser classifications: DEXTER, CORRAL and RABID for US forces, while GCHQ stuck to PEARL, THUMB and ZEAL'.[109] Only up to a point. The US Army as well as GCHQ used PEARL (having earlier christened it CIRO PEARL) and THUMB as lower-grade names, as much as a year after the BRUSA agreement which West sees as settling the names. ZEAL was not restricted to GCHQ, for the US Navy used it as an early variant for ULTRA; ZYMOTIC was another, shared by the British. Several of these stood for signals intercepted but not broken, and for traffic analysis, for which PINUP later emerged as a joint US Army and Navy name.

Churchill and his entourage had coined several whimsical explanations for early Enigma information. At first it was a mythical agent BONIFACE. When it was seen that MI6 was not then in high regard, it was 'information recovered from a waste-paper basket', until the capacity of the alleged waste-paper basket began to disturb the credulity of even the most gullible. Churchill called Ultra 'the geese who laid the golden eggs' or 'the chickens who were laying so well', a doubtful compliment to the Wrens (Women's Royal Naval Service) who helped to produce it; it is true that 'they never clucked or cackled'. Much later he was still asking 'Where are my eggs?'

Elsewhere Ultra was alluded to as 'Uncle Henry', from 'Always believe what your Uncle Henry tells you' in *Three Men in a Boat* by Jerome K. Jerome.[110] Even Bletchley Park was 'BP' to its inmates, before there was a risk of confusion with British Petroleum, and elsewhere 'Station X', 'War Station Room 47', 'HMS Pembroke' for the Wrens and 'Mousetrap' for the Australians.

'ULTRA' came into existence in June 1941 and even its parentage is contested. Winterbotham, writing in 1974, says that he initiated the inter-service discussions which produced it. Beesly states that Commander Colpoys, of the naval Operational Intelligence Centre, suggested ULTRA, 'about the only Latin he could remember', thus displacing 'HUSH, Most Secret' with its charming nursery-rhyme echoes.[111] An earlier naval name had been HYDRO. But for the Navy Ultra covered actual signals and documents only, their contents being known as 'Special Intelligence' or 'Z'. For GCHQ, 'Z' was the lowest grading and 'ZZZZZ' the highest.[112]

PART THREE

A TANGLED WEB

14

Clandestine Groups and their Signals

I have briefly touched on the use of spies and captured documents; we must not forget the role played by the groups that operated behind the lines in Burma and elsewhere in south-east Asia, with the original task of organising sabotage and guerrilla activities, and an extra responsibility, added later after acrimonious controversy, for collecting intelligence. There was a link with signals intelligence: signals were their lifeline, and signals security was even more crucial for their survival than it was for any military unit.

The Americans had a simple arrangement in the area: the OSS (Office of Strategic Services) looked after all their clandestine groups, whatever their function, while the OWI (Office of War Information) dealt with propaganda. For the same functions in the same area the British had no fewer than ten secret organisations, five of which had no hand in sabotage, the training of guerrillas or the getting of intelligence. That leaves five which did:

1. ISLD (Inter-Services Liaison Department; the local cover-name for SIS, MI6 or intelligence-gathering or espionage)
2. Force 136 (the local name for SOE, Special Operations Executive)
3. V Force (fighting patrols gathering intelligence close behind the main enemy positions)
4. Z Force (fighting patrols gathering intelligence deeper inside enemy-held territory)
5. Burma Intelligence Corps (providing guides and interpreters for these and other operations)

The title of the first of these, Inter-Services Liaison Department, may suggest that it performed a co-ordinating role. Nothing could be further from the truth. It was not merely secret, like its partners, but ultra-secretive and totally unwilling to co-operate with them.

For several years it refused to allow the aircraft of the RAF Special Duty Squadrons to combine its loads with those of any other organisation. This folly culminated in having a special mission flown from Calcutta to Rangoon to drop *one* radio set for ISLD, on a night when any of nine other aircraft in the area on similar duties could have done it. The dangerous inanity of this mission was all the more acute since over 200 airmen lost their lives in these operations as against only five among those they dropped, both during the drop and on the ground. It was largely the scandal provoked by this one flight which brought the absurdity into the open and resulted in the overdue setting-up of P Division to co-ordinate all such operations within SEAC.[113]

There were other difficulties. Both the long-term objectives and even the current priorities of these groups were fiercely argued. It proved impossible to reconcile conflicting demands for the getting of intelligence, the training and arming of guerrillas, the committing of sabotage, the spreading of propaganda and the nurturing of political subversion, largely because in London too there was no unanimity over policy. The War Office, the Foreign Office, the India Office, the Colonial Office and the Ministry of Economic Warfare were often at loggerheads – to say nothing of the three Service ministries. SOE in particular, wherever it operated, suffered from being cajoled into adding to its traditional roles of guerrilla-training and sabotage the almost incompatible task of intelligence-gathering.

Nor was this a new problem. From the 1930s the General Officers Commanding and the Governors in Malaya and Burma, and the Commander-in-Chief, Far East, had left a trail of delay and discouragement. The head of SOE in London said, 'It is most tantalising to see ... how His Majesty's Representatives have vetoed any preparatory work, cried for help from SOE the moment trouble started, and then complained if we did not deliver the goods'.[114]

It is not surprising that this legacy of regional mismanagement often meant slapdash recruitment, short-sighted training and poor equipment, with results that ranged from admirable to abysmal. Moreover their ultimate aim was not clear. Cruickshank puts it in a nutshell: 'Who was the real enemy – the invading Japanese or the colonial power they had thrown out?' The question vexed not only the local inhabitants and some British, but many Americans, who saw no reason why they should intervene to throw out the Japanese merely to enable Britain, France and the Netherlands to regain their lost empires. Their doubts were not merely those of a former colony which sympathised with anti-colonial sentiment; they were exacerbated in Indo-China because Roosevelt and De Gaulle disliked and mistrusted each other. In consequence the Americans refused to support any French-led resistance to the Japanese in that country, even though the USA and France were nominally allies against the Axis. In the words of General Browning, Mountbatten's Chief of Staff at SEAC, 'Those' (the Americans and the French) 'were the two at war in Indo-China. The Japs were not in it'.[115] Ironically this led to the USA's supporting a Communist leader whom they met later on the other side of the fence: Ho Chi Minh. We did very much the same in Malaya.

Burma was at least spared a downright clash of policies, but the discrepancy in attitudes spilled over so that co-operation there between SOE and OSS rested more on their local military commanders than on any identity of views between their governments on long-term objectives. There were also some immediate difficulties, for example between the US and RAF air forces when aircraft were used not on orthodox but on clandestine missions. It has been asserted that the USAAF actually shot down three RAF Liberators which were lost in early 1945 while flying missions to Indo-China. The evidence is shaky, and the area where they crashed suggests that ten-tenths cloud, severe icing and violent turbulence, all too common over Burma, were to blame.[116]

But an American B-29 Superfortress was shot down by the RAF on the night of 20 December 1944, when it did not conform to a flight plan, failed to give the correct IFF response, and – presumably by mistake – dropped bombs near Chittagong. It was thereupon judged to be a Japanese bomber, declared hostile, and shot down by two Beaufighters. This episode finally persuaded the USAAF to co-operate fully in those activities which they had been keeping secret, to the relief of local American fighter patrols which had had similar problems with these unidentified aircraft.

The activities of Force 136 have been described in several excellent accounts, but some practical details call for comment. Communication was always a central problem. Radios were scarce and batteries, vital in a country where mains electricity hardly existed outside the towns, scarcer still. In Burma and elsewhere SOE had ingenious methods of recharging them: by pedalling a bicycle or turning a crank by hand, by wind power, by a good fire in a brazier, by petrol or, wonder of wonders, by a steam engine.[117] Many of these devices unfortunately tended to wear out quickly in tropical conditions.

Crypto security was generally good. Most daily needs were met by a code-book consisting of three-number groups for phrases or even complete sentences: an excellent way of keeping messages short and thus reducing the risk that enemy direction-finding stations might intercept and triangulate on the transmitter. These 'crack' signals could convey in three groups or less such messages as 'We are safe and establishing a hideout' or 'Send radio and spare batteries'. It is odd that this principle was not more widely applied. Messages as short as this were so unlikely to be intercepted at all that they were sometimes sent without recipherment, and were helped to merge with their background by borrowing the operating procedures used by radio amateurs ('hams') or by ships of any nationality: QRK = How clear is my signal? and QRV = Are you ready?

Longer messages, and those not covered by the crack signals, were drafted in plain text, enciphered at first on a book of cipher keys but after 1943 on an OTP. Two things were needed:

i. A cipher table, in the form of a rectangular silk handkerchief which could be rolled up and hidden in a brush handle, bicycle pump or handlebar. It contained 26 by 26 (676) letters set out alphabetically along top and side, each coupled with a random letter (see illustration).

ii. A set of keys, each used only, set out on small sheets of rice-paper or film; half for enciphering outgoing and half for deciphering incoming messages. Each carried 500 five-letter groups.

The procedure is as follows:

1. Write out the message, as short as intelligibility permits. Punctuation (STOP, X or XXX) is used only when really needed:

DROP SNAKE TEAM DZ PRIMROSE PLUS SPARE BATTERY MANGO

SNAKE is the cover-name for this operation. DZ is 'dropping-zone', identified by the agreed name PRIMROSE. MANGO is the agent's cover-name. Now write this out in five-letter groups, adding nonsense letters if it ends in mid-group:

DROPS NAKET EAMDZ PRIMR OSEPL USSPA REBAT TERYM ANGOX

2. Select and write out the key for the day, allowing one spare group at the start. If this is FVZTL it will be transmitted with one letter wrong (e.g. FVZTB), to show that you, along with your cipher, have not been captured and forced to transmit under duress. If captured you would send FVZTL correctly. MANGO says the same; if captured you would, if necessary, admit to the name

```
A  B  C  D  E  F  G  H  I  J  K  L  M  N  O  P  Q  R  S  T  U  V  W  X  Y  Z

AvAfAkAdAgAnApAxAuArAoAeAmAhAaAqAiAcAlAwAsAbAjAyAtAz
BeByBjBnBdBvBbBcBgBpBmBoB1BsBiBfBrBzBuBxBkBaBqBtBhBw
CrCzCmC1ChCgCeCbCdCcCwCsCuCfCxCpCtCaCoCjCvCyCkCiCqCn
DwDnDtDaDbDzDgDeDcDdDhDiDfDrDkDxDqDoDvDsDmDpD1DuDyDj
EbEhErEkEeEwEcEdEvEsEqEaEyEuEnEoEjEtEpEfE1EiEgEaEmEx
FzFaFiFmFvFrFfFgF1FnFtFqFdFcFwFbFuFhFyFeFjFoFpFxFaFk
GiGjGzGhGaGcGdGfGbGgGyGmGtGqGoGuGnGxGsGvGpGwGeGkGrG1
HqHeHsHgHcHpHkHiHtHhHdH1HjHaHmHzHyHfHxHuHoHnHwHrHbHv
IgIwIfIjIzImIyIhIkIiIrIdIxItIbInIaI1IqIpIuIeIoIcIvIs
JyJgJbJiJuJoJ1JnJjJkJpJtJhJzJsJwJeJrJmJcJfJqJaJvJxJd
KxKrKaKeKtK1KhKkKiKjKvKnKpKmKdKsKoKyKzKqKbKuKcKgKwKf
LuLqLwLcLmLkLjLzLfL1LsLhLbLyLrLvLpLiLaLtLeLxLdLnLoLg
MnMxMcMfM1MiMwMuMpMmMbMgMaMkMhMyMvMsMjMzMdMrMtMqMeMo
NmNdNpNbNsNaNoNjNnNfNuNkNwNvNeNiNgNqNtNyNxNhNrN1NzNc
OsOvOyOqOoOjOnOtOxOuOaObOzOwOgOeOkOdOcOrOhOfOiOpO1Om
PtPsPnPzPrPhPaPqPmPbPjPwPkPxPpPcP1PvPePiPgPdPfPoPuPy
QsQvQyQqQoQjQnQtQxQuQaQbQzQwQgQeQkQdQcQrQhQfQiQpQ1Qm
RcRkReRxRpRfRqRrRyRaRiRvRsRdR1RtRbRjRwRoRzRmRnRhRgRu
SoSpShSwSnSySuSsSqStS1ScSrSbSjSkSzSmSgSdSaSvSxSeSfSi
TpTuTdTyTkTtTxToThTsTfTjTgTiTvTrTcTeTnT1TwTzTmTbTaTq
UlUtUqUvUjUuUsUmUaUoUnUxUcUeUyUgUfUwUbUhUiUkUzUdUpUr
VaVoVxVuVfVbVzVwVeVvVkVrVqVnVtV1VmVpVdVgVcVaVyVjViVh
WdWiW1WsWqWeWmWvWwWyWcWpWnWoWfWjWxWuWrWaWtWgWhWzWkWb
XkXmXvXrXyXqXtXaXoXxX2XuXiXpXcXdXwXgXhXbXnX1XaXfXjXe
YjYbYoY-tYxYsYiYyYrYwYgYzYeY1YuYmYhYkYfYnYqYcYvYaYdYp
ZfZcZgZpZiZdZvZ1ZzZeZxZyZoZjZqZhZsZbZkZmZrZtZuZwZnZa

A  B  C  D  E  F  G  H  I  J  K  L  M  N  O  P  Q  R  S  T  U  V  W  X  Y  Z
```

A typical cipher table used in conjunction with one-time keys by Force 136 and similar clandestine groups

PEANUT and use that in any message you were forced to send. Either security check, let alone both, will reveal to your base what has happened.

3. Leaving FVZTB on its own, write out the remaining key-groups exactly above the message-groups, and repeat FVZTB at the end:

```
FVZTB  GBJCA  ODNXV  MHEKP  SWQRU  LYTPI  HABBG  TSVEL  NJUPZ  CIXRY  FVZTB
       DROPS  NAKET  EAMDZ  PRIMR  OSEPL  USSPA  REBAT  TERYM  ANGOX
```

4. Now use the key and the rectangular one-time table together to encipher the text, taking the top and bottom lines *one pair of letters at a time*. The top line shows the column in the table, the bottom line

shows the row – the same method as 6633 (Number 27 in Chapter Seven). The first pair is GD. In column G, row D, the letter shown is 'g', so write down 'g'. The next pair is BR, giving 'k', and so on:

FVZTB GBJCA OXNXV MHEKP SWQRU LYTPI HABBG TSVEL NJUPZ CIXRY FVZTB
DROPS NAKET EAMDZ PRIMR OSEPL USSPA REBAT TERYM ANGOX

fvztb gkuno edmaz yxlhh enasz bffcf mopsp opagj iszmo knkdj fvztb

5. Having enciphered the message, keep the bottom line, the signal text, and destroy the rest. It is not always made clear that the table printed on a silk handkerchief is not itself 'one-time', though clearly an agent would have required an embarrassingly large stock of silk handkerchieves, each fastidiously destroyed after being used once, to maintain signals security. It was the keys, instantly eatable or ignitable, that provided the 'one-time' element; the handkerchief lived on.

6. At the agreed transmission time, transmit the message on the specified frequency using international operator's procedures. The short nine-group signal given as an example, making eleven groups in all, would take about two minutes to encipher or decipher and two minutes more to check; transmitting it would take under a minute – probably nearer half a minute. No clandestine station was supposed to transmit for more than five minutes (120 groups) on one frequency, or more than a total of twenty minutes daily, which greatly lessened the danger of having the transmitter pinpointed by the enemy. Even in occupied France, with its large population, good communications and a very sophisticated German direction-finding system, it was reckoned that 10–15 minutes were needed to close in on a transmitter. Since the times, places and frequencies of transmission were staggered in a subtle pattern, the five-minute limit offered good protection. In the Far East the transmission would normally be more conspicuous to an eavesdropper, despite the precautions which I have mentioned, but the operator would generally be in a far more remote area.

7. When your signal is received at the base station the staff will note that the first and last groups carry the authenticating one-letter error and that the agent's cover-name is the one confirming that all is well. The signal can be checked to make certain that the operator's idiosyncracies of transmission match the samples recorded before you left. These can vary widely, particularly with common groups like AR 'message ends', which often appear rather slickly, with the dots shortened. Numerals, which have a pattern of their own,

162

are sometimes exaggerated. Some operators lengthen final dots, while others shorten them, 'turning morse symbols into Wagnerian spondees or Mozart dactyls'.[118] Agents were encouraged to reveal the existence of this check if they were captured, in the hope of discouraging the enemy from trying to mimic their transmitting style. Similar methods were used to identify enemy operators' characteristics and even the variations in the typical sound of different radio sets.

8. In order to disguise the significance of sudden increases in traffic before an important operation, 'phantom' operators at the base station would send dummy messages at other times so as to maintain a better balance – something which Montgomery's operators in north Africa should have known about. The Germans were often able to guess at the date of his movements by changes in the volume of his signals.

9. When the aircraft came to drop its load of radio, ammunition, food or reinforcements a further device was used to draw attention away from the real purpose of the flight: while still flying low it would drop leaflets in nearby settlements and villages. One dropping-zone only two miles from a Japanese post was regularly supplied for five months before the enemy became aware of it. To the same end, markers could be laid out to guide an aircraft towards a bombing target nearby, which it would attack after making the drop.

One aspect of these signals again raises the question of deception: how is the home base to know if the agent has been captured or not? The method which I have described came into general use within the various sections of SOE during 1943, relying on double verification inside the message: the one-letter error in the first and last groups, and the correct choice of agent's name. It replaced a system which, though slightly more cumbersome, could and should have been foolproof, but was discarded after the disastrous episode, called *Englandspiel* by the Germans, in which successive SOE agents were rounded up as soon as they arrived in the Netherlands. The story has been told often, and I will touch only on the security aspect of it.

The reason given for abandoning the earlier system, namely that it was insecure, is charitable to those in London who handled it so ineptly for so long. The facts suggest that they could have bungled either system. The earlier one had relied on two forms of security check. First came the regular check: a free operator was to make single-letter mistakes at specified points in the signal, but if transmitting under duress was to make none: obviously the right way round. Later it was realised that the enemy might know or guess that this check existed; henceforth the operator was to have a 'bluff check' to confess to, and a 'true check' to keep dark. The second and 'random' check, in reserve, was for the home station to transmit a question. If the reply was relevant and logical, then the agent was presumed captured. If it was wholly irrelevant, all was well. If Colombo asked, 'Have you contacted Hassan?' and received the answer 'Hassan is here', or anything else in that vein, it knew the worst. Only the inappropriate 'We are moving south tomorrow' showed that things were going well. The snag is that this all means extra traffic, and any unnecessary signal adds to the risks. Each method depends on the agent's keeping cool and on the base operator's being alert and ensuring that the controller is told of any missing checks and immediately acts on them. That is where the *Englandspiel* went so shamefully wrong.

An outstanding example of an agent who kept his head was Captain Ibrahim bin Ismael, who was landed on the east coast of Malaya late in 1944 with three other Malays; one of them, the radio-operator, not only had the ciphers with him but had written down the security checks, against every rule in the book. These clearly showed the pattern of logical and illogical answers to questions. Ibrahim managed, by force of personality, to persuade the Japanese that for security these were written down the wrong way round, and they believed him.

When 'Have you met Miriam?' came up, he sent, 'Yes, I've met Miriam', which allayed the suspicions of the Japanese and simultaneously alerted Colombo to his capture. For the rest of the war they exchanged messages which managed always to contain plausible reasons why the planned drop of arms, equipment and another agent – all destined to fall into enemy hands – had to be postponed yet again. 'Ibrahim was put in for a Japanese decoration for helping them, as well as a British one for not having done so.'[119] It seems only fitting that Captain Ibrahim later rose to become a General and Chief of the Malayan armed forces after the war.[120]

15

General Slim and Signals Intelligence

The Burma campaign bequeaths us two puzzling legacies. Both have been identified by Louis Allen, whose penetrating and compassionate account, *Burma, The Longest War*, sheds so clear a light on that war. Although, on the evidence available, I find myself disagreeing with his conclusions, he has done us a service in pointing out the discrepancies which led him to form his suspicions.

The first puzzle is this: if we consider the volume and value of signals intelligence, yielding comprehensive and up-to-date information on the enemy's positions, resources and intentions, and often the very orders he is giving and receiving, it seems clear that even without intelligence from any other source sigint must have served General Slim, commanding 14 Army in Burma, as well as any other Allied HQ. We now trip over an apparent contradiction.

Slim first refers to a shortage of intelligence in late 1943:

> Improving as our intelligence was since 1942, it was far from being as complete or accurate as that in other theatres. We never made up for the lack of methodically collected intelligence, or the intelligence organisation which should have been available to us when the war began. We knew something of the Japanese intentions, but little of the disposition of their reserves, and practically nothing about one of the most important factors that a general has to consider – the character of the opposing commanders.[121]

Later, as the Japanese assault on Imphal gathers momentum in January 1944, he returns to the subject. 'We knew the attack was coming, for throughout January and February, besides the general reinforcement of the Burma theatre by fresh Japanese formations, there were increasing local indications on 4 Corps front. I had not at my disposal the sources of information of the enemy's intentions that some more fortunate commanders in other theatres were able to invoke'; and he goes on to emphasise his reliance on patrols and the 'documents, diaries, marked maps and even operational orders' that they could bring in. 'All these clues, painstakingly fitted into the mosaic of our intelligence at Corps and Army Headquarters, began to give us a general picture of the enemy's intentions.' [122] Similarly General Scoones, then commanding 4 Corps, complains in a letter in June 1944 about 'the amount of money and manpower which we are wasting on these hush-hush organisations and which, so far as I am concerned, produce nothing useful'.[123] And he instances the move of most of the Japanese 151 Regiment to the Bishenpur front during the Imphal battles without their being identified until they reached the front line – though he inflates them to the size of '53 Division ... or elements of it'.

What are Slim and Scoones getting at? Louis Allen takes it to be signals intelligence, pointing out that when Slim's book was published in 1956 it was still forbidden to refer to Ultra, so we could not expect him to be more specific.[124] This is perfectly true, though our consequent unenlightenment can point us in any direction. But is he right? Neither could Evans, following Slim in 1969, nor the official history, completed in the same year, have supplied an answer: the existence of Ultra, and even its name, remained secret until 1974 with the exception of one vague allusion by Malcolm Muggeridge in an article. Or is Slim referring to the other 'hush-hush organisations', the twelve British and American clandestine groups competing and rarely co-operating within Burma?

His remarks could, on the face of it, mean either. The covert comparisons with other, luckier theatres could read like a dig at sigint, and so could 'hush-hush'. Equally they could be aimed at Force 136 and the other groups, which often raised the hackles of generals who wanted them doing something more obviously profitable, and coming directly under their command. The word 'organisations' points more ominously at the clandestines since it emphasises the plurality of whatever Scoones was grumbling about, and sigint was singular in all senses.

But how could Slim be carping at sigint? In doing so he would be going dead against clear statements by Winterbotham in 1974 and Lewin in 1982. Both were written soon after it was permitted to mention codebreaking, and both refer to Ultra quite specifically. Slim is quoted as telling Winterbotham how valuable Ultra has been:

166

> The real triumph had been the information which led up to the final attack by the Japanese at Imphal and Kohima. It had become very evident from Ultra that the Japanese supply position was desperate ... and that the Japanese air force in the area had dwindled so as to be practically useless.

Winterbotham, who was anything but a complacent man, had gone out specifically to see that the distribution of Ultra was working well in SEAC and elsewhere, and he was quick to sort out any problems that he found. Far from finding any in 14 Army when he visited General Slim and Air Vice-Marshal Alec Coryton at Slim's HQ at Comilla, he received a bouquet. They 'were well satisfied with the information which was being received, and were conforming to all the security rules. The type of Ultra information received from the Japanese was much the same as that received from the German Army in Europe: operational and movement orders, strength returns and locations which not only formed useful targets for the air force but gave General Slim *a complete order of battle of the Japanese force*' (my italics). 'There were, too, some strategical signals giving a wider overall picture of Japanese operations in the whole of the south-east Asia area. General Slim told me that the intelligence from Ultra about the Japanese forces had been invaluable throughout the campaign ...', and so on.[125]

It is impossible to reconcile the dissatisfied tone of Slim's and Scoones' remarks, and especially their envious comparisons with other theatres, with the 'real triumph' and 'well satisfied' and 'invaluable' comments made to Winterbotham. Either he is telling a series of thumping lies – which nobody has suggested and no evidence supports – or they are talking about two totally different things.

Quite apart from Winterbotham's evidence, Scoones' remarks about the unidentified arrival of part of one regiment during the Imphal battles, and the 'producing of nothing useful' cannot be referring to sigint, of which it is now known that 'the movement of four divisions into Burma in preparation for the drive into India, which began in March 1944, was discovered from Army Ultra far in advance of the beginning of the attack, and a number of indications that an attack was impending were obtained'.

Then why did Lewin's book on the campaign, published in 1976, two years after Winterbotham's, not clarify the point? He just missed the bus. He explains in *The Other Ultra* (also known as *The American Magic*) published in 1982 that

It is now evident that at the time of the 1944 offensive at Imphal, and the long-range penetration by Wingate's Chindits behind the enemy lines in Burma, Magic supplied precise intelligence about the reorganisation of the Japanese command structure on the Burma front and critical information about the flow of Japanese reinforcing divisions from further east. The exact nature of this intelligence could not be deduced from the British Official History, nor was it available to the author when he was preparing ... the official biography of the commander of the Fourteenth Army.[126]

He uses the American term Magic rather than Ultra because this later book is largely about the Pacific War and American code-breaking successes, and it sounds very much as if he too had been puzzled by the apparent contradictions.

Fortunately there is other evidence to clinch the issue. Slim's first complaint, made during the Imphal and Kohima battles, was far more specific than his book reveals: he was without essential information on Japanese activities in the rear of their forward areas and on their lines of communication. He proposed an expansion of Z Force – fighting patrols which gathered intelligence in such areas – to provide some twenty patrols which could operate over a very large area of central Burma, from Mogaung near Myitkyina in the north to Henzada, less than 100 miles north of Rangoon, in the south; in other words an area roughly the size of England, Scotland and Wales put together.

O'Brien later discussed Slim's reasons for making this proposal with General Browning, Mountbatten's Chief of Staff, who was given the job of 'settling the various clandestines into more effective unity'. Slim had, Browning said, appreciated Force 136's work but reckoned that they should be supplying more tactical intelligence direct to the Army. 'The amount of useful information reaching his forces was simply not worth the manpower and resources being utilised by Force 136' – Scoones' phrase again. 'He demanded a better system of co-ordination between the clandestines, with emphasis being directed towards helping the regular army forces. If they could not provide the goods they should be disbanded.'[127]

This was no recent foible of Slim's. Even during the retreat of 1942 he had written:

Apart from the absence of air reconnaissance ... we felt terribly the want of light, mobile reconnaissance troops, who could get out into the jungle, live there, and send back information. Our attempts to form such units did not have much success. The extreme inefficiency of our whole intelligence system in Burma was probably our greatest single handicap.[128]

Slim complained again to Mountbatten in September 1944, barely one month before his enthusiastic praise of sigint to Winterbotham, about the unproductive (in intelligence-gathering terms) record of the clandestine forces, and claimed that there was no intelligence coverage in Burma at all. The plural word 'forces' again echoes Scoones' word 'organisations'. Also note the phrase 'in Burma'; the clandestines worked there, but most sigint was produced outside the country. There were only two Z patrols even then, and neither had yet gone into Burma. He went on: 'Had we a P Division representative as promised three months ago, it is probable that I would have been able to plan on much better information than I now enjoy', a remark notably like his earlier and more ambiguous comments. P Division was formed belatedly to co-ordinate the work of the multifarious clandestine organisations, but would have had no say whatever in the production of sigint.

Later still Slim suggested that Force 136 should cease to operate in Burma and should be replaced by their broader US equivalent OSS. P Division pointed out in answer to Slim's scheme that Force 136 had sent in over 500 reports during the first half of 1944 – to SEAC, not to Slim direct – and a further 19 in the last six weeks; it was in any case originally formed 'to set Burma ablaze' as in Europe, by training and arming guerrillas and by sabotage, and not for intelligence-gathering.

Protracted negotiations followed, satisfying nobody but offering a compromise by which Force 136, without coming under direct military control, being merged with Z Force or entirely losing its traditional roles, should henceforth have intelligence as its main function and should conform to 14 Army rather than SEAC in the battle area.[129]

This evidence shows beyond doubt that it was not sigint but Force 136, and possibly others of the clandestine groups, that Slim had in his sights – whether that was a proper target or not. With Scoones the issue becomes clearer still; as a mere corps commander he was not an authorised recipient of Ultra and could not have known of its existence, let alone labelled its assembly-line a 'hush-hush organisation'. Even if he had heard of it orally, and merely spoken of it slightingly, he could not have referred to it in his letter without a gross breach of the Ultra rules mentioned in Chapter Twelve. He would have heard of Force 136 and could say so without similar restrictions. Any sigint passed on to him would have been well laundered so as to conceal its source. If it is suggested that Slim had been illicitly revealing that source to Scoones, we must note that Winterbotham specifically stated, 'I found Slim and Coryton ... were conforming to all the security rules'. There is not a scrap of evidence to suggest that Slim alluded to Ultra for Scoones' benefit by any nod, wink or hint whatever. Only Slim and Coryton would therefore have been able to assess the quantity, quality and utility of sigint in their operational area. Similarly I think we may throw out any unworthy notion that Slim might have been buttering up Winterbotham. A man who could say to Churchill, in the triumphal year 1945, about the approaching general election, 'I'll tell you one thing, Prime Minister. My men won't be voting for you' needs no further proof of frankness, especially since Winterbotham was, as a Group Captain, considerably junior to General Slim.

It does seem curious that Slim should have found Mountbatten, of all men, apparently so reluctant to spare more men for the Z patrols that Slim coveted. There never were enough skilled people available to meet such demands, but this one appears to have foundered paradoxically.

Finally we may add a human consideration. Slim always valued on-the-spot tactical intelligence highly. His creed was 'Get out of HQ, look at the terrain, talk to the men doing the job, see for yourself'. Neither sigint nor captured documents nor clandestine intelligence-gatherers could ever satisfy his thirst for first-hand local knowledge. In September 1944 he wanted twenty Z patrols but got only the promise of two. Allen puts his finger on the significance of this: 'It is characteristic of Slim that he should value direct information, taken on the spot, of this kind, which might often be less useful or detailed than that provided by captured documents'.[130]

Over and over again in his account of the campaign we find Slim in the heat of action: visiting bridgeheads, chatting to a busy gunner, watching aircraft being serviced at forward airstrips, talking to Indian troops in Hindi and to Gurkhas in Gurkhali, looking over Cowan's shoulder as he directs the attack on Meiktila, and listening in on the tank signals net, 'always an interesting and often a worthwhile thing to do'.[131] He gently chides Rees for going too far ahead of his troops, yet approves when Rees is congratulated by his corps commander for 'shooting a goal when the referee wasn't looking', by capturing Shwebo although it had been earmarked for another division.

In the opening paragraph of his book on the Burma campaign he mentions a division as the largest formation 'in which every man can know you'. He has been commanding a division in the Iraq desert where 'you can see your man', and when he is told to fly to India for another job, 'My heart slumped. "I don't want another job. I want to stay with my division." '

Slim cannot quell this schoolboy enthusiasm in himself. While he is watching the assault on Gangaw his light aircraft 'accidentally' flies south over enemy-held territory. During the battle for Pegu, near Rangoon, 'I told my pilot to fly south *as I wished to see for myself*' (my italics) 'the country over which 17 Division would have to operate'. In consequence they run into anti-aircraft fire which means the loss of a leg for one of his staff officers travelling in the same aircraft, and he later reproaches himself bitterly. A similar episode, when his party goes so far forward that it comes under fire from a British tank, produces the jaunty comment, 'I felt like a schoolboy who had dodged his masters and was playing truant for the day'.[132]

None of this happens because he feels any need to interfere with his divisional commanders' decisions – on the contrary he trusts and encourages them to sort out the details for themselves. No breathing down the neck, such as he had himself endured from Irwin at the start of his command in Burma. It was simply that he did not feel that he was doing his job if he stayed in the remoter HQ area and relied on second-hand information. His appetite for first-hand intelligence precisely tallies with his demand for more troops to collect it: if there cannot be more Z patrols, then use Force 136 which is already in the right position to supply it.

I would agree fervently with Allen on a kindred subject: forward army formations in Burma were starved of Japanese linguists while the sigint organisations were relatively well provided. He mentions their scarcity immediately after putting forward his view that Slim is slating the sigint people for under-using their allegedly lavish resources. The provision for both purposes was inadequate, and the ration of two linguists for each division – one translator for captured documents and one interrogator – is simply ludicrous.[133] That was particularly true for the formations who bore the brunt of the rapid assault which won the Burma campaign. Even if no more could have been spared for those in the Arakan and NCAC areas, a strong case could be made for arguing that some officers should have been detached from WEC and its sister units and assigned to the forward divisions to double their resources.

16

Phuket Island

While I was at WEC Delhi we deciphered a 6633 message in the summer of 1945 reporting a British landing on Phuket Island, off the west coast of the long Kra isthmus – now an international beach resort famed for its water-sports and seafood delicacies. We assumed that GHQ, down the road, would be glad to have this up-to-the-minute situation report from the enemy, and rang up to give them the news. There was a tense silence; then a horrified voice said 'We can't possibly discuss that. It's Top Secret', and rang off.

Almost every piece of paper that a codebreaker or any intelligence officer handles in his duties is Top Secret, so this was hilarious as well as depressing evidence of a dead-headedness that has been known to afflict some staff officers in large headquarters remote from the battle-front. That may account for the dottier side of the Phuket story – but is there a darker side as well?

The strategic importance of Phuket Island, with its harbour and airfield halfway between Rangoon and Singapore making it an ideal stepping-stone in any re-occupation of Malaya, had long been appreciated. There had been a British plan to seize it before the Japanese invasions began, so as to deny them its use. Officialdom withheld its approval until it was too late, understandably enough since it was in Thai territory. Its convenient position was recalled later, and its capture had been on and off the agenda of the Combined Chiefs of Staff for some time. Its seizure by the Allies would paralyse Japanese lines of communication by land, sea and air, so that when SEAC began its next offensive operation in southeast Asia the enemy would be unable to move troops to the threatened area. The timetable given in the official history *The War against Japan*, Volumes 4 and 5, may be summarised as follows:

October 1944   Phuket harbour is raided by two British midget submarines, which return safely after sinking one merchant vessel and damaging another.

February 1945   SEAC conferences discuss the possible seizure of Phuket as a first step in an advance on Singapore via the Kra isthmus. It will need two divisions and one commando brigade. This operation, code-named ROGER, is confirmed for 1 June, followed by a landing in west Malaya in October 1945 (ZIPPER) and the capture of Singapore (MAILFIST) whether Rangoon is captured before the monsoon in early May or not. Troops are allocated by late February; plans are to be ready by 1 April.

The idea, to quote Sir Andrew Gilchrist, who was himself intimately involved, was to land on Phuket, capture the island and establish a perimeter of about fifteen miles on the neighbouring mainland, the object being to keep the airstrips free from enemy artillery fire. Fighter aircraft would go into action first from aircraft-carriers and then from the landing-ground on the island; in the course of a few weeks large heavy-duty strips would be laid out on Phuket from which twin-engined and four-engined bombers could operate.

February–March 1945   Photographic reconnaissance of Phuket Island is carried out by aircraft from a sizeable carrier force.

March 1945   It is agreed to postpone ROGER until the fall of Rangoon is imminent. SEAC will probably use part of the ROGER force for the amphibious seizure of Rangoon (DRACULA).

April 1945   Only a small part of the ROGER force will be detached for DRACULA, but ROGER and ZIPPER will be delayed by between six and nine weeks.

3 May 1945   SEAC decides to cancel ROGER but to bring forward ZIPPER from October to August.

24–26 July   Under the heading 'sweeping mines from approaches to possible Allied landing-places': The area off Phuket is swept for the loss of one mine-sweeper in an operation covered by 'the battleship *Nelson*, the cruiser *Sussex*, two escort-carriers and four destroyers'. Also there are air strikes on targets in the Kra isthmus. For the first time in south-east Asia ships are attacked by *kamikaze* aircraft. Three Japanese aircraft are shot down, but the mine-sweeper is sunk.

The clear implication is that Operation Roger never took place. A Japanese view is that it did take place but was a costly failure: 'a massacre'. This Japanese account, right or wrong, deserves some consideration. Their signal was sent without the slightest reason to suggest that it was being intercepted, broken and understood; it was true eavesdropping. It did not speak of a small reconnaissance party but was couched in terms that suggested a large-scale landing. Louis Allen interrogated several high-ranking Japanese officers immediately after the war, and their unanimous verdict was that several hundred Allied troops got ashore but were virtually wiped out. By then almost all Japanese officers were discussing such matters frankly and accurately.

One curious feature in the official account is that Phuket Island, after being taken off the invasion agenda in early May, should have had its approaches mineswept by a force which included a protective screen of no less than one battleship, one cruiser and four destroyers as well as two escort-carriers. This is enough to lead a sceptical and perhaps land-lubberly mind into wondering if minesweeping was all that was proposed.

And why does this entry appear under the heading 'sweeping mines from approaches to possible Allied landing-places' when the landing had allegedly been cancelled twelve weeks before? Why sweep mines at all if no landing is planned, let alone with so impressive a naval accompaniment?

The scale of Operation Roger was to have been large. Two codebreakers from Delhi were told in late April that they would be part of it, and it is interesting to wonder what special reasons there were for having codebreakers so much further forward than was usually thought prudent under the Ultra rules. What were they to have done? They themselves had no idea. They were briefed and departed on 'immediate embarkation leave' on 8 May (VE Day), five days after the reported decision to cancel the operation.

Is it possible to believe that with Rangoon captured and the Japanese so badly placed on all fronts they could still have defeated us in this relatively small yet massively supported operation? It is hard to swallow but not too hard to believe. There was Operation Tiger on a Devon coast, a débâcle where over 700 US troops training for the Normandy landings were killed by German E-boats only just off the English coast, as late as April 1944.[134] In case it is assumed that the official history of the SEAC operations might have concealed the truth for some reason and for a few years only, I must stress that the Tiger affair was not revealed, apart from local gossip which was strictly against orders, until an American writer took the lid off the affair in 1985. Moreover the Far Eastern history, in places, does more than conceal Ultra as the source of some information. It repeats the cover-stories of the time by explaining the torpedoing of some Japanese naval vessels as the result of chance sightings, when they were the result of Ultra. This untruth may have been necessary, but we should be aware that it existed. There was also a sinister pointer in south-east Asia, and it occurred even after the Japanese surrender. Operation Zipper, the amphibious assault on the west coast of Malaya, for which Roger would have provided valuable experience, went ahead as planned on 9 September, exactly one week after the Japanese Emperor had ordered all resistance to stop, and three days before Mountbatten formally accepted the surrender, in Singapore, of all enemy forces in south-east Asia. Slim says of this merely that 'the landing ... over the beaches ... went in ... as a tactical operation. There was no resistance, and even if there had been, I think the operation would have been a success, for the Japanese plans, *as we afterwards discovered*' (my italics) 'were based on our landing elsewhere.'[135] Slim omits to mention the shambles of the landings, about which even the official historian speaks frankly, and the phrase 'as we afterwards discovered' is uncharacteristically disingenuous. As Spencer Chapman points out, 'When Operation Zipper landed ... there was only one battalion – 1,000 men – of Japs in that area to oppose them. All the rest – thanks to the Japanese habit of believing what they are told – were hundreds of miles further north in Kedah, where they thought the landing would take place'.[136] In other words Force 136 had successfully contrived that one battalion with at most two dozen aircraft would have opposed two divisions supported by two battle-ships, four cruisers, six escort carriers and 15 destroyers, plus 18 squadrons of RAF fighters and bombers and 180 naval fighters. This force was only just over twice the size of that marshalled for the naval operations off Phuket Island – surely a much easier nut to crack.

The Japanese had complied fully with their instructions and there was no opposition. That was just as well, for the landing was a fiasco. Both selected landing areas proved totally unsuitable. Near Port Dickson a further reconnaissance had to be made before a suitable beach could be found, fifteen miles away on the other side of the town. The landings there began three days behind schedule. At the other beach near Morib conditions were hopeless. In the words of the official history: 'A sand bar, running parallel to the beaches a mile off-shore, presented an obstacle over which even minor landing-craft could not pass at low water. The American transfer system, used in the Pacific where landings were often made over coral reefs divided by a deep lagoon from the beaches, had to be adopted.' Troops, vehicles and supplies all had to be transferred from one landing-craft to another, a mile out to sea. Moreover the coastal roads were flooded and many were impassable.[137]

The Advanced HQ of 224 Group RAF paints an even gloomier picture:

> Conditions on the beaches were chaotic, vehicles drowned in scores as there were no decent exits from the beaches, and roads became choked with ditched tanks which tore up the road surfaces and grass verges. A lack of vehicles ashore made the movement of stores impossible.

The ultimate disgrace ensued when a message had to be passed to the local Force 136 party telling them 'to break cover, find the local Japanese commander, and borrow his transport to get them out of trouble'.[138] The official account goes on stoically: 'Despite the chaos on the beaches there is little doubt that, had it been necessary to take Malaya by force of arms, Operation Zipper would eventually have achieved its object', and goes on to list the overwhelming disparity of forces. 'It is equally true that ... the invasion forces would have been very roughly handled and at least pinned to the beaches for some time. It is even possible that the troops landed on the Morib beaches might have had to be withdrawn.'[139] To say that it is fortunate that there was no resistance – even some help – is to put it very mildly.

Clearly the preparatory work – secret landings at night by small reconnaissance parties, up-to-date soundings and the sampling of beaches – had been botched. There was no shortage of time, for over four months had elapsed since Zipper's date had been fixed. Equally there was no shortage of talent, because the commandos and frogmen who had been so skilful and resourceful in preparing for the Irrawaddy crossings not long before, in all too predictable an area, were now freely available, and in larger numbers: a whole Amphibious Support Regiment of Royal Marines, and 3 Commando Brigade.

Poor mapping was an embarrassment to the Allies elsewhere in the Pacific. The US operational maps of Leyte in the Philippines were 'almost devoid of terrain detail' although they had spent forty years there. The maps and charts of the Gilbert Islands, under British rule since 1892, were 'distorted, unoriented and without soundings in the lagoons'.

But all the miscalculation and desperate improvisation for Zipper took place not far from Kuala Lumpur, in a generously-mapped area which many British settlers in Malaya knew well. If such a blunder could occur in so well-charted an area against no resistance, a far worse disaster could have taken place at Phuket, in an obscure corner of a long peninsula equally remote from British colonial territories and from the Thai capital, against a garrison guarding a valuable harbour and airfield, and already alerted by a submarine raid and by photo-reconnaissance – above all when such fanaticism had been shown elsewhere in the face of a powerful and skilfully-handled advance in Burma. Does the presence of so large a naval force, including a battleship and its screen, indicate that something larger than a mine-sweeping operation was in mind? Does the stupefying remark of the staff officer, 'That's Top Secret; I can't discuss it', imply that news of a failure had already reached New Delhi?

Not necessarily. There is room for a conspiracy theory, but no real proof. One reason is that any operation against Thai territory would have been a gross violation of Thai neutrality, which would have given full scope to Japanese propaganda about 'Britain's perfidious and imperialistic ambitions'. We had been flying over Thailand and dropping both British and Thai members of Force 136 there, but that was part of an internal Thai resistance and liberation move-ment. A military landing conducted by foreign troops would be a totally different matter. Is it then possible that the manifold sea and air operations of July 1945 were locally misinterpreted as a prelude to a landing, and that the story spread, uncorrected, through the Japanese military hierarchy? That too seems unlikely; minesweep-ing and bombing are simply not so easily mistaken for actual landings.

Gilchrist explains that the Army had regarded Roger as a very risky operation from the start, and wanted Force 136 to organise sabotage, mobilise guerrillas and provide local intelligence well beforehand. They had been working in the area since 1944, and had made Chan Island, 100 miles north of Phuket, an important base both for this purpose and for trans-shipping equipment and guerrillas between India and Thailand. They now mounted Operation Priest to meet SEAC's new need, and landed a pre-liminary party on Phuket by flying-boat. Soon afterwards, however, Mountbatten decided to cancel Roger, since Japanese resistance was rapidly weakening and he could go straight for Malaya (Zipper) and Singapore (Mailfist) without it, at the same time advancing Zipper by two months as we have already seen.[140] In a book recently published in Bangkok, Haseman goes on, 'When Lord Mount-batten cancelled the overall invasion plan the agents of Operation

Priest turned their efforts to recruiting cadre for offshore training and collecting intelligence'.[141]

Sir Andrew Gilchrist has kindly explained to me that he was misinformed about the reason for cancelling Roger, and discovered the truth only after his excellent book *Bangkok Top Secret* was published. Mountbatten took up the point, and revealed that the real cause was the shortage of landing-craft – a chronic problem for SEAC – and Gilchrist points out that no mention of landing-craft is made in the official history's list of naval forces used on 24–26 July.[142]

The explanation is precise and relevant, but some nagging questions remain. Why was the proper explanation, which involved no secrets, not given in the official history? If one is sceptical enough one can suggest that the editor omitted the landing-craft to disguise both the attempted landing and its failure. I do not myself believe that, but I can understand why others might. A further consideration strengthens the official version: if there had been an attempted landing, the Priest team would know all about it from their ringside seat (that includes Gilchrist) and the news would have emerged by now from them and from the local populace. But it looks as if there is an answer, although it must raise a few eyebrows. Bickham Sweet-Escott, himself an experienced SOE man, describes what happened:

> We received an indignant message from one of our people on the west coast of the Siamese mainland near the island of Phuket, that the Siamese general to whom he was attached was complaining that we had broken faith with the Siamese. The British fleet, the message said, was manoeuvring within sight of the island without his having been previously informed. He wished to know whether this meant that the Allied invasion of Siam (with which his forces would be co-operating) was about to begin.

SEAC HQ denied all knowledge of any such operation, and it was eventually discovered that the Navy had been ordered by the Admiralty to carry it out without reference to SEAC and without even telling them the news: an extraordinary aberration.[143] At least this provides two further pointers: the Thai general would have known if a landing had been attempted, and the Navy would not have had troops to put ashore if SEAC knew nothing of its intentions – unless they had embarked the Marines. I think we should have heard about it if they had.

The whole episode is bizarre, to say the least.

17

Deception in the Burma Campaign

Earlier chapters have contained several examples of the combined use of sigint and deception, usually with sigint both monitoring the effects of deception already practised and suggesting the next episode. Although I had no hand in any deception scheme I have been interested in the subject ever since I learnt that my father had been involved in a particular version of deception in the 1914–18 war, serving as radio-operator on a Q-boat, the *Helvetia*. This was a converted and disguised trawler whose job was to discourage German U-boats from attacking unarmed fishing vessels in the North Sea. When a U-boat hove in sight and ordered them to abandon ship the *Helvetia*'s crew, who had been carefully trained, gave a convincing imitation of panic. They lowered the ship's boat so ham-handedly that one end was submerged while the other dangled in the air with davit jammed. They rushed to and fro excitedly. The SOS message was bungled, and with luck the U-boat drew nearer to watch the pandemonium. When they were within range the order was given: one pull at a lever collapsed the hinged sections of the deckhouse, revealing a gun whose team hoped to sink the enemy before he sank them.

In Burma there were many attempts at tactical deception, not always successful, and one outstanding piece of strategic deception in which signals played a small but useful role and sigint was once again employed to monitor the result. First we must study the man at the centre of the stage.

Peter Fleming, who was in charge of D (Deception) Division in South-East Asia Command, was a man of vivid and whimsical talents and great theatrical flair. He approached his task with relish and savoured even the most trivial detail. 'He showed me the items with some pride, drawing attention to the worn state of the map case, to the hair-oil stains around the inner rim of the hat band, to the old crease markings on the map. All went to prove that these were genuine used articles, he said; they had thought of everything, right down to the rumpled squeezes of the toothpaste tube. "Good, isn't it?" he kept saying enthusiastically.' It had cost D Division six bottles of Scotch to persuade the brigadier who owned the unusual map case, which Fleming had instantly coveted, to part with it, and if Fleming had not caught sight of it at a meeting he might never have conceived this operation.[144]

His imp of mischief was at work as early as 1942 when three pro-British Karen tribesmen were parachuted, complete with radio, just north of Rangoon, as agents. They were captured and 'played back' by the Kempeitai, and when questions arrived from Calcutta bogus answers were concocted by Japanese GHQ. 'For a time the questions were genuine, asking about the code-names of units, the effects of Allied bombing or the whereabouts of Subhas Chandra Bose', the Congress leader who collaborated with the Japanese.

> Then a signal came through directing the agents to spread propaganda to the effect that the Japanese Emperor was a monkey and had a tail. Saruta [the lieutenant in charge of the operation] suspected that Calcutta had tumbled to what was happening, but GHQ in Rangoon continued to believe that the playback was safe, and the system continued in Saruta's house until October 1944, when GHQ, dissatisfied with the feeble results of the operation, took the agents out of Saruta's hands.[145]

This appears to tally with the account of Fleming's agent code-named Brass, who was invited to pass on the message that the ruling family had 'short, furry tails of which they were inordinately proud'.[146]

On the purely verbal level, having invented the wholly fictitious 33 Division, ostensibly due in Ceylon, he lovingly labelled them 'The Thirsty Thirty-Third'. Another imaginary British division, 12 Infantry Division, had a much longer fantasy life nearer home. It was conjured up to give the impression that a larger force existed in Egypt than we actually possessed, and it lasted so well that Hans-Otto Behrendt, in his excellent book which appeared as recently as 1980, not only very honestly leaves it in two German intelligence appreciations of the time, but still does not seem to have realised that it existed only on paper.[147]

Peter Fleming's biographer, Duff Hart-Davis, quotes a remark by Fleming about one of his schemes:

> I do not think it will be easy for the Japanese service chiefs to

begin to suspect. The idea ... which depicts us bickering with our allies is entirely alien to their mentality. We have a number of senior officers on our side who would be incapable of seeing the point ... if it was explained to them. It is safe to assume that their counterparts exist in Tokyo.[148]

But he was not simply a droll stuntman. He perceived that the whole point of strategic deception is 'to make your enemy take – or refrain from taking – a particular course of action, and thereby to improve your chances of defeating him. Merely to gull him – to implant in his mind a false idea of the situation – is only half the battle; it is not enough, even, that he should 'do something about it'. He must do what you want him to do'.[149] This opinion accords remarkably with Dudley Clarke's motto 'It matters nothing what the enemy THINKS; it is only what he DOES that can affect the battle'.[150]

This important principle is often ignored. Fleming himself forgot it in the intoxicating delight of bamboozling the enemy. The sheer brilliance of a scheme could carry him away. After speaking of Japanese willingness to swallow 'the most outrageous and implausible fabrications' he decides that they are 'too slow-witted to make even the most obvious deductions from the information they have been fed'. He sees this as a proof of incompetence, which is a curious piece of reasoning: since when has gullibility been a virtue, or the ability to see through a sham a sign of incompetence?

The explanation seems to be that Fleming had taken umbrage: many of his deception ploys were not noticed by the enemy, or if noticed they were ignored – which may be evidence of negligence, but only of neglecting to be deceived. All this ran counter to his personality. He was immersed in The Great Game and felt piqued when his opponent seemed to be showing less than proper appreciation of his best moves. He needed a more responsive audience.

Whether right or wrong, the Japanese reaction to many of the traditional devices had been to ignore them. During the Burma retreat another 'lost' map-case, ostensibly belonging to General Wavell, had been creatively left in a crashed jeep. Senior Japanese officers interrogated after the war were sure that it had never been noticed, let alone taken seriously. As Cruickshank drily puts it: 'The Japanese failed to act logically on the misinformation presented to them'. Fleming is right to remind us that we had plenty of senior officers ourselves who were unable to grasp such subtleties. One who visited Bletchley Park during the war, and displayed great interest in the work on Enigma and in the results it produced, showed mounting consternation as his visit continued and eventually gave voice to it: 'But surely all this stuff is *in German*?'

One spectacular event which must have given the organisers great artistic satisfaction, but probably did no more than mystify or entertain the Japanese while it lasted, was staged after the crossings of the Irrawaddy had begun. It was a typically colourful and whimsical array of parlour tricks, for which 357 Special Duty Squadron of the RAF, long experienced in dropping men and supplies accurately in all weathers, were called in. The central event was the simulated mid-air explosion of an imaginary aircraft, which disgorged 'bucket seats, engine cowlings, unopened parachutes, kitbags of personal belongings and' (predictably) 'one haversack containing divisional orders and maps concerning the crossing at the decoy site'.[151] Were no bodies, or remnants, also disgorged? What was supposed to have happened to the occupants, the owners of the kitbags, the wearers of the unopened parachutes, when the hypothetical aircraft exploded? Were they supposed to have been vaporised, or to have walked away?

The central theme was repeated when 7 Division carried out a spurious crossing near Pakokku, the first stage of which served as a feint and the second, by double bluff, as the real thing. It was accompanied by the usual paraphernalia: visits by mock staff officers with red hats and red tabs, the questioning of villagers about currents and sandbanks, and yet another 'lost' map. On another occasion four Dakotas dropped special firecrackers and other devices 'conspiring to give the impression of a parachute bridgehead landing which was giving rise to an untidy and complicated battle'.[152]

All these events, picturesque though they must have been, appear to have found the Japanese inattentive. The most striking and strikingly successful deception of the whole campaign was utterly different. It was no tactical sideshow, relying on pyrotechnic wizardry, but a central feature in Slim's masterly change of strategy towards the end of the campaign, and a decision which effectively guaranteed the success of his plans. To explain its nature and significance I must summarise the military background.

In December 1944 Slim's 14 Army was to use 4 Corps (two divisions plus one tank brigade) to threaten Mandalay from the north, while 33 Corps (two divisions, one infantry brigade and a tank brigade) was approaching it from the north-west. Both corps were starting from the general area of the River Chindwin, from

Tamu in the north to Kalewa in the south. They would converge near Shwebo, one of the few areas in Burma with sufficiently flat and open ground for tanks to operate freely, and there Slim hoped to meet and destroy the enemy, whom he expected to make their stand well north of the Irrawaddy.[153] That had indeed been the plan of General Kawabe, commanding Burma Area Army (Biruma Hōmengun). Kawabe had recently been replaced by Kimura, however, and almost at once it emerged that he had abandoned Kawabe's ideas. Natural obstacles like mountain gorges, which would earlier have been tenaciously defended, were only lightly held. Ground and air observation, sigint and other intelligence all told the same story: the enemy were not after all digging in to the north of the Irrawaddy but preparing to move back across it and to use it as a formidable natural barrier to be defended from the other side.

This was an unwelcome discovery for Slim. His object was not to gain ground by pushing them back but to destroy them as soon as possible, and well before the monsoon arrived in six months time, preventing any major movement of troops on either side, and probably allowing the Japanese time to bring in reinforcements and prolong the campaign for a further year. He therefore recast his plans, and Operation Capital became Operation Extended Capital. 33 Corps, consisting of 2 and 20 Divisions, 268 Brigade and 254 Tank Brigade with its elderly Lee-Grant and Stuart tanks, was already moving well towards Mandalay from the north-west. Further away 19 Division from 4 Corps was threatening the city from due north. It had already forced a crossing of the Irrawaddy, which there is twice the average width of the Rhine. Fortunately 7 and 17 Divisions, the rest of 4 Corps, were not yet committed.

Slim's master-stroke, as Kimura later called it, was to detach these two divisions and switch them secretly from the extreme east of the front to the extreme west, adding to them 255 Tank Brigade with the newer Sherman tanks, easily the best available to either side in this campaign. This force would move undetected along the tiny tracks of the Kabaw and Gangaw valleys, 100 miles to the west, would storm the Irrawaddy well clear of Mandalay, and would then make a lightning dash, led by its armoured column, for Meiktila. This road, rail and administrative centre was 80 miles south of Mandalay, exactly athwart the Japanese communications, and its capture would paralyse the defensive capability of all the troops along the Irrawaddy line. It was a plan in the tradition of General Guderian, the first commander to apply on any scale the concept of

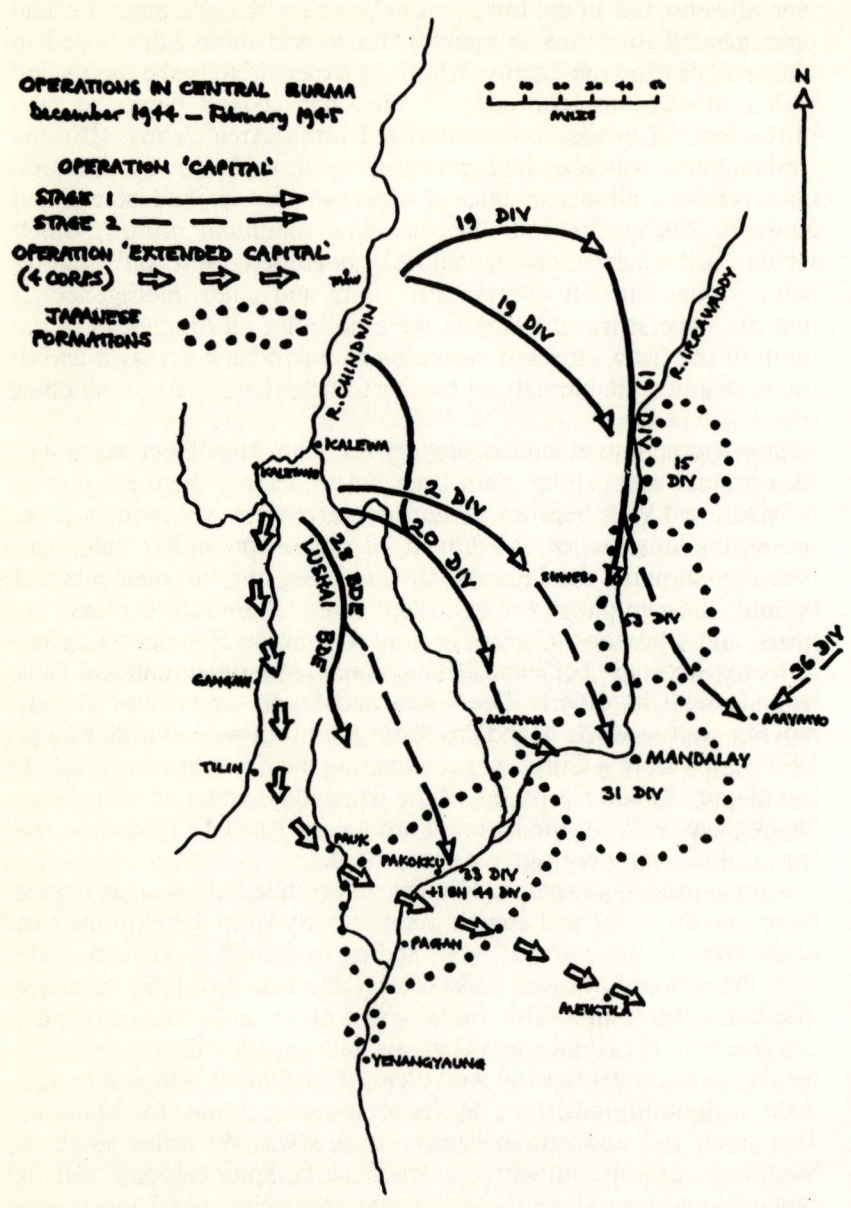

Map showing operations in Central Burma, December 1944 – February 1945

deep penetration by tanks, supported by infantry and aircraft, far enough into and behind the enemy's main positions to make them untenable. The remarkable difference would be that, in contrast to Guderian's massive and seasoned Panzer divisions, trained for years in these specialised and demanding tactics, the extreme difficulty of Burmese terrain had given Slim's tank crews precious little opportunity to operate at all, except spasmodically and in ones and twos – the exact negation of the proper use of armoured strength. The question of co-operation with aircraft had thus hardly arisen, and as the monsoon approached would be at the mercy of some of the worst flying weather in the world. Finally, the sudden change of plan meant wholesale improvisation, and the forward units would be at the end of a precarious supply line, sometimes little more than a track, stretching back 700 miles to the nearest railhead. General Marshall appropriately commented that this was 'the most ambitious operation yet waged on the end of an airborne supply line'.

While 4 Corps was preparing to take this new and hazardous route, 19 Division, still in the east of the combat area, would pass from 4 Corps to 33 Corps, and if the Japanese identified it, that would support their natural assumption that the rest of 4 Corps was there too – an obvious deduction to make from the speed and ferocity of the British and Indian advance. But much more would be needed to guarantee the secrecy of the right hook which was to envelop the enemy from the west: that called for a comprehensive and foolproof deception scheme. Let me first describe the technical problems which 4 Corps now had to face, and some of the ingenious ways in which their route, along narrow valley tracks as far as the Irrawaddy, could be made more passable for their heavy transport, since the same natural difficulties also helped to shape the deception measures:

1. They had to improvise a new track by covering the dust with hessian cloth impregnated with bitumen, and rolling the result. Thus a technique already used for improvising airstrip runways produced a surface which could be laid at the rate of a mile a day. More surprisingly still, it proved capable of taking a thousand vehicles a day even through the monsoon, which was capable of washing most things away. When bulldozers were first used in Burma they helped to clear the landslides, caused by monsoon rains, down into the ravines; the landslides retaliated by clearing the bulldozers down too.

2. They built completely new sections of track by cantilevering them out from the cliff-face, and built seven new prefabricated Bailey bridges in five miles in 23 days.

3. They worked out one-way-traffic rules to make sure that one 50-ton tank transporter, edging round a precipice, did not meet another bringing a tank back for repair. The gradients were often so steep that tanks had to tow their own transporters.

4. Under the guidance of 'Elephant Bill' Williams and his team, elephants were brought in to fell giant teak trees, build bridges, clear spaces for airstrips every 50 miles, and collect timber for 500 river barges, designed by a peacetime furniture manufacturer and assembled on the river bank at Kalewa.[154]

5. They floated petrol supplies down the river in rafts of drums lashed together.

The strategic deception scheme, with its somewhat revealing cover-name Cloak, was wide-ranging, and was probably conceived by Slim and his staff rather than by Peter Fleming.[155] A central feature was to build on the presence of 11 East African Division in the Kabaw-Gangaw valley area throughout the previous monsoon, assuming that the Japanese had identified them. Although it had now been pulled back, it was replaced in the advance-guard of 4 Corps by 28 East African Brigade in the hope that one unit of East Africans might be mistaken for another, and would suggest 'no change in this sector'. 4 Corps were to show no insignia on uniforms or vehicles until they reached the river; then they were to show the familiar 11 East African Division badges and insignia.

Even one report of a cloud of dust thrown up by the large mechanised columns travelling along these tiny tracks would have raised the alarm; the RAF were therefore ordered to prevent any enemy aircraft from entering the area; if they did, they were not to get away afterwards. In the same way, to avoid disclosing what tanks and artillery were in the valley area, an enemy position at Gangaw, which was known to be strongly held, was to be attacked by bombers alone. One final touch: any date associated with these operations was to be a month later than that of the real event.

The signals deception scheme was intended to mislead the Japanese in a similar fashion. They might learn that Tamu had been the starting-point for 19 Division, then still part of 4 Corps. Very well: to strengthen the illusion that the rest of 4 Corps was still with 19 Division, let 4 Corps HQ appear to be at Tamu still. When the rest of 4 Corps HQ moved south, a bogus Corps HQ stayed behind at

Tamu, complete with HQ vehicles making plausible dummy runs, with its signals unit using the same call-signs and frequencies as before, and maintaining the volume of signals traffic that would befit the presence of a second corps north of Mandalay. To bring this illusion closer to reality, Slim ordered that every signal between 19 Division and its new parent, 33 Corps HQ, was to be passed all the way back to Tamu and then all the way forward again. To quote Slim's dry comment, 'This ... was a real annoyance to corps and divisional commanders, and its enforcement a test of patience and discipline, but it paid an excellent dividend'.[156]

In addition to this genuine but re-routed signals traffic, dummy signals brought the total up to a realistic level. The bogus HQ was also entrusted with several delicately-worded 'minor breaches of radio security' in which staff officers gave short, indiscreet and tantalising messages in clear speech, as if by mistake – a rather risky ploy unless enacted with very great care.

To return to the impending river crossing: once the forward units reached the Irrawaddy area with its open banks, complete surprise could no longer be maintained, but it was still important to keep the enemy guessing about the details. The object of the deception then became twofold: first, to sell the enemy the idea that the objective on the far bank was the oil refinery at Yenangyaung, a plausible goal some 50 miles due south; second, to keep him guessing about the exact points and times at which the crossings would take place, by staging multiple feint and practice crossings.

This aspect of the deception plan was all the more necessary because of the physical and military hazards entailed in crossing it. These were some of the longest opposed river crossings attempted in any theatre of operations during the Second World War. At several places in the stretch west of Mandalay it was over 2,000 yards wide, six times as wide as the Thames at Waterloo Bridge. It flowed fast and its notorious sandbanks, which could easily engulf an army vehicle up to its axles, were constantly shifting. Frogmen and commandos were brought in to carry out nightly surveys. The near bank was low and under close observation from the far bank with its cliffs one hundred feet high. Some of the Japanese gun positions, like those on Okinawa, were tunnelled deep into the foot of these cliffs, so that only a direct hit from point-blank range could silence them.

To make matters worse, 4 Corps was desperately short of river craft, and such outboard motors as they had were noisy, feeble and reluctant to start. Harvard aircraft, notoriously noisy themselves, were brought in to fly along the river over the crossing-points to drown the noise for as long as possible. Some of the villagers were persuaded to paddle their boats to take men across, but understandably they were cautious about so rapid a change of occupying army, and when firing started from the far bank they were naturally prone to panic.

One small detail remains to be mentioned: two of the real crossing-points selected were at the exact junctions of pairs of Japanese formations – again a gift from good intelligence – because 'the Japanese rarely seemed properly to interlock their junction-points'.[157] Part of 20 Division crossed at the boundary between the enemy 31 and 33 Divisions. 7 Division made for the junction of 15 and 28 Army, and were richly rewarded, while halfway across, by seeing the troops on the far bank hastily marching away in both directions, presumably bemused by the complexity of the feint crossings.[158]

We must not forget that quite apart from this mystification the biggest single reason for the Japanese to assume that the only threat to Mandalay was from the north, was that that threat was all too real in its own right. Rees, the 19 Division commander, took literally Slim's order to take risks and move fast. He refused to allow his transport or his men to stop. When after three days and nights his brigadier used his radio-telephone to say that his men were exhausted and his vehicles needed repair, Rees told him to keep advancing through the night. When his tanks or trucks were stuck on steep slopes they were winched up. When the tanks were held up by a deep river channel, he told the engineers to heave three 3-ton trucks on their side, and send the tanks across on top of them.[159] The division's headlong progress, with infantry riding on the tanks, heightened the misleading message which Slim wanted to give.

4 Corps moved just as fast once they were across the river. The armoured spearhead – a formation unique in the Far East though familiar nearer home – was formed of two mobile infantry brigades, two Sherman tank regiments, an armoured-car group and a battery of self-propelled guns. Whenever they ran into an obstacle, RAF liaison officers travelling in jeeps with the leading units used radio to call down strike aircraft, waiting in the 'cab-rank', to deal with it.[160] They were to bypass really strong defences, and were to make no effort to keep the road open behind them; 7 Division would follow to reopen it.

The rest of the campaign is military history in its own right. To summarise: after the heroic defence but ultimate fall of Meiktila,

Rangoon Liberator

SPECIAL EDITION

Wednesday, August 15, 1945   Price Annas 2

JAPAN SURRENDERS UNCONDITIONALLY

S.E.A.C., Hqs, August 15 : (07:05) hrs :—At 7-10 last night the Japanese Minister in Switzerland left a note with the Swiss authorities. At mid-night (G. M. T.) Mr. Attlee made his dramatic announcement and we are able to tell you that Japan has unconditionally surrendered.

LAST OF OUR ENEMIES LAID LOW

Mr. Attlee broadcasts text of Japanese Reply

Japan has surrendered. The official announcement of the Japanese surrender was made just under three hours ago this morning simultaneously in London, Washington Moscow and Chungking.

The Allied Commander who will receive the Japanese surrender is Gen. MaArthur. President Truman has asked Mr. Byrnes, the American Secretary of State, to send an order to the Japanese through the Swiss Legation to bring the war to an end on all fronts. They must send emissaries at once to give Gen. McArthur full information about the Japanese Armed Forces everywhere in the Pacific. President Truman, in announcing the surrender of the Japanese at a Press Conference, said that the agreement has yet to be formally signed. The victory in the Far East will be proclaimed only after the formal signature. High ranking British, Russian and Chinese officers would represent their countries at the signing ceremony.

British people at home and overseas heard the voice through a broadcast from Mr. Attlee, the Prime Minister. He began his broadcast with these dramatic words. "JAPAN HAS TODAY SURRENDERED. THE LAST OF OUR ENEMIES IS LAID LOW." The Prime Minister then gave the text of the Japanese reply to the Allied note communicated to the Japanese Government last Saturday. The reply runs:—

1. His Majesty the Emperor has issued an Imperial Rescript regarding Japan's acceptance of the Provisions of the Potsdam Declaration.

2. His Majesty the Emperor is prepared to authorise and ensure the signature by his Government and the Imperial General Head-quarters of the provisions of the Potsdam Declaration.

3. His Majesty is also prepared to issue his Commands to all the Military, Naval and Air forces of Japan and all the forces under their control wherever they are located and to issue such other orders as may be required by the Supreme Commander of the Allied Forces for the execution of the above terms.

Signed—TOGO.

Broadcast Of Great Importance From Tokyo

Tokyo has announced, after a long silence, that a broadcast of unprecedented importance will be made in 12 hours' time, i. e., at noon to-day Japanese Time.

the main feature of the campaign was a two-pronged assault on Rangoon by both corps, operating – at times on half-rations because of supply problems – along parallel salients some 300 miles long and each barely a mile wide at best.[161] Rangoon fell when these pincers from the north were joined by a synchronised amphibious attack by 15 Corps from the south, in the first week of May, precisely as the monsoon arrived to bog down further movement by drowning much of the surrounding plain to the depth of several feet. The campaign, apart from long and arduous clearing-up operations, effectively ended three months before Hiroshima.

It is difficult or impossible to assess the actual success of the deception scheme. Slim's verdict that 'It must have worked. We won the battle' is generous but illogical. What matters is that to make sure of winning the battle he had to have the deception scheme; he could take no chances. The scheme was admirably planned to reinforce what he knew that the Japanese were ready to believe on direct evidence: that the essential threat to Mandalay was from the north *alone*.

There is no unanimity about what the enemy made of 4 Corps' advance when they did recognise it, or when that recognition occurred. Four Japanese generals – the chief of staff of Southern Army, the commander of Burma Area Army, the commander of 15 Army and the commander of 33 Division, disagreed in evidence after the war about what was known and what was deduced from it. Their communications were by then in a poor state, having come under particularly heavy air attack, and this cannot have helped. It is always difficult to tell, in such instances, how much is known at the time and how much is wisdom after the event, not merely in the sense of self-deceit, but also because in fast-moving battles of this sort reliable and up-to-date intelligence assessments are hard to come by. Lord Carver, who served with tanks throughout the north African campaign, commanded a tank brigade in north-west Europe, and later became Chief of the Defence Staff, has described how, in the very fluid tank battles in the desert in 1941 and 1942, 'both sides often had only a hazy idea not only where the enemy tanks were, but where their own were also'.

Despite the RAF's efforts there *was* a report from a Japanese aircraft which had seen 'a long line of vehicles on the road from Tilin to Pauk', at the extreme southern end of the Gangaw valley. The Japanese comments on this sighting are unenlightening, and in any case so late a report was virtually useless, since once past Pauk they would have come under direct observation from the far bank.

Connoisseurs of deception are apt to give higher marks for schemes which conjure things into existence than for those which conjure them out of existence, and admittedly the latter is easier. Slim owes us no apology: this is not a comparison of pure art forms but of practical ways of shortening and winning a war, when deception and intelligence are the servants of the commander, not his masters. Intelligence helps him to shape his plans, deception can help him to carry them out successfully, and intelligence again can monitor that success. Slim's scheme permitted and persuaded the enemy to concentrate his attention on a genuine and mesmerising threat which he perceived as the only one, while it concealed a greater threat which he was too preoccupied to take seriously even when he belatedly recognised it.

Lewin's assessment is worth quoting:

> The Japanese were so completely misled, that the way Slim mystified Kimura, the concealment of 6 Panzer Army's location before the Ardennes offensive, and the persuasion of the Germans at the time of D-Day that a phantom Army truly existed in south-east England may perhaps be accounted the three most interesting examples of military deception in the second world war.[162]

It looks as if we should now add to that list, despite the scarcity of colourful detail, the successes of the Soviet Union's military deception (*maskirovka*) in 1944 and 1945.[163]

There was no opportunity and no need for Slim to create a fictitious army, and such fictions are apt to go wrong. Whether the story is true or apocryphal, the message is valuable: that the Germans painstakingly built a decoy airfield, with dummy aircraft, fuel bowsers, hangars and control tower all beautifully made of wood, to distract attention from the real thing. On the day it was completed the RAF, who had been keeping a quiet eye on what was happening, showed their appreciation by dropping one wooden bomb on it.

Select Bibliography

Only books that are fairly readily accessible appear in this list; others are included in the Notes which follow.

Allen, Louis, *Burma, the Longest War* (London: Dent, 1984)

Andrew, Christopher, *Secret Service: the Making of the British Intelligence Community* (London: Heinemann, 1985); in US *Her Majesty's Secret Service* (New York: Viking, 1986)

Andrew, C.M. (ed.) *Codebreaking and Signals Intelligence* (London: Cass, 1986)

Andrew, C.M. and Dilks, D.N. (eds.) *The Missing Dimension* (London: Macmillan, 1984)

Andrew, C.M. and Noakes, J.M. (eds.) *Intelligence and International Relations, 1900–1945* (University of Exeter, 1987)

Beesly, Patrick, *Very Special Intelligence* (London: Hamish Hamilton, 1977)

Behrendt, Hans-Otto, *Rommel's Intelligence in the Desert Campaign* (London: William Kimber, 1985)

Bennett, Ralph, *Ultra in the West: the Normandy Campaign of 1944–5* (London: Hutchinson, 1979)

Bennett, R., *Ultra and Mediterranean Strategy 1941–5* (New York: Morrow, 1988; London: Hamish Hamilton, forthcoming in 1989)

Calvocoressi, Peter, *Top Secret Ultra* (London: Cassell, 1980)

Clayton, Aileen, *The Enemy is Listening* (London: Hutchinson, 1980)

Cruickshank, Charles, *Deception in World War Two* (Oxford University Press, 1981)

Cruickshank, C., *SOE in the Far East* (Oxford, 1983)

Evans, Lt.-Gen. Sir Geoffrey, *Slim as Military Commander* (London: Batsford, 1969)

Foot, M.R.D., *SOE: The Special Operations Executive 1940–46* (London: BBC, 1984)

Gilchrist, Sir Andrew, *Bangkok Top Secret* (London: Hutchinson, 1960)

Hart-Davis, Duff, *Peter Fleming, a Biography* (London: Cape, 1980)

Hinsley, Professor Sir Harry, *et al.*, *British Intelligence in the Second World War*, Vols. 1, 2, 3, Parts 1 and 2 (London: HMSO, 1979–88)

Hodges, Andrew, *Alan Turing, the Enigma of Intelligence* (London: Counterpoint, 1983)

Hooper, David, *Official Secrets: the Use and Abuse of the Act* (London: Secker & Warburg, 1987)

Hoyt, Edwin P., *The Invasion before Normandy: the Secret Battle of Slapton Sands* (London: Robert Hale, 1985)

Jones, R.V., *Most Secret War: British Intelligence 1939–45* (London: Hamish Hamilton, 1978)

Kahn, David, *The Codebreakers* (London: Weidenfeld & Nicolson, 1966; New York: Macmillan, 1967)

Kirby, Major-Gen. S.W. *et al.*, *The War against Japan*, Vols. I–V (London: HMSO, 1956–69)

Kozaczuk, Wladyslaw, *Enigma* (London: Arms and Armour Press, 1984; University Publications of America, 1984)

SELECT BIBLIOGRAPHY

Lewin, Ronald, *Slim, the Standard-Bearer* (London: Leo Cooper, 1976)

Lewin, R., *Ultra Goes to War* (London: Hutchinson, 1978)

Lewin, R., *The Other Ultra* (London: Hutchinson, 1982; also known as *The American Magic* (London, Penguin Books, 1983)

Lorain, Pierre, *Secret Warfare* (London: Orbis Publishing, 1984, translated and adapted by David Kahn)

O'Brien, Terence, *The Moonlight War* (London: Collins, 1987)

Robertson, K.G. (ed.) *British and American Approaches to Intelligence* (London: Macmillan, 1987)

Slim, Field-Marshal Viscount, *Defeat into Victory* (London: Macmillan, 1956)

Spector, Ronald H., *Eagle against the Sun* (New York: Macmillan, 1984; London: Penguin Books, 1987)

Spencer Chapman, F., *The Jungle is Neutral* (London: Chatto and Windus, 1949)

Sweet-Escott, Bickham, *Baker Street Irregular* (London: Methuen, 1965)

Welchman, Gordon, *The Hut Six Story* (London: Penguin Books, 1984)

West, Nigel, *GCHQ: The Secret Wireless War, 1900–86* (London: Weidenfeld & Nicolson, 1986)

Winterbotham, F.W., *The Ultra Secret* (London: Weidenfeld & Nicolson, 1974)

Issues of the quarterly journal *Intelligence and National Security* (London: Frank Cass) are also highly relevant.

Notes

1. Peter Calvocoressi, *Top Secret Ultra* (London: Cassell, 1980) p.3.
2. Christopher Andrew, 'F.H. Hinsley and the Cambridge Moles', in Richard Langhorne (ed.), *Diplomacy and Intelligence during the Second World War* (Cambridge, 1985) p.36.
3. Ibid., p.34.
4. Ronald Lewin, *Ultra goes to War* (London: Hutchinson, 1978) p.117.
5. R.V. Jones, *Most Secret War* (London: Hamish Hamilton, 1978) pp.61–2.
6. I am grateful to Alexis Vlasto for this delightful story.
7. Neil Webster, George Steiner and Hugh Trevor-Roper, quoted in R.A. Denniston, *The Professional Life of A.G. Denniston* in K.G. Robertson (ed.), *British and American Approaches to Intelligence* (London: Macmillan, 1987) p.115.
8. David Kahn, 'Codebreaking in World Wars I and II', in Christopher Andrew and David Dilks (eds.), *The Missing Dimension* (London: Macmillan, 1984) pp.155 & 149.
9. Lewin, *Ultra goes to War*, p.17.
10. Kozaczuk, *Enigma* (Arms and Armour Press, 1984) p.240, note 3.
11. Winterbotham, *The Ultra Secret* (London: Weidenfeld & Nicolson, 1974) p.15.
12. F.H. Hinsley *et al.*, *British Intelligence in the Second World War*, Vol. 3, Part 1 (London: HMSO, 1984) p.479, and Gordon Welchman, *The Hut Six Story* (London: Penguin Books, 1984) pp.177–9. Two photographs of the *Geheimschreiber* appear in Calvocoressi, op. cit., between pages 86 and 87; a brief appraisal of the machine in Lewin, op. cit., pp.130–3, and a summary of GCHQ's attack on its traffic in Hinsley, op. cit., Vol. 3, Part 1, pp.477–82. I am asked to emphasise that I am not revealing first-hand information.
13. Andrew Hodges, *Alan Turing, The Enigma of Intelligence* (London: Counterpoint, 1983) pp.299–300.
14. Letter from John Prentice, of the sixth Bedford Japanese course.
15. Letter from John Evans, formerly a signals officer in the Far East.
16. Letter from Robin Gibson, formerly of WEC Delhi.
17. *Operational History of Japanese Naval Communications, December 1941–August 1945* (US Department of the Army, 1953; reprinted Aegean Park Press, no date) pp.91–4.
18. Hinsley, op. cit., pp.483–7.
19. I am very grateful for the help of Bernard Bellingham, Carmen Blacker, F.W. Clayton, Eric Copson, Jack Dalglish, Anthony Fitton Brown, Robin Gibson, Michael Herzig, John Horwood Smart, Cyril James, David Kahn, Toshiaki Kohara, John Martin, Hugh Melinsky, Sean Morgan, Bennie Polack, John Prentice, Frank B. Rowlett, Richard Rutt, David Sissons, Hugh Skillen, Barry Smallman, Alexis Vlasto, Brian Warmington, Maurice Wiles and several colleagues who wish, or are compelled, to remain anonymous.
20. David Kahn, *The Codebreakers* (New York: Macmillan, 1967) p.590.
21. Ibid., p.589.
22. Nigel West, *GCHQ* (London: Weidenfeld & Nicolson, 1986) p.171.

23. Cipher A. Deavours and Louis Kruh, *Machine Cryptography and Modern Cryptanalysis* (Dedham, MA: Artech House, 1985), Chapter VI *passim*.
24. Hinsley, op. cit., Vol. 3, Part 2, pp.779–80 (footnote).
25. Lewin, *The Other Ultra* (London: Hutchinson, 1982); also known as *The American Magic* (London: Penguin Books, 1983) pp.196–7.
26. D.M. Horner, 'Special Intelligence in the South West Pacific Area in World War Two', *Australian Outlook*, Vol. 32, No. 3 (December 1978), pp.315–6.
27. This and later signals and intelligence summaries, listed under SRH references, are from material in the US Army Military History Institute, Carlisle Barracks, Pennsylvania, in the SRH Histories series: SRH-258 *Japanese Army Air Forces Order-of-Battle 1945* pp.143–6.
28. SRH-287 *Movements of Japanese Forces* Series A, Nos. 1, 2, 3 and 4, *passim*, and SRH-219 *Ultra material in the Blamey Papers, passim*.
29. Horner, op. cit., p.323.
30. SRH-219 p.12.
31. The daily US MAGIC Summary was started about March 1943.
32. SRH-258 pp.054–5.
33. Horner, op. cit. p.322, quoting MAGIC Summary SRS 35 of 7 April 1944.
34. SRH-287 Series A, No. 1.
35. SRH-287 Series A, No. 2.
36. Ronald H. Spector, *Listening to the Enemy* (Wilmington, DE: Scholarly Resources, 1988) quoting from *Army–Navy arrangements regarding ULTRA* by Col. Carter W. Clarke, p.188.
37. Horner, op. cit., p.323.
38. SRH-254 *Examples to illustrate information obtained from cryptanalysis*, pp.004–5.
39. Kahn, *The Codebreakers*, pp.595–601.
40. Carl Boyd, 'Significance of MAGIC and the Japanese Ambassador to Berlin: (II) The Crucial Months After Pearl Harbor', *Intelligence and National Security*, Vol. 2, No. 2 (April 1987), pp.314–6.
41. Ibid., pp.312–3.
42. Hinsley, op. cit., Vol. 3, Part 1, pp.519–26.
43. Ibid., pp.515–7.
44. Ibid., pp.352–3.
45. SRH-254, pp.005–6.
46. SRH-211 *History of the Signal Security Agency*: Vol. 3 – The Japanese Army Problems: Cryptanalysis (prepared under the direction of the Chief, Army Security Agency) pp.013–022. I am most grateful to colleagues at the Faculty of Oriental Studies, University of Cambridge, for the admirable illustration of the typical form of such a text.
47. Aileen Clayton, *The Enemy is Listening* (London: Hutchinson, 1980), p.155.
48. Colonel John C. Hartley, Australian Department of Defence, 'The Japanese Attack on Darwin, 19 February 1942: A Case Study in Surprise at the Operational Level' (paper presented at the Third International Conference on Intelligence and Military Operations, US Army War College, May 1988), pp.38–40.
49. Christopher Andrew, 'The Growth of the Australian Intelligence Community and the Anglo-American Connection' (paper presented at the Third USAWC Conference), p.10.
50. Hartley, op. cit., p.41.
51. Rear Admiral (Retd) J.F.W. Nuboer, 'A History of Afdeling I (Intelligence), Naval Staff, Batavia, Netherlands East Indies, from August 1934 to January 1938', in *The Cryptogram*, Vol. XLVII, No. 2, March–April 1981, *passim*.
52. West, op. cit., p.174.
53. Field-Marshal Viscount Slim, *Defeat into Victory* (London: Macmillan, 1956) p.272.
54. SHR-196 *Reports on the Activities of Dr Marshall Stone in the China, Burma and*

China Theaters, 29 January–31 March 1945, p.004.

55. Letter in *The Guardian* of 29 November 1985, reprinted in *Intelligence and National Security*, Vol. 1, No. 2 (May 1986), p.280.
56. Kahn, *The Codebreakers, passim.*
57. Kahn, *Codebreaking in World Wars I and II*, pp.155–6.
58. Clayton, op. cit., p.100.
59. Christopher Morris, 'Ultra's Poor Relations', *Intelligence and National Security*, Vol. 1, No. 1 (January 1986), reprinted as *Codebreaking and Signals Intelligence*, pp.114–15.
60. Clayton, op. cit., pp.244–5.
61. Noel Currer-Briggs, 'Some of Ultra's Poor Relations', *Intelligence and National Security*, Vol. 2, No. 2 (April 1987), p.277.
62. Kahn, *The Codebreakers*, p.467.
63. 'Private Signals for knowing each other by Day'
    On odd days:
    'The ship or vessel that first makes the signal, shall hoist a Spanish jack at the foretopmasthead and an English ensign at the mizen peak, with one gun. To be answered by a Dutch ensign at the maintopmasthead, and an English jack at the mizen peak, with two guns.'
    On even days:
    'The ship or vessel that first makes the signal, shall hoist a French jack at the maintopmasthead and a Dutch ensign at the mizen peak, with three guns. To be answered by an English ensign at the foretopgallant masthead, and a French jack at the mizen peak, with four guns.'
    After which, both ships were to hoist their proper colours. Further sets of signals using lights, false fires and passwords to be hailed and answered, were laid down for night recognition. The order, signed by Admiral Leonard Horner, on HMS *Perseus*, and intended for Captain Darby, commanding HMS *Pylades*, was dated 13 November 1782.
    What *were* they up to?
64. Kerckhoffs, *La Cryptographie Militaire* (Paris: Baudoin, 1883 and later reprints).
65. Kerckhoffs was probably the first person to grasp the significance of what is now called 'reciphering' a code or cipher text by a separate key which can be changed whenever necessary without altering the system. He explained how the crypt-analyst could create a 'superencipherment' (nowadays 'build a depth') of different messages reciphered on the same key, and illustrated the principle that the greater the depth, the easier and securer the solution became. Kahn, on pages 236–7, usefully gives letter-by-letter examples of a principle which, as Kerckhoffs shows, applies equally to word-by-word key-breaking. His principles were later embodied in the celebrated St. Cyr system, which was taken up by the French army.
66. Geoff Jukes, 'The Soviets and Ultra', *Intelligence and National Security*, Vol. 3, No. 2 (April 1988), p.237 and *passim*, together with 'A Comment on Jukes' Hypothesis' by P.S. Milner-Barry, ibid., pp.248–50.
67. Gordon Welchman, *The Hut Six Story* (London: Penguin Books, 1984) p.131.
68. Calvocoressi, op. cit., p.15.
69. West, op. cit., p.222.
70. Jones, op. cit., pp.420–1.
71. Lewin, *Ultra goes to War*, pp.313–20, gives a good summary. There are fuller accounts in Ralph Bennett, *Ultra in the West* (London: Hutchinson, 1979), *passim*, and T.L. Cubbage, 'The Success of Operation Fortitude', *Intelligence and National Security*, Vol. 2, No. 3 (July 1987), pp.327–41.
72. Letter from Robin Gibson.
73. Slim, op. cit., pp.611–2.
74. The poem is by Humbert Wolfe.
75. Hans-Otto Behrendt, *Rommel's Intelligence in the Desert Campaign* (London:

William Kimber, 1985) p.75.
76. Spector, op. cit., p.188.
77. Calvocoressi, op. cit., p.4.
78. Kahn, *The Codebreakers*, p.264.
79. Ibid., p.469–70.
80. Harold Deutsch at 'The Ultra Conference', November 1979, quoted by David Kahn in *Cryptologia*, January 1979, p.4.
81. In a BBC series 'The Profession of Intelligence', written and presented by Christopher Andrew, on 16 August 1981; quoted in *The Missing Dimension*, op. cit., pp.1–2: 'My calculation is that supposing we had had none or little as compared with the vast amount we did have, the war would have lasted about three years longer than it actually did.'
82. Horner, op. cit., p.316.
83. Spector, op. cit., p.170.
84. Winterbotham, op. cit., p.89.
85. Spector, op. cit., pp.178–9.
86. Lewin, *The Other Ultra*, pp.150–1.
87. SRH-046 (a) Procedure governing the handling of ULTRA DEXTER intelligence in the China–Burma–India Theater, March 1944, *passim*; (b) Regulations for maintaining the security of Special Intelligence in Pacific and Asiatic Theatres of Operations, 1944, *passim*.
88. John Ferris, 'The British Army, C³ (Command, Control and Communication) and Signals Security in the Middle East and North Africa, 1940–2' (paper presented at the Third USAWC Conference) p.2.
89. SRH-196, p.017.
90. Letter from Eric Copson, formerly of WEC Delhi.
91. Information from Dr Tony Clayton of the Royal Military Academy, Sandhurst.
92. Louis Allen, *Burma, the Longest War* (London: Dent, 1984) pp.413–4.
93. Letter from Robin Gibson.
94. *Operational History of Japanese Naval Communications*, pp.85–6; Kahn, *The Codebreakers*, p.590.
95. *Operational History*, p.90.
96. Ibid., p.91.
97. John Chapman, 'Japanese Intelligence 1918–1945: A Suitable Case for Treatment' in C.M. Andrew and J.M. Noakes (eds.), *Intelligence and International Relations 1900–1945* (University of Exeter, 1987) p.167 and *passim*.
98. J.W. Bennett, W.A. Hobart, J.B. Spitzer (eds.), *Intelligence and Cryptanalytic Activities of the Japanese during World War II* (SRH-254) (Aegean Park Press, 1986) pp.6–12; Kahn, *The Codebreakers*, p.579 (footnote).
99. Ibid., pp.12–23; information from Louis Allen.
100. Kahn, *The Codebreakers*, p.582.
101. SRH-258, pp.234–5.
102. Letter from Major-General Shlomo Gazit, Head of Israeli Military Intelligence, 1974–79.
103. Andrew, Introduction to *The Missing Dimension*, p.13.
104. Information from the diaries of Captain Oswald Tuck, R.N.; from the School of Oriental and African Studies, University of London; and from the recollections of fellow-students and myself. I am grateful to Robbie Stamp for allowing me to refer to his research into this subject.
105. SRH-196, p.013.
106. Clayton, op. cit., p.251; West, op. cit., p.126.
107. Letter from Professor Sir Harry Hinsley.
108. Kahn, *The Codebreakers*, p.601.
109. West, op. cit., p.203.
110. Lewin, *Ultra goes to War*, p.64.
111. Patrick Beesly, *Very Special Intelligence* (London: Hamish Hamilton, 1977)

p.100.
112. Lewin, *Ultra goes to War*, p.124.
113. Terence O'Brien, *The Moonlight War* (London: Collins, 1987) pp.68, 76–7 and *passim*.
114. Charles Cruickshank, *SOE in the Far East* (Oxford, 1983) quoting Sir Frank Nelson, p.81.
115. O'Brien, op. cit., p.310.
116. O'Brien, op. cit., pp.107–8 and 356.
117. Pierre Lorain, *Secret Warfare*, translated and adapted by David Kahn (London: Orbis Publishing, 1984) p.62 and *passim*; M.R.D. Foot, *SOE* (London: BBC, 1984) is also a mine of information on the whole subject and its background.
118. Lewin, *Ultra goes to War*, p.116, quoting Group Captain Shephard.
119. Foot, op. cit., pp.135–6.
120. O'Brien, op. cit., pp.112–14.
121. Slim, op. cit., p.221.
122. Ibid., p.289.
123. Allen, op. cit., p.395.
124. Ibid., pp.394–6.
125. Winterbotham, op. cit., pp.169–70.
126. Lewin, *The Other Ultra*, p.244.
127. O'Brien, op. cit., pp.115–16.
128. Slim, op. cit., p.120.
129. Major-Gen. S.W. Kirby *et al.*, *The War against Japan, Volume IV* (London: HMSO, 1965) pp.30–3; Cruickshank, op. cit., pp.169–71.
130. Allen, op. cit., p.395.
131. Slim, op. cit., pp.447–8.
132. Ibid., pp.405–6, 504–5, 446–50.
133. Allen, op. cit., p.396.
134. Edwin P. Hoyt, *The Invasion before Normandy* (London: Robert Hale, 1987) *passim*.
135. Slim, op. cit., p.532.
136. F. Spencer Chapman, *The Jungle is Neutral* (London: Chatto & Windus, 1949) p.373.
137. Kirby, op. cit., Vol. V (1969) pp.269–70.
138. Bickham Sweet-Escott, *Baker Street Irregular* (London: Methuen, 1965), p.264.
139. Kirby, op. cit., p.270.
140. Andrew Gilchrist, *Bangkok Top Secret* (London: Hutchinson, 1960) pp.165–183.
141. John B. Haseman, *The Thai Resistance Movement during the Second World War* (Bangkok: Chalermnit Press; undated, but 1976 or later) p.139.
142. Letter from Sir Andrew Gilchrist.
143. Sweet-Escott, op. cit., pp.251–2.
144. O'Brien, op. cit., pp.47–9.
145. Louis Allen, 'Japanese Intelligence Systems', in *Journal of Contemporary History* (London: Sage, Vol. 22, 1987), p.553.
146. Duff Hart-Davis, *Peter Fleming, a Biography* (London: Cape, 1980) p.283.
147. Behrendt, op. cit., p.90 and Index p.246, and comments by Sir David Hunt in *Intelligence and National Security*, Vol. 2, No. 2 (April 1987) p.382.
148. Hart-Davis, op. cit., pp.273–4.
149. Ibid., p.265.
150. Quoted as Appendix I to Michael Handel, 'Strategic and Operational Deception in Historical Perspective', *Intelligence and National Security*, Vol. 2, No. 3 (July 1987) p.89.
151. O'Brien, op. cit., p.171.
152. Ibid., p.172.
153. Lt.-Gen. Sir Geoffrey Evans, *Slim as Military Commander* (London: Batsford, 1969) p.184.

154. Slim, op. cit., pp.397–404; J.H. Williams, *Elephant Bill* (London: Hart-Davis, 1950) *passim*.
155. Kirby, op. cit., Vol. IV, Appendix 20, pp.501–5.
156. Slim, op. cit., p.395.
157. Ibid., p.420.
158. Ibid., p.431.
159. Allen, op. cit., pp.405–6.
160. Kirby, op. cit. Vol. IV, p.254 (footnote).
161. Graphic yet exact description by Louis Allen in a paper presented to the Study Group on Intelligence, London, 24 June 1988.
162. Lewin, *Slim the Standard-Bearer* (London: Leo Cooper, 1976) pp.214–5.
163. David M. Glantz, 'The Red Mask: The Nature and Legacy of Soviet Military Deception in the Second World War', in *Intelligence and National Security*, Vol. 2, No. 2 (July 1987), *passim*.

Index

INDEX

'West, Nigel', 69–70, 96, 107, 153
Western Wireless Sub-Centre; *see*
    Bangalore
Wiles, Maurice, 21–2
Wingate, Orde, 79, 168
Winterbotham, F. W., 26, 100, 117,
    153, 166–7, 170
Wireless Experimental Centre; *see*
    Delhi

Wireless Experimental Depot; *see*
    Abbottabad

Yamamoto, Admiral Isoroku, 69,
    86, 127
Yardley, Herbert, 96–7
Yugoslavia, 114–15

Z patrols, 157, 168–9
Zipper, Operation, 77, 173, 175–7